Wordsworth Translated

Continuum Reception Studies series:

Wordsworth Translated

A Case Study in the Reception of British
Romantic Poetry in Germany 1804–1914

John Williams

continuum

Continuum International Publishing Group

The Tower Building	80 Maiden Lane
11 York Road	Suite 704
London SE1 7NX	New York, NY 10038

www.continuumbooks.com

British Library Cataloguing-in-Publication Data
A catalogue record for this book is available from the British Library.

ISBN: 978-1-4411-3121-8 (paperback)

Library of Congress Cataloging-in-Publication Data
A catalog record for this book is available from the Library of Congress.

Typeset by Newgen Imaging Systems Pvt Ltd, Chennai, India
Printed and bound in Great Britain by the MPG Books Group

Contents

Acknowledgements

I first have to thank a small army of translators who made invaluable additional comments on the texts that came their way: Nicola Armitt, Bettina Barber, Thorsten Hauler, Stefan Manz (who also shared his research on Anglo-German exchanges unreservedly), Mariella Sutherland, and (alphabetically last, but by no means least), Teresa Zhult. I am also indebted to Susan Reed at the British Library, to staff at the Swanley Public Library, and to Wendy Creed who, with characteristic energy and good cheer, hunted down some key texts for me. Encouragement and advice came from Elinor Shaffer, Myriam Salama-Carr, Eleoma Joshua, Nick Jacobs, and Susanne Schmid; advice specifically on translation studies came from Zoë Pettit, while Mick Bowles helped with eighteenth-century German philosophical sources. John Powell Ward cheerfully set Coleridge to one side to help me seek out unattributed extracts from Wordsworth's poetry. As usual, my family had to put up with everything! I would like to dedicate this book to all these people, on the understanding that any faults that emerge are entirely my responsibility.

1 The Eighteenth-Century Context

Introduction

> *I travell'd among unknown Men,*
> *In Lands beyond the Sea;*
> *Nor England! Did I know till then*
> *What love I bore to thee.*
>
> Wordsworth 1983, 103

British poetry was widely read in Europe throughout the eighteenth and nineteenth centuries. It was frequently translated, but it was also published to be read in English. This book offers a case study in the processes of reception, focusing on William Wordsworth's reception in nineteenth-century Germany. Set alongside several poets of his generation, Wordsworth may seem an unusual choice. Burns, Byron, Moore, Scott, and Felicia Hemans are among those whose work appears to have been considerably more widely disseminated in Germany than that of Wordsworth. In twenty-first century Germany, knowledge of Wordsworth has all but disappeared. For this reason alone it is worth rediscovering the interest he did excite in the century prior to the First World War. Researching Wordsworth's reception in Germany also reveals intriguing and important insights into the interplay of German and British culture during the nineteenth century.

It is necessary first, however, to consider the eighteenth-century context for Wordsworth's reception. This will be done by identifying key intellectual preoccupations of the eighteenth-century Enlightenment in Germany, and then by assessing certain aspects of the contribution which English literature and literary theory made to the development of German literature as it began to flourish in the course of the eighteenth century.

Aufklärung

> 'I have portrayed matters of religion as the focal point of enlightenment, i.e. of man's emergence from his self-incurred immaturity.'
>
> Kant, 'What is Enlightenment?' in Reiss 1991, 59

Formed in Berlin in 1783, the Wednesday Club ('Mittwochsgesellschaft') was a society dedicated to the promotion of Enlightenment ideals. It was also a secret society because it sought freedom for its members to express frankly their views on the burning social and political issues of the day. Among these were education, censorship, law reform, and the persistence of superstition. The society consisted of over 20 members, including Justus Möser, Moses Mendelssohn and Johann Erich Biester, editor of the influential journal *Berlinische Monatsschrift*. Though the formal existence of a society was never acknowledged, Biester published accounts of some of the debates in his journal, along with contributions from Thomas Jefferson, Benjamin Franklin, and Mirabeau, in addition to essays from the regular German members. Emmanuel Kant (1724–1804) was a founder member, and in 1784 he published his essay, 'Was ist Aufklärung?'.

Thomas Munck has summarized Kant's understanding of Enlightenment as being 'the process of discovery, and active and critical engagement of the individual' (Munck 2000, 7). Kant privileges the importance of the pursuit of knowledge over its attainment; he is passionate about the coming together of individuals to seek enlightenment through frank and open debate, contrasted with a notion of enlightenment defined by the establishment of fixed ideas and positions. Munck concludes:

> Such an approach may at times make for a very broad and inclusive definition of enlightened ideas, complete with internal contradictions and inconsistencies of detail. But it may also help us to recognize the framework of geographic comparison and international cross-fertilisation which was itself one of the most important contemporary sources of inspiration. (Ibid., 7)

Two particularly important points emerge from this passage. Firstly, we note the existence of 'contradictions and inconsistencies'. The contradictions and inconsistencies of Kant's text (which fuel a creative tension throughout) are more broadly observable in a Europe which, while it was host to a movement that sought to extend the boundaries of wisdom and knowledge and banish the regressive, superstitious beliefs and practices of an unenlightened past, was also a place where war, generally pursued with ferocity, cynicism, and a savage disregard for any civilized values whatever, was a recurring consequence of political ambitions fuelled by nationalist and imperialist ambition. Secondly, and still relevant to the contradictions inherent in Enlightenment thought, Munck refers to the fact that 'international cross-fertilisation' was 'one of the most important contemporary sources of inspiration'. Looking back across the century from the 1790s in his 'Letter 113' of the *Briefe zu Beförderung der Humanität*, Herder sketched out a roll call of some of the chief English and Scottish writers admired by his compatriots: Shakespeare, Milton, Addison, Swift, Thomson, Sterne, Hume, Robertson, Gibbon, Richardson, Young, Fielding, Ferguson, Smith, Stewart, Millar, and Blair (Price 1968, 168–72). Herder is heir to the cosmopolitan spirit that informed a quest for knowledge intended ultimately to rescue humanity from its social and physical ills. In a similar mood of optimism, Nicolas Cochin's frontispiece of 1764 for the *Encyclopédie* of Diderot and D'Alembert depicts the spirit of rational, secular wisdom descending from the clouds to an expectant multitude in the manner of a Renaissance religious set piece. When set alongside representations of the Assumption or Christ's Ascension, however, we can appreciate that the process has been subversively reversed and secularized. Fourteen years later, in a similar vein, Fragonard painted the *Apotheosis of Benjamin Franklin*, in which the political revolutionary casts out worldly error and corruption in the manner of a Michaelangelo God the Father.

This is evidence of the way political boundaries and religious creeds might be construed as provisional in the interests of ensuring that people would no longer languish as slaves of superstition, prejudice, and religious bigotry. For Herder, however, who studied theology at Königsberg University (where he was taught by Kant), as for his contemporary, Johann Georg Hamann, also a theology student at Königsberg, the secularizing views of the French *philosophes* held little if any attraction. Religion was firmly embedded in German traditions of thought and self-expression, not least because it was the sixteenth-century Lutheran Bible that had provided Germans with a common language of East Middle German through which they might develop a sense of shared identity. Herder's failure to jettison his religious beliefs prompted the atheistical William Taylor (1765–1836), an enthusiastic advocate of German poetry, to write of Herder in 1828 that 'His trains of ideas, like gliding fenfires, are seen to shine, more than to illuminate' (Taylor 1828 I, 41). Language was perceived to be a crucial issue within the debate about how ideas came to be formed and disseminated, and this resulted in a somewhat different attitude on the part of contributors to the German *Aufklärung* when compared to the secularizing and cosmopolitan tendencies of other Enlightenment thinkers. Hamann wrote, 'With me the question is not so much: What is reason? But rather: What is language?' (Berlin 1956, 274). Herder questioned a common Enlightenment view that language was no more than a vehicle for expressing ideas that were already in existence. As Andrew Bowie has pointed out, the fact that Herder is working at a time when 'there is no real political entity called Germany', helps to explain how he comes to concentrate (in opposition to much Enlightenment thought) on the dynamic qualities of language: 'the . . . ways in which language can build culture and identity' (Bowie, 2003, 51). In his *On Recent German Literature. Fragments* (1766–8) Herder seems to suggest that, rather than look forward to the evolution of a unified language of Enlightenment wisdom, people are given the option of exploring other worlds by their acquisition of other languages, and thus have the opportunity of 'translating' new thoughts and new ideas into their own cultures. This is an issue that confronted German writers anxious to develop their own national literature as they sought a political and cultural identity: what precisely did they seek as they looked to France or (as was increasingly the case as the eighteenth century progressed) to England for texts to 'translate'?

This is a 'translation' issue that M. H. Abrams pursues in *Natural Supernaturalism* with reference to Herder and Gotthold Ephraim Lessing (1729–81), another theology student, but one who soon transferred his energies to literary production. In 1776, in *The Oldest Documents of the Human Race*, Herder 'translated the Biblical account of Eden, the fall, and the restoration into his version of universal history; for the Scriptural story, he said, though told with a simplicity appropriate to children, embodies the true history both of the entire human race and of each member of the race' (Abrams 1971, 202–3). In Lessing's essay of 1780, 'The Education of the Human Race':

> [he] translated the scriptural revelation of man's fall and redemption into a secular history of mankind's progressive education in reason and morality, assimilated external Providence to an imminent historical principle, equated the stages of

civilization to stages in the maturation of an individual, and represented the educational process in the persistent metaphor of a laborious journey on the long road toward perfection.' (Ibid., 201–2)

Abrams links this powerful and complex influence of Christian thinking in German Romanticism specifically to the means by which Wordsworth worked out his 'Programme for Poetry'; he argues that Wordsworth saw himself as:

> . . . the latest in the line of poets inspired by the 'prophetic Spirit,' and as such has been granted a 'Vision' which sanctions his claim to outdo Milton's Christian story in the scope and audacious novelty of his subject. The vision is that of the awesome depths and height of the human mind, and of the power of that mind as in itself adequate, by consummating a holy marriage with the external universe, to create out of the world of all of us, in a quotidian and recurrent miracle, a new world which is the equivalent of paradise. (Ibid., 28)

As Herder, in the last year of his life, turned the pages of his copy of Wordsworth's *Lyrical Ballads*, what was happening as he translated the poems he saw there? Crabb Robinson noted that Herder 'agreed with Wordsworth as to poetical language', and that there was also 'a general sympathy between the two in matters of morality and religion' (Robinson 1967, 154). Was translation in this instance essentially the same process as that implied by Abrams when he described both Herder and Lessing as 'translating' the scriptures into 'universal history', and into a 'secular history of mankind's progressive education in reason and morality'?

George Steiner has also discussed the profound significance of religion upon the development of linguistics and the activity of translation. In *After Babel* (1975) he comments specifically on the way Hamann, in the 1760s, undertook a comparative examination of the French and German languages. Hamann, he affirms, based his method on the following belief taken from his own linguistic culture:

> Hebrew verb forms are inseparable from the niceties and strict punctualities that mark Jewish ritual. But that which a language reveals as being the specific genius of a community, the language itself has shaped and determined. The process is dialectical, with the formative energies of language moving both inward and outward in a civilization. (Steiner 1998, 80)

Herder, Steiner goes on to argue, took what he calls Hamann's 'fantastications' a step forward into the Enlightenment, but for all that, 'the theory of a divine act of special bestowal was never far from Herder's thoughts' (Ibid., 81). A religious strand was inextricably woven into a habit of thinking, at the heart of which lay an interrogation of language. The history of the way in which translation became perceived as an imperative undertaking in Europe, Steiner reminds us, revolves to a significant degree around the drive to disseminate the Christian faith:

> In the two centuries between the reign of Pope Nicolas and Urquhart's Rabelais (1653), the history of translation coincides with and informs that of Western thought and feeling. No 'original' composition was more creative of new intellectual, social possibilities than were Erasmus's version of the New Testament (1516) or the Luther Bible (1522–34). (Ibid., 259)

Theology remained a central preoccupation for German writers of the Enlightenment, from the time when French classicism was a dominating influence, through the vogue for sensibility, the *Sturm und Drang*, the so-called *Frühromantik*, Romanticism, and Weimar classicism. Friedrich Schleiermacher (1768–1834), who became Professor of Theology at Halle University in 1804, was a major influence on German Romanticism, combining his fervent religious faith with an appeal to the primacy of feeling, contemplation, and intuition. Jeremy Munday notes that 'Schleiermacher is recognized as the founder of modern Protestant theology and of modern hermeneutics, a Romantic approach to interpretation based not on absolute truth but on the individual's inner feeling and understanding.' He also quotes Kittel and Polterman's view that 'practically every modern translation theory – at least in the German-language area – responds, in one way or another, to Schleiermacher's hypotheses. There appear to have been no fundamentally new approaches' (Munday 2001, 27–8). However, if students go to *The Oxford Companion to German Literature* for a brief guide to Schleiermacher's achievement, while they find a clear statement of the way religion lay at the heart of his 'Romanticism', they find there no hint at all of the way the issue of translation is inextricably bound up with the development of his ideas.

There is very little in the matter of the previous few paragraphs which looks compatible with the secularizing Enlightenment vision of the contributors to the *Encyclopédie*. One reason why Wordsworth attracted German minds throughout the nineteenth century was without doubt the religious, pietistic strain discernible in so much of his poetry.

English Literature and Eighteenth-Century German Culture

'In days of yore, there were Englishmen here, who passed their time pleasantly enough, and some of whom I remember with esteem and regret.'

> Goethe to R. P. Gillies in
> Zonneveld, 2004, 326

In the early years of the eighteenth century, French literature rigidly based on classical models exerted a powerful influence over German writers. However, in the course of seeking out the original classical sources, an enthusiasm for the work of English writers evolved. Addison, Pope, and Thomson recommended themselves because of their association with French classicism, and they remained popular throughout the century. Johann Mattheson produced the first German imitation of *The Spectator* in 1713–14. Luise Gottsched translated *The Spectator* in 1739 and *The Guardian* ten years later directly from the English and not, as had previously been the case, from French translations. With the increasing popularity of Shakespeare, however, the hegemony of French formal rules began to fall away.

A passionate debate developed around the relative merits of classicism that informed the evolution of German literature on through the nineteenth century. Luise Gottsched's husband, Johann Christoph (1700–66), strenuously insisted on the primacy of the French classical model for German writers. He was initially opposed by Johann Bodmer (1698–1783) and Johann Breitinger (1701–76). A significant part of their opposition to Gottsched's prescriptive classicism was expressed through their recommendation of English literary models rather than the French. Among his many translations of English poetry, Bodmer published a prose translation of Milton's *Paradise Lost* in 1750–52, and in the latter years of his life numerous ballads from Thomas Percy's *Reliques of Ancient English Poetry* (1765).

There could be little doubt whose side Friedrich Wilhelm Zachariä was on in this debate. His poem *Tageszeiten* was published in 1756, and in it he stressed what was by then a commonplace conviction relating to the racial and linguistic common ground between the British and the Germans. The French are Gallic slaves, held in thrall by their grammatical rules, while German Saxon blood flows in the veins of free British bards:

> Und warum ists falscher Geschmack, dem Britten zu folgen?
> Ist er nicht näher mit uns verwandt, als Galliens Sklaven,
> Denen Gebrauch und Grammatik die stäksten Flügel beschneiden?
> Deutsches sächsisches Blut schlägt in Brittanniens Barden.

Milton, widely translated and admired in Germany, is described by Zachariä as reincarnated in poets like Bodmer and Klopstock:

> Grosser Milton, wer könnt, auch bey uns dich schöner verewgen,
> Als ein Bodmer und Klopstock durch ihre göttlichen Lieder!
> (Price 1968, 27)

England received many visitors from Germany, including Christian Wernicke (1661–1725), Albrecht von Haller (1708–77), and Karl Moritz (1756–93), while Caspar Wilhelm von Borcke (1704–47), for a time head of the Prussian Legation in London, was one of the earliest translators of Shakespeare, producing an entirely versified rendering of *Julius Caesar* in 1741. Helferich Sturz (1736–79) and Georg Lichtenberg (1742–99) met with Johnson, Macpherson, and Garrick while in England. Lichtenberg and Sturz, Roger Paulin notes, were of the same generation as Johann Joachim Eschenburg (1743–1820), 'Germany's first real Shakespeare expert' (Paulin 2003, 115). This was a generation 'for whom English is not a mysterious language read properly by a few, but the essential key to a literary culture encompassing Shakespeare and Ossian, but so many central texts of European sensibility and empiricism besides' (ibid., 119). Christlob Mylius (1722–54) arrived in England in the early 1750s with plans to write a comprehensive history of English literature, an ambition cut short by his early death. Friedrich von Hagedorn (1708–54), Justus Möser (1720–94), and Johann Hamann (1730–88), were all decisively influenced by visiting England, and specifically the London in which were to be found Pope, Thomson, Richardson, Gray, Young, and Mallett.

The English writers' engagement with their own cultural history was a source of inspiration to German writers like Herder, Goethe and Möser, committed to establishing a German cultural identity. This was reflected in many of the journals and in works like Thomas Warton's *History of English Poetry* (1774–81) and Samuel Johnson's *Lives of the Poets* (1779–81) – a recurring point of reference for the Eschenburg generation after 1774 – and in Percy's *Reliques of Ancient English Poetry* (in Bodmer's translation). *Von deutscher Art und Kunst* of 1773 included essays on Shakespeare and Ossian by Herder, *Von Deutsche Baukunst* by Goethe, and *Deutsche Geschichte* by Möser. *Von Deutsche Art und Kunst* is generally taken to be the manifesto of early German Romanticism, the *Sturm und Drang*, a topic that continues to be controversial (see Beiser, 2003);

but however these developments are described in relation to German cultural history, the influence of English writers was clearly deeply ingrained, and would thus continue despite the consequences of the French Revolution and its aftermath.

The importance of religious themes, of a pietistic, moralizing tradition, clearly drew German writers and translators to specific English writers. What was true of people, was true also for certain locations. In the case of Zürich, Lawrence Price notes that the affiliation with England dated back to the sixteenth century, when English Protestants fleeing from the persecutions of Queen Mary sheltered there. English Divines translated by Bodmer, Waser, Tobler and others include John Tillotson, Jeremy Taylor, Isaac Barrow, James Hervey, and Richard Hurd. Edward Young's edition of letters by Elizabeth Singer Rowe, *Friendship in Death*, was translated into German by Johann Mattheson (1681–1764) in 1734. Mattheson (already noted here for his German *Spectator*) was from Hamburg. Along with Leipzig, Zürich, and Göttingen, Hamburg was an important centre for the dissemination of English literature. Mattheson remains best known for his translations of one of the great eighteenth-century English moralist novelists, Samuel Richardson. His *Pamela* appeared in 1742, *Clarissa* in 1748, and he published *Sir Charles Grandison* in 1754. He translated Rowe's *Devout Exercises* (published in England in 1739) in 1754. Price suggests that in mid-eighteenth-century Leipzig, Klopstock, Cramer, Giseke, and Ebert 'celebrated Elizabeth Rowe almost as much as Young' (Price 1968, 149). In his *Tageszeiten* of 1756, Zachariä points to the influence of Rowe on the poetry of Christoph Wieland (1733–1813): 'Die unsterbliche Rowe singt aus dem fühlenden Wieland' (Price 1968, 27). Young's pietistic *Night Thoughts* (1742–5) found numerous translators, including Herder, Wieland, Gerstenberg, Lenz, Ebert, Klopstock, Hamann, Bodmer, and Cramer. Writing to Young in 1759, Samuel Richardson reported the receipt of letters in praise of *Night Thoughts*, adding, 'In Germany, they revere Dr Young in his works more than they do those of any other British genius' (Young 1971, 499).

Price writes that 'in the attempt to imitate the English models, new concepts were added to the German language; friendship, religious fervour, patriotism, sentimentality, religious introspection, a feeling for popular poetry' (Price 1968, 20). Embedded here are two preoccupations that, when it came to reading the first generation of the English Romantic poets, might have been expected to recommend Wordsworth for close inspection. Besides a generally religious tenor to the work, the recurrence of a solitary wanderer motif helps to explain why 'The Solitary Reaper' and the Lucy poems were to feature regularly as anthologized pieces, and why *The Excursion*, with its humbly born but theologically minded itinerant narrator, also attracted attention. Frederick Beiser argues that in Germany 'The heart of romantic social and political thought is their ideal of community', pointing out that this has its origins in classical sources, 'especially Plato and Aristotle' (Beiser 2003, 36). Hamann had written 'Togetherness ["Geselligkeit"] is the true principal of reason and language . . .' (Berlin 1956, 274), and Wordsworth was seen to be writing not only about life in rural communities, and the beliefs and experiences of people living in such communities, he was also understood to be playing a dominant role himself in fostering a community of poets in a corner of England that boasted a landscape of forests, mountains, and lakes with which German readers could immediately identify.

Central to much of the theoretical material that was being discussed in mid-eighteenth-century Germany was the role of language. In 1758 the fourth number of Gotthold Ephraim Lessing's *Theatralische Bibliothek* included Friedrich Nicolai's history of English drama. It argued for the paramountcy of English drama in the modern age. Lessing (1729–81) contributed extracts from Dryden's essay 'Of Dramatick Poesie' (1668), and Paulin comments that this 'was a convenient way of confirming things closest to Lessing's heart'

> that naturalness and freedom from the unities and other artificial constraints (such as rhyme), even if this entailed the loss of traditional distinctions between tragedy and comedy, were part of the dramatist's resources in presenting strong passions and, through them, of moving the human heart. (Paulin 2003, 84)

Edward Young's *Conjectures on Original Composition* (1759) was translated into German in 1760. This was followed in 1763 by Joseph Warton's 'An Essay on the Genius and Writings of Pope' (1756). Young's enthusiasm for spontaneity, 'the unruliness of genius . . . the force of creative imagination' (Ibid., 141) was enthusiastically received, not least by Heinrich Wilhelm Gerstenberg (1737–1823), who published *Letters on the Curiosities of Literature* in 1766–7 extolling the quality of genius, specifically as it manifested itself in Shakespeare (Ibid., 140). His writings anticipate the *Sturm und Drang*, and of his contemporaries, he singles out Lessing and Herder for particular praise. Writing on Young's *Conjectures*, Herder commented:

> Why does a flame of fire leap at us when reading Young's work on original composition, such as we do not feel with mere compilations? Because Young's spirit is present in all of it, speaking as it were from his heart to our hearts, as an electric spark is transmitted. (Ibid., 136)

It is easy to appreciate, therefore, the appeal of Warton, who privileged the power of inspiration in the raw over 'wit' and 'sense' in his account of the development of English poetry.

Assessing the significance of the British theorists on Herder, Price writes:

> Herder openly defended the *Conjectures* and the same year [1766] he copied passages from them into his notebook. The following year he quoted Young twice directly and after that but rarely . . . Much weightier was the combined influence of Lady Mary Montagu, Samuel Johnson, Henry Home, John Brown, and Richard Hurd. Baumgarten and Mendelssohn were in some respects the predecessors of Home, but it was Home who first advocated the subjective and psychological conception of poetry as an approach to literary criticism. Herder mentions Home as early as 1766. (Price 1968, 295)

Crabb Robinson's assertion that Herder and Wordsworth had much in common does seem to be well founded. If we return to Herder's *Shakespeare* essay of 1773 in *Von deutscher Art und Kunst*, Roger Paulin has argued that it is possible to track the development of a frame of mind that accords increasingly with the preoccupations that begin also to emerge from Wordsworth's poems in *Lyrical Ballads*. Herder begins this essay with Young's *Conjectures* clearly in mind, as well as Gerstenberg's *Briefe über die neure deutsche Literatur*. He then moves on to be influenced by Henry Home's ideas on what we have seen Price summarize as the 'subjective and psychological conception' of how the critic should relate to his subject. He is also clearly aware of Samuel Johnson's literary criticism, of John Brown writing on poetry and music, of Hurd, and of Elizabeth Montagu's *Essay on the Genius and Writings of Shakespeare*. As Herder developed his historicism, he began to connect an early form of folk expression, endemically 'simple' (as with the Greeks, Ossian, and the early balladeers reproduced in Percy's *Reliques of Ancient English Poetry*), to an expression of the same essential truths expressed through the mind of an inspired genius. Here we have also a theory that may be used to help us understand what motivated Wordsworth not only to write about the unsophisticated peasant child in 'We Are Seven', and the Highland girl in 'The Solitary Reaper', but also to attempt to capture something of their actual utterance. Both poems were frequently reproduced in German anthologies. The Highland girl sings in a language Wordsworth has to translate intuitively, taking the music as his guide, 'Will no one tell me what she sings?':

> The music in my heart I bore,
> Long after it was heard no more.
>
> (Wordsworth 1983, 185)

Herder would have understood this. Consider now the way Paulin summarizes Herder's *Shakespeare* essay, 'language and poetry, and their product and culture, grow organically out of time and place, following the genetic processes of nature itself and tapping the resources of life in being' (Paulin 2003, 149). We might equally apply this belief to the thinking that informs Wordsworth's 'The Solitary Reaper'.

Goethe's classical turn in the late 1770s, and indeed his avowed disinterest if not dislike of Wordsworth, is of little significance for the broader picture of Wordsworth's reception in nineteenth-century Germany. The influence of Goethe's views on later critics who came to assess the reception of the British Romantics, however, is not to be underrated. Pointner and Geisenhanslüke have commented on the remarkable power of Goethe's pronouncements, particularly with respect to the ascendancy of Byron (Cardwell 2004, 240). The fact remains that Goethe's views were far from universally accepted, even if there was an unwillingness to contradict the great man openly. German readers were able to see that Wordsworth's disconcerting tendency to 'simplicity' was offset by a philosophical profundity that harked back to traditions of classical thought with which they were familiar. His poetry was imbued with an engagement with the forces of nature, and with a language that sought to replicate the processes of nature through deeply religious and patriotic fervour. Yet for all that, they could also see that Wordsworth remained very aware of the historical moment and of the political issues at stake; they could relish the political sonnets in which he defied the Imperial ambitions of Napoleon, and indeed lauded one of their heroes, Andreas Hofer.

When we consider Friedrich Schlegel's ideas on the concept of 'romantische Poesie' at the turn of the century, it becomes further evident why the range of Wordsworth's poetry was to catch the notice of German readers in the course of the second decade of the nineteenth century. Schlegel, along with his brother August Wilhelm, Schelling and Novalis, revert to Plato and Aristotle to explore the word 'poetic' as meaning to make, or create, something. Amelia, a character in Friedrich Schlegel's *Gespräch über Poesie* (1800) is driven to ask at one point, 'Is everything then poetry?' (Beiser 2003, 16). With Schlegel – and others – challenging the notion of 'poetry' as confined within a single literary genre, we can in consequence appreciate the attraction of a poet who could write in 'Simon Lee, The Old Huntsman', lines that seem to offer to redefine what the 'gentle reader' understands as the literary identity of 'poetry':

> O reader! Had you in your mind
> Such stores as silent thought can bring,
> O gentle reader! You would find
> A tale in every thing.
> What more I have to say is short,
> I hope you'll kindly take it;
> It is no tale; but should you think,
> Perhaps a tale you'll make it.
>
> (Wordsworth 1992, 67)

The English cult of pietistical sentimentality continued to strike a deep chord within German literature, and when, in the 1790s, F. Schlegel, Schelling, and Novalis were developing their views on 'romantische Poesie', it bore fruit in the idea that 'poetry' should be understood as a comprehensive term defining an aesthetic ideal drawing upon all aspects of life. The creativity of the artist was an expression of the universal power or energy behind all things; what Herder called 'die Urkraft aller Kräfte' (Beiser 2003, 21). These ideas found their way back into the English Romantic movement in the context of the pantheism that so engaged Coleridge through the 1790s. The natural world was thus central to the aesthetic ideal, as was the quest for self-revelation; this is a form of 'Bildung' – self-knowledge – that rests also on social integration, on a sense of community, and in no small degree on the relationship of language and translatability to ideas of society and personal identity. As we have seen, Beiser argues that this took Schlegel and others back to classical sources, to Plato and Aristotle, in the process creating a tension between Christian and Classical cultural models. This becomes clearly apparent in the poetry of Friedrich Hölderlin (1770–1843):

> My Master and Lord!
> O you, my teacher!
> Why did you keep
> Away? And when
> I asked among the ancients
> The heroes and
> The gods, then why were you
> Not there? And now my soul
> Is full of sadness as though
> You Heavenly yourselves excitedly cried
> That if I serve one I
> Must lack the other.
>
> ('The Only One', *Der Einzige* in Hamburger 2004, 537)

These issues remained deeply embedded in German cultural life for the next century, and the assimilation of English literary sources since the early eighteenth century played a key role in their development. With this in mind, we continue to see why, of all English poets, Wordsworth should retain a fascination for the heirs of Hamann, Herder, Schlegel and Novalis. Wordsworth's poetic subjects took him beyond traditional 'poetic' subject matter to include common people such as the solitary reaper, Simon Lee, and the protagonists of *The Excursion*, while *The Excursion* also gave its readers reason to reflect on the consequences of a new age of industry and factory labour. Wordsworth was manifestly religious in his celebration of the natural world; he wrote about community and alienation, and it was these themes, combined with his strong sense of the past and its continuity with present religious and political strife that commended him to German readers throughout the nineteenth century.

After 1850, alongside recurring lyrics of *Bildung*, Wordsworth could be seen devoting a major work, *The Prelude*, to the same theme. His verse was rarely free from political engagement, and he was known as a poet with a strong communitarian spirit. It is, therefore, small wonder that 'The Solitary Reaper' and 'We are Seven', a poem of *Bildung* set in a rural community, should be regularly chosen for anthologizing. It is equally not surprising that from the late 1830s Ferdinand Freiligrath identified the themes of politics and nature that coexist in 'Yew Trees' and that are dramatically represented in the extracts from *The Excursion* that he chose to anthologize. Bearing in mind Beiser's point that German Romanticism remained indebted to classical ideas, it is also important to be reminded that both Wordsworth's poetry and his political beliefs retained very clear indicators of his attachment to the Classical models he had absorbed in his schooldays at Hawkshead and continued to cherish. The tensions epitomized in Hölderlin between Christianity and Classical sources were clearly discernible in much of Wordsworth's poetry, not least *The Excursion*, which maintained its position as a major work in the eyes of German Wordsworthians from Jacobsen in 1820 to Felix Güttler in 1914.

The reception of Wordsworth in Germany is contextualized by a view of art that strove for inclusiveness, that identified the importance of origins in primitive folk traditions (such as those to be found in Percy and Ossian), that recognized a profoundly spiritual strand within the inspirational experience of the artist, and seized upon the natural world – its forests, its lakes, and its mountains – and love of country, as also being central. Wordsworth was seen in many ways to embody in his poetry, as in his life, precisely these qualities, though he could frequently do so in tantalizingly obscure, convoluted ways calculated to render the process of translation a major challenge.

2   Revolution and War: Germany, the 'New English Poetry' and Wordsworth's Arrival on the Printed Page

England and Germany: The Context of Romanticism

'"Liberty and Equality!" is the cry. The quiet citizen reaches for his weapon . . .'
Schiller, The Lay of the Bell in Forster 1957, 276

This chapter is concerned with the period in Germany's history which sees the remarkable flowering of cultural life within a nation for which nationhood remained as yet little more than an idea. Writing of de Staël's *De l'Allemagne* (1810), John Isbell suggests that 'In 1810, Germany did not exist. Staël's first job was to invent it' (Isbell 1994, 6). Isbell's eagerness to emphasize the extent of de Staël's unreliability as a chronicler of German cultural history, however, led him to underestimate the extent to which nationhood was emerging as an influential aspiration at the end of the first decade in nineteenth-century Germany. In 1806 the Prussian army had been defeated at Jena-Auerstädt. 'Romanticism' was in consequence defiantly defined in the context of nationalist aspirations. Political leadership was supplied by Friedrich Wilhelm III of Prussia. At the heart of this movement was the new Berlin University, founded in 1810 by Wilhelm von Humboldt. Johann Gottlieb Fichte was already teaching in Berlin and became its first rector. Fichte's was a defining voice in the changing intellectual climate, demanding in his *Reden an die deutsche Nation* of 1807–8 total subservience in the arts to the nationalist cause, in the process insisting on the centrality of the German language to the project. Drawing on Kant and Schiller, Fichte affirmed that 'no individual must be treated as a means, but only as an end in himself, a free agent' (Silz 1929, 10). Those joining him at Berlin included Friedrich Schleiermacher, Friedrich Schelling, Karl Solger and Friedrich Wolf. It is through Schleiermacher in particular that we can see how a nationalist agenda lay at the heart of the development of translation theories that were destined to influence the nature of cultural relations through to the present day. Still best known for his work as a theologian and philosopher, it was Schleiermacher's hermeneutics that informed his essay of 1813, *Über die verschiedenen Methoden des Übersetzens.*

Just one year earlier, 1812, the year of Napoleon's disastrous Russian campaign, Theodor Körner, Ernst Moritz Arndt, Baron de la Motte Fouqué and Friedrich Jahn, followed Fichte's call to the point of taking up arms against the enemy, as did the artists Friedrich Kersting (1785–1847), Philipp Veit (1793–1877) and Ferdinand Olivier (1785–1841). Between 1812 and 1814 Caspar David Friedrich produced some of his most overtly political canvasses, including *The Tomb of Arminius, Tombs of the Fallen in the Fight for Independence* and *The Chausseur in the Woods*. *The Chausseur* shows an unhorsed French soldier staring into an impenetrable German pine forest, watched by a raven. With an eye to French censorship, reviewers of Friedrich's paintings – who included Arnim and Brentano – pointed out the patriotic messages embedded in these and other works (Wolf 2003, 31–41). Fichte also inspired Heinrich von Kleist (1777–1811), for whom the debacle of Jena proved a turning point in his political thinking. His play of 1808, *Die Hermannsschlacht*, though published posthumously, reflects the steady development of a sense of German nationalism through the last decades of the Napoleonic Wars. Kleist had been nurtured in the beliefs of the German Enlightenment. His disillusionment prompted the composition of a series of remarkable and disturbing stories, terminating in his suicide in 1811.

Heidelberg in particular became a refuge for German nationalism during this period, attracting leading Romantics from Jena, including Creuzer, Brentano, Arnim, Voss, Thibaut and Klüber. Heidelberg, Jon Vanden Heuvel explains, was where Görres developed his idea that 'all culture is national, and must be understood in national terms':

> The German language provided the key to the German national spirit . . . Görres embraced a romantic nationalism, an appreciation of that which German culture had passed down over the ages. The cultural inheritance, he believed, was a guide-post for what Germany ought to be. (Heuvel 2001, 123)

Lilian Furst, however, while noting the nationalist strand in Heidelberg Romanticism, comments also on the way writers became involved in exploring 'the irrational aspects of life – the so-called "nocturnal sides of nature"', producing 'a host of supernatural and fantastic stories, such as those of Tieck, Kleist, and Hoffmann' (Furst 1969, 40).

One explanation of the way a nationalist spirit evolved during this period may well have been the disparate nature of the German states. This is what Friedrich Perthes (1772–1843) believed, in contradiction to Goethe's contention that Germany needed a capital city to promote a unified literary culture. In 1816 Perthes, a book dealer in Hamburg, pointed out that where the English looked to London and the French to Paris for their culture, the Germans looked to '*Germany*': '. . . the most splendid intellectual blossoms and the deepest ponderings arise in hundreds of German cities and villages' (Kontje 1998, 96–7).

The growth of nationalist aspirations in Germany meant that cultural relationships between Germany and Britain began to undergo significant changes from the 1770s onward. Although the direct influence of British writers became less marked, the extent to which German culture had absorbed English language texts since the early eighteenth century ensured that there would be an important strand of British influence running through the complex evolution of German literature, criticism and philosophy. It is, however, worth noting at this point that a contemporary estimate puts the figure of literate Germans in 1775 at 20,000 out of a population of 20 million, while in 1800, Jean Paul estimated that the number had risen to 300,000, (Saul 2000, 208–9). Johann

Wolfgang Goethe (1749–1832) swiftly came to epitomize the coming of age of German culture at this time. While Goethe's importance remains paramount, Nicholas Saul questions the degree of centrality it has. Goethe's major works, he agrees, 'embody the conflicts of the age refracted through his own experience', but he concludes that 'this kind of monolithic model no longer explains what we know of the literary situation [in Germany] and its development.' Nicholas Boyle, he notes, 'has gone so far as to present Goethe himself as the great outsider of his own time.' Saul looks elsewhere for the basis of an overview of the literature of this period in Germany, suggesting that 'literature's role from 1790 to 1830 was in general to respond creatively to historical events, both political and cultural' (Saul 2000, 202–3).

It is with this in mind that we should reflect on how the new 'Romantic' writing in Britain attracted German readers. When Saul argues that German literature after 1790 finds its identity in terms of 'political and cultural' events, what he has primarily in mind are the consequences of the French Revolution. These were the Revolutionary wars of 1792–1807, the collapse of the Holy Roman Empire, the French occupation of Prussia in 1806, the fight for German liberation between 1812 and 1815, the founding of the German Federation in 1815, and the onset of a period of reactionary government epitomized in the Karlsbad Decrees of 1819. Looking back to this period from 1826, Heinrich Heine, in 'The Emperor and the Drummer', characterized it as a time when 'there was a great deal of promotion among princes; old kings got new uniforms, and new kingdoms were cooked up and sold like hot cakes ...' (Heine 1943, 229). This brings us to the end of the period considered in this chapter, a moment marked by the publication in 1820 of Friedrich Jacobsen's extensive review of English poetry during this period, his *Briefe an eine deutsche Edelfrau, über die neuesten englischen Dichter.*

The major cultural event of the period for Germany which, according to Saul, shaped its literary evolution, is secularization, 'the decline and fall of traditional religion following the challenge to externalized religious authority by secular reason which is Enlightenment's signature.' Sacred institutions were formally abolished in 1803 and Saul draws attention to the way that German literature throughout this period 'always resonates with the sense of religious loss' (Ibid., 203). Steven Ozment describes how this was brought about: All but three Rhenish ecclesiastical principalities were secularized: 45 of 51 free imperial cities ceased to exist; and the larger states cannibalized the private lands of the imperial knights. Also vanishing for ever were 112 small southern and western states, most absorbed by Baden, Bavaria, Württemberg and Hesse-Darmstadt (Ozment 2005, 158). The loss suffered in 1803 was profound; three years earlier Görres, Eickemeyer and Linz had been in Paris to deliver a 'scathing indictment of French rule in Germany'. Görres returned before the others and in despair wrote in his report: 'for the present generation, freedom is lost' (Heuvel 2001, 88–9).

The political and social circumstances were manifestly different from those in England, therefore. However, as M. H. Abrams argues in *Natural Supernaturalism*, during this period there remain important parallels between Britain and Germany to be perceived in the spread of 'Natural Supernaturalism' (Abrams 1971, 11–16). Through his study of the nature of Wordsworth's religious convictions, Abrams argues that German writers found in his poetry a voice that resonated with many of the issues that formed the legacy of their own political and religious upheavals of 1789–1815 and their aftermath. Görres writes of the German tendency to value the inner life ('Innerlichkeit'), as opposed to the Frenchman's preference for 'externals' which renders them (the French) fickle and unreliable (Heuvel 2001, 90–1). Wordsworth's Preface to the 1800 edition of *Lyrical Ballads* might therefore be expected to have far more to offer a German than a French reader. After a long list of reasons for choosing 'Low and Rustic life' as a setting for many of the poems, Wordsworth concludes by claiming that, 'in that situation the passions of men are incorporated with the beautiful and permanent forms of nature.' Permanence perceived through a process of mature contemplation ('my habits of meditation') on 'the essential passions of the heart' is a key motif throughout the Preface and closely resembles the German 'Innerlichkeit' (Wordsworth 1992, 743–4). A somewhat more ironic reflection on the outcome of the German perception of the 'inner life' as it related to liberty came from Heine, who in 'Liberty and National Character', written in 1830, commented that when 'The German' began to reflect (in the manner of the English and the French) that liberty might be worth having, 'his philosophers wisely taught him to doubt the existence of such things' (Heine 1943, 61).

When he was in his late twenties, Wordsworth – like Kleist – went through the painful process of jettisoning his commitment to secular, rational, radical politics, turning instead to an ideal of social and political reform that incorporated a faith in spiritual and numinous forces manifest in the natural world. His play *The Borderers* (1796) rehearses the torment of transition; *The Ruined Cottage*, begun in 1796 and eventually incorporated into *The Excursion* of 1814, begins to articulate the credo that German readers were beginning to encounter in poems dating back to Wordsworth's *Lyrical Ballads* collection, first published in 1798. They would recognize in Wordsworth's profound attachment to religion the basis of their own philosophical traditions, though the fact remains that 'supernaturalism' had been rendered 'natural' in ways that signified profound change. In England and Germany, Abrams argues, so-called 'Romantic' writers 'undertook . . . to save traditional concepts, schemes and values which had been based on the relation of the Creator to his creatures and creation.' This was to be done by reformulating such concepts, schemes and values 'within the . . . human mind or consciousness and its transactions with nature' (Abrams 1971, 13).

Considerations such as these help to explain why the portrayal of German writing during this period as essentially apolitical has been the subject of repeated scrutiny. Mary Fulbrook argues that the a-politicization of German culture should be understood as a consequence of circumstances where the impulse to political and social reform could be followed through by members of the professional classes like von Humboldt, rather than by 'independent critical intellectuals as in France' (Fulbrook 2004, 91). Ozment, comparing German and French society at this time, emphasizes the difference by explaining that, compared to France:

> There was no comparable, commercially successful, property-owning German bourgeoisie to attack, nor masses of *sans culottes* ready to hurl themselves against the rich and privileged. (Ozment 2005, 155)

It is less surprising than it might at first seem, therefore, that Edmund Burke's *Reflections on the Revolution in France* of 1790 sold more copies in Germany when it first appeared than it did in England. Saul argues that while Novalis embraced Burke's conservatism, his acceptance of the Revolution as a phase of natural evolution on the part of humanity toward perfection renders him at the same time 'modern and progressive' (Saul 2000, 233). This invites comparison with Wordsworth's changing view of Burke, charted most specifically through revisions he made to *The Prelude* after 1805. Wordsworth's evolving views on Church and State are also expressed in sections of *The Excursion* and other poems made available to German readers by the time Jacobsen published his *Letters* in 1820. These include *The White Doe of Rylstone*, set in the sixteenth century, which in turn prompts a comparison with the Romantic medievalism of Novalis, an influence on Friedrich and Dorothea Schlegel, Zacharias Werner, Johann von Görres, Adam Müller and Clemens Brentano.

In order to understand further the relationship between English and German literature as it had evolved by 1820, it will be helpful to take an overview of the appearance of a series of German literary movements which were partly a reaction against English literary infiltration from the 1770s and partly complemented contemporary English imports. Cultural historians have mapped this period by identifying first the appearance of the *Geniezeit* or *Sturm und Drang* movement, the 'manifesto' for which is frequently cited as the collection of essays published by Herder in 1773, *Von deutscher Art und Kunst*. The movement acquired its most familiar name from the title of a play of 1777 by Friedrich Klinger, characterized by extremes of emotion and excessive celebration of freedom and nature. The former was particularly evident in Goethe's novel of 1774, *The Sorrows of Young Werther*, in which the hero commits suicide as a result of unrequited love – but not before he has exclaimed, 'Ossian has ousted Homer from my heart' (Goethe 2006, 107). Goethe's verdict on Werther remains ambivalent; he appealed to a readership thirsting for emotional excess, but as the novel proceeds, Werther's infatuation is portrayed as increasingly obsessional – a weakness to be denigrated rather than a virtue to be applauded. In 1774 German readers were also able to compare the fate of Werther with that of his British *doppelgänger*, Harley, the hero of Henry Mackenzie's *The Man of Feeling*, written in 1770 and translated into German by C. G. Lessing. Harley's death is less violent than Werther's, however; a broken heart alone is sufficient to finish him off. It was Mackenzie's paper on the German Drama delivered to the Royal Society of Edinburgh in 1788 that first introduced Schiller to the British public through *Die Räuber* (Mackenzie was working from the French translation by Friedel and De Bonneville based on the version prepared for performance at Mannheim). The play was described as 'one of the most uncommon productions that modern times can boast'; Schiller's characters were 'drawn from the sources of an ardent and creative imagination' and expressed themselves 'with a language in the highest degree eloquent, impassioned and sublime' (Rea 1906, 8).

Sturm und Drang is frequently differentiated from the Romanticism that followed by a brief early romantic, or *Frühromantik* phase. German Romanticism, then, flourished under the influence of Herder and the brothers August Wilhelm and Friedrich von Schlegel. A. W. Schlegel moved to Jena University in 1795 and was joined there by his brother in 1796. Classicism was championed at this time by Goethe in nearby Weimar. The difficult relationship between these two camps is epitomized by the awkward but productive relationship that ran through the 1790s (against the background of an increasingly fraught political situation) between Schiller, the reformed disciple of *Sturm und Drang*, and Goethe. The fall of Napoleon has been seen as signalling the onset of the so-called *Biedermeier* period that ran from 1815 to 1848, in which literature and the arts reflected 'withdrawal into the private sphere of the home and family . . . the respect for traditional, middle-class values such as stability and order, moderation and modesty, and the preservation of the status quo' (Saul 2000, 292). If R. P. Gillies is to be believed, 'Herr Advocat Jacobsen', the anglophile author of the *Letters . . . on the New English Poetry*, was the very model of the *Biedermeier* German (Gillies 1851, 270). Embedded within this broadly defined context are evolving preoccupations destined to shape the way the new British Romantic Period writers were to be selected, interpreted and – in both the critical and linguistic sense – translated into German. If we look at early nineteenth-century Journals such as the *Jenaische allgemeine Literatur-Zeitung*, it becomes very clear that well established eighteenth-century writers such as Defoe, Richardson, Percy, Young and Hurd remained important and respected points of cultural reference. The next generation, however, beginning with Goldsmith and Macpherson's *Ossian* and including women novelists such as Sophia Lee, Ann Howell and Phoebe Gibbs, were every bit as eagerly sought after, both as imports and as models for aspiring German authors.

The weave between German and British literary cultures is thus a complex one. Herder's intense nationalism reflected in the aspirations of *Sturm und Drang* writers might seem to leave little room for the recognition of external influences. At first sight his enthusiasm for the German Middle Ages, volubly reinforced by Friedrich Klopstock's portrayal of the German forests as the home of the tribal Druids, gave rise to what we might consider an intrinsically German institution, the *Göttinger Hainbund* of 1772. This was a brotherhood of German students at Göttingen University, who swore eternal friendship, pledging their poetic output to the rejuvenation of the Fatherland. Included in the Bund were H. C. Boie, F. W. Gotter, J. H. Voss, L. C. Holtz and J. M. Miller. But even here it transpires that the influence of English literature is not far away. Göttingen University was founded in the 1730s; Leipzig, Hamburg and Zürich were already established centres of English influence, the Leipzig publisher, J. G. Beygang 'owned a *Cabinet de Lecture* with over two thousand French, English and Italian works', while J. C. Seiler's catalogue for 1780 included 59 English volumes (Brown 2005, 32). Göttingen was soon to rival them in this respect. Haller and Michaelis were Anglophiles and Lichtenberg – a regular visitor to England – encouraged a steady stream of visiting English students, the best known of whom was to be Coleridge who arrived in 1799, the year after Lichtenberg died. Many of the *Göttinger Hainbund* poets coached English writers in German and gave English lessons to Germans at the University (Price 1968, 32–3). It is from Göttingen that the earliest reference in print to Wordsworth's poetry was to emanate in 1804.

In 1773, in the *Göttinger Musenalmanach*, the literary vehicle of the *Hainbund*, Gottfried Bürger, one of the most distinguished members of the group, published his ballad of *Lenore*. The origin of this most German of *Hainbund* ballads may be traced back to the ballad of 'Sweet William's Ghost', published in Percy's *Reliques*. Here is an instance of the intersection of nationalist folk poetry with the ideal of World Literature. Bürger, who unsuccessfully sought a private tutoring post in

England, worked regularly on translations from Macpherson's *Ossian* and Percy's English and Scottish ballad collection.

The success of Bürger, both in Germany and England, underlines the significance of the ballad as a poetic form for the changing nature of Anglo-German literary exchanges. Just as it had become incorporated into the fabric of British Romanticism through the work of Percy, Chatterton, Macpherson and others, so in Germany it was a continuing preoccupation as *Sturm und Drang* and the *Hainbund* gave way to *Frühromantik* and from thence to the so-called *Hochromantik* associated with Jena and subsequently Heidelberg. Schiller remained indebted to the folk ballad tradition encouraged by Herder, steeped in Shakespeare, Ossian and Percy. Around him, beyond the territory of the *Klassik/Romantik* debate, Pope, Dryden, Defoe, Richardson, Sterne and Goldsmith continued to be popular, alongside English sentimental and Gothic novels.

As the century drew to a close, however, few things better illustrate how complex Anglo-German literary relationships were becoming than the way Schiller's *Die Räuber*, enthusiastically commended by Mackenzie in 1788, fell from grace. The trail leads eventually back to Wordsworth and the way his changing political views were reflected in his play, *The Borderers*. Given Schiller's nomination for honorary citizenship of Revolutionary France on the strength of *Die Räuber*, it is not surprising to find the *Anti-Jacobin* leading the English charge against Schiller and all things German. In 1798 its readership was offered a play called *The Rovers*, a parody of *Die Räuber*, which stressed what might be termed the 'Robin Hood' aspect of Schiller's plot, representing it as a sanctioning of robbery and immorality on the grand scale. A year later, another parody was aimed jointly at Schiller and his compatriot, August von Kotzebue (1761–1819): *The Benevolent Cut-Throat* was by 'Klozboggenhaggen', translated into English by 'Fabius Pictor' (Rea 1906, 12). There might also be an ironic reference here to Benedikte Naubert's novel, *Elisabeth, Erbin von Toggenburg* of 1789 (Brown 2005, 105–7). It was Kotzebue's *Das Kind der Liebe* of 1790, translated into English as *Lovers' Vows*, that Jane Austen used in *Mansfield Park* to warn her readership of the dangers of incipient immorality being imported across the English Channel. Schiller parodies of the late 1790s are still to be found pulling in appreciative London audiences in 1811, when the *Gentleman's Magazine* approvingly reviewed *The Quadrupeds of Quedlinburgh*, a revival of the genre at the Haymarket (August 1811, 186).

In 1795 Wordsworth began work on his play, *The Borderers*; in addition to its predictable indebtedness to Shakespearean tragedy, *Die Räuber* was a major influence. Unlike Mackenzie, Wordsworth had the benefit of A. F. Tytler's English translation of 1792 (Stokoe 1926, 30–1). *The Borderers*, written at a turning point in his commitment to radical politics, takes Schiller's idea of a band of Bohemian robbers who rob the rich to help the poor and introduces a villain who exposes their leader as unrealistically idealistic and thus vulnerable to being misled (as easily misled as was Goethe's Werther by his enthusiasm for Ossian). The plot of *Die Räuber* turns on the relationship between two brothers, the heroic Karl von Moor and the villainous Franz. Although Franz eventually pays for his misdeeds, Karl is made to realize that despite his good intentions, he has been helping to undermine rather than uphold the right order of things. What made the strongest impression on Schiller's readers, however, was the robbers' battle against the oppression of the poor by a rich and powerful minority.

In Wordsworth's play it is the disastrous subversion of the fraternal band of Borderers by an Iago-like villain that dominates the action. The need for a fairer world is not denied, but the hero is not equipped to deal with the powers of darkness that surround him. In Schiller there exists from the first, no matter how 'Jacobin' *Die Räuber* might have appeared, a conservative tendency that in later years would begin to reassert itself. The same might be said of Wordsworth and this was noted approvingly by his nineteenth-century German readers. The complexity of the situation at the turn of the century may be illustrated further by considering a recurring theme in *Sturm und Drang* ballad writing, setting it against an example from Wordsworth's poetry of the late 1790s: that of brothers and comrades.

In *Die Räuber* Karl Moor is set against his brother Franz. In Goethe's *Götz von Berlichingen* (translated into English by Sir Walter Scott in 1799), Goethe supplied Götz, a sixteenth-century Knight who fights for freedom, with a weak and worldly opposite number, Weislingen, who was once Götz's schoolfellow. Götz trusts him, only to be betrayed. By 1800 Wordsworth was of a mind openly to attack *Sturm und Drang* in his Preface to the second edition of *Lyrical Ballads* with a withering reference to 'frantic novels, sickly and stupid German tragedies, and deluges of idle and extravagant stories in verse' (Wordsworth 1992, 746–7). It is therefore interesting to see that in the 1800 edition of the *Ballads* he includes 'The Brothers, A Pastoral Poem', composed shortly after his return from Germany in 1799. From his account of his meeting with Klopstock in Hamburg in 1798, we learn that Wordsworth had given considerable time to reading and assessing the merits of German poetry (Wordsworth 1974, 89–98). 'The Brothers' may be interpreted as a corrective to the German poets whose work he was now beginning to criticize, including Klopstock, Bürger, Wieland and Schiller. Wordsworth's brothers are forced apart by domestic tragedy which also suggests a measure of social injustice. The stronger of the two boys decides to seek his fortune as a sailor. There is no hint of revolutionary pyrotechnics in this low key, melancholy tale of stoic endurance.

Complaining bitterly about the *Anti-Jacobin* attack on German literature, not least about its attack on Goethe's private life, Henry Crabb Robinson wrote in defence of German literature in the *Monthly Register* for 1802–3, and it was from around this time that a renewed interest in the subject began to emerge with men like Coleridge, Gillies and William Taylor paving the way (with Crabb Robinson) for later nineteenth-century enthusiasts. In Wordsworth, despite the disclaimers, the influence of Bürger's *Lenore* and *Der wilde Jäger* has been noted in 'Ellen Irwin' and 'Hartleap Well' respectively, and between Friederike Brun's *Die Sieben Hügel* and Wordsworth's 'The Seven Sisters'. William Taylor wrote on and translated German literature for the *Monthly Review* throughout this period and eventually published his *Historic Survey of German Poetry* between 1828 and 1830. The *Scots Magazine* of 1813 carried an article in praise of German culture and, though Schiller's reputation remained dented by the *Anti-Jacobin*, in 1814 the same number of the *Quarterly Review* that carried Charles Lamb's sympathetic account of Wordsworth's *The Excursion* included an article guardedly approving of Schiller. All his dramas, we read, 'abound in situations of terrific effect, all are filled with profound and philosophical reflections'. In *William Tell* 'the enthusiasm of the nation in favour of liberty is represented in colours the most captivating'. However, for the reviewer, a problem remains that goes beyond the individual ability of Schiller: 'The characteristics of the Germans are genius and invention, but they are extremely deficient in taste' (vol.12, 1814–15, 145). There is an echo here of de Staël's comment on German writers in a letter of 1803: 'there is poetry in their soul but no elegance of form. (Fairweather 2005, 298).

In the case of Wordsworth's *The Excursion*, critical arguments over its merits were influenced to a degree by the same political differences that divided the nation's view of German writers. Lamb's endorsement of the poem in the *Quarterly* was all but drowned out by Francis Jeffrey's contemptuous rejection of it in the *Edinburgh Review*. Jeffrey had long since made the case that Southey, Coleridge and Wordsworth were closet Jacobins, whose productions were at best risible, at worst seditious. It was easy to assume that German writers like Schiller were tarred with the same brush. Germany, still a disparate collection of states, responded to the Revolution and to Napoleon's subsequent advances in a way that was indecisive well after the outbreak of war between England and France in 1793. The British Nation could not afford to foster the infiltration of writers who appeared likely to endorse anything other than outright defiance of the foreign invader.

It was the indeterminate nature of Germany's response to Napoleon's France, however, that made it possible for Wordsworth, his sister Dorothy and Coleridge, to travel to Germany late in 1798. They had been evicted from their rented Somerset home because the owners were informed of their allegedly radical opinions and contacts. Their avowed reason for choosing to go to Germany, apart from the fact that the war debarred them from any other affordable European destination, was to learn enough of the language to be able to do the same as Thomas Holcroft, Walter Scott, A. F. Tytler and others were doing, making money by translating fashionably risqué German texts for the English market.

Their initial destination, Hamburg, contained a strongly anglophile element that included William Remnant's highly successful English book shop, where Dorothy purchased a copy of Percy's *Reliques* to keep her company in a strange land. It is not difficult to imagine Wordsworth and Coleridge wandering through Remnant's 'English Library' and reflecting that with *Lyrical Ballads* in the press, here was an opportunity to do some business in the near future. Missing the Wordsworths by only a few months, Thomas Holcroft arrived in Hamburg intending to use it as a place to launch a Journal, *The European Repository*. Holcroft, along with John Thelwall, had been put on trial for his life on charges of treason in 1794. It was the visits of Thelwall to his friends Wordsworth and Coleridge in Somerset that had suggested to local patriots that Nether Stowey and Alfoxden harboured a nest of dangerous political radicals. Thelwall's friend Joseph Gales avoided arrest in 1794 by escaping to Germany, before he set sail for the United States in 1795 (Goodwin 1979, 333). Holcroft translated much German literature into English and noted that 'The admiration of the Germans for English Literature and their contempt for the French are well known' (Holcroft 1926, 306). But despite the evident popularity of the English in Hamburg and Altona (Holcroft paints a far more flattering picture of the place than did either of the Wordsworths or Coleridge), his new venture failed to prosper.

The authors of *Lyrical Ballads* had arrived in a country whose poets, not least among them Klopstock, understood the ballad form as not only the epitome of indigenous art, but also as a key to the root of all art. Britain, though it did not have the same motivation as the fledgling German Nation, had been exploring the same territory and in the process been instrumental in inspiring German writers. We have seen how Wordsworth stalled in pursuit of radical reform in the mid 1790s, and in the process took up Schiller's *Die Räuber* along with Shakespeare as a model for creating his own dramatic structure within which he could debate the issues. Schiller too found himself driven to re-examine his initial response to social and political change, and duly abandoned literature for philosophy in an attempt to understand where his creative energies should lead him. In the process, his writing on aesthetic theory in the mid-1790s produced a body of work that would prove as ubiquitous for European Romanticism as Herder's *Von deutscher Art und Kunst* of 1773. With Schiller's *Ästhetischer Briefe* we see further evidence of why in subsequent years Wordsworth, as much as any British poet, should draw to himself a German readership.

Johann Gottfried Herder, Friedrich Schiller and Wordsworthian Preoccupations

'The romantic genre is, however, still in the process of becoming; indeed, this is its essence: to be eternally in the process of becoming and never completed.'
Schiller, *Athenäum Fragment 116* in Strathman 2006, 44

Herder, even more than Lessing, inspired his fellow writers to build their work on the basis of German culture, encapsulated for him in the language of Martin Luther and grounded in an idealized perception of a vigorous feudal heritage of the kind enthusiastically described by Justus Möser.

This determination for national revival is nowhere more evident than in Herder's enthusiasm for folk songs and tales. While Goethe, under his tutelage, was instructed to seek out evidence of orally perpetuated German ballads, Herder's quest took him further, in the process endorsing the continuing German engagement with British literature and culture. Michael Burleigh notes that the major German literary and philosophical figures of the late eighteenth century (Goethe, Kant, Lessing, Schiller and also Herder) were cosmopolitans; and this element of universalism was a preoccupation that a period of intense German cultural nationalism never wholly suppressed (Burleigh 2005, 151–2). It was a phenomenon to which many nineteenth-century miscellanies and anthologies appealed and to which – as Andrew Piper has recently controversially argued – Goethe himself aspired in a visionary way as he prepared his final Collected Works (Piper 2006, 124–38). 'World Literature' was what Herder had in mind when in *Von deutscher Art und Kunst* he claimed that Shakespeare was 'the interpreter of nature in all her tongues', but this remained 'World Literature' construed in a very Germanic way (Williams 2001, 11).

While foreign texts could still provide a literary model to ensure commercial success, as was the case with Benedikte Naubert's use of the English novel of sensibility from the 1770s, the demands of establishing a 'German' cultural identity tended to mean that texts taken from elsewhere had their national characteristics minimized in translation, even though they might still be exalted to the status of 'World Literature'. A major battlefield upon which contending imperialist ambitions confront each other is that of linguistic dominance and nascent Germany was, in this period, being drawn into the fray on these terms. It is all the more interesting to note, therefore, that we shall be considering the way in which Wordsworth – unlike Shakespeare and contemporary poets such as Byron, Moore and Hemans – became noted for his resistance to being understood in any terms other than that of a profoundly English poet. Wordsworth's German readers were frequently to be confronted by his patriotism; this was of course laudable, not least because his patriotism often expressed itself in the denunciation of Napoleon, but beyond this lay a deeply felt 'Englishness', and this was to be of the utmost importance in establishing the relatively unusual and revealing relationship that evolved between Wordsworth's poetry and his German readers and translators. What is almost certainly the first attempt to initiate that relationship was made by Henry Crabb Robinson, who arrived in Germany in 1800 with *Lyrical Ballads* in his luggage, poetry that claimed to investigate 'how far the language of conversation in the middle and lower classes of society is adapted to the purposes of poetic pleasure'; in short, this was poetry about, and for, the 'folk' (Wordsworth 1992, 738).

Interest in folk ballads is central to an understanding of the way Anglo-German cultural relationships evolved. Herder published his first collection of folksongs, *Volkslieder*, in 1788–9; it was reissued in 1807 as *Stimmen der Völker in Liedern*. The *Volkslieder* prepared the way for numerous similar ventures, notably Ludwig Arnim and Clemens Brentano's collection of 1805, *Des Knaben Wunderhorn*, a seminal text for German Romanticism and an inspiration to Arndt, Görres, Fichte, Kleist and others. Herder had taken to heart Hamann's conviction that poetry was 'the mother tongue of the human race' (Robertson 1953, 300). He published his *Volkslieder* of 1788–9 with a view to exposing the primitive, enduring structures of poetry, which he had come to see as a window into the process of human history, a process he began to map out in his *Ideen zur Philosophie der Geschichte der Menschheit* (1784–91). In this he remained, like Hamann, deeply indebted to his reading of Young and Hurd. Poetry, Herder wrote, had to be discovered in its natural form, before 'art came and extinguished nature' (Williams 2001, 68). 'Poetry' was a term applied to all artistic creativity; it identified a continuity between nature and art. It followed that '*all* forms of human creativity are simply appearances, manifestations and developments of the creativity of nature itself . . . what Herder called "die Urkraft aller Kräfte"' (Beiser 2003, 21). From poetry, a pure, unalloyed source of human expression, might be traced the evolution of man in society. This aspiration, summarized in German cultural history as *Bildung*, was to play an important part in the way Wordsworth's poetry was perceived by German readers.

Bildung was an ideal that consisted 'in the development of not only our characteristic human powers, which we all share as human beings, but also our distinctive individual powers, which are unique to each of us' (Ibid., 27). Beiser goes on to argue that *Bildung* was a concept that permeated *Aufklärung*, *Sturm und Drang*, *Frühromantik*, *Romantik* and *Klassik* in equal degrees. Poems by Wordsworth such as the ballad style 'We Are Seven', 'The Thorn' and 'The Solitary Reaper' (less generically a 'ballad' itself, though its subject is folk song), and the epic length *Excursion* and *The White Doe of Rylstone*, offered themselves as exercises in the exploration of the linked development of man as both an individual and a social animal subject to the forces of history and, in so doing, placed particular emphasis on the importance of childhood. Goethe's *Heidenröslein* was commended by Herder for the way it reproduced the child's artless voice. Though in content a very different poem, it is possible to appreciate in the light of this why Wordsworth's 'We Are Seven' consistently appealed to German translators and anthologists, along with 'To a Highland Girl' and 'The Solitary Reaper', a poem that laments the passing of a lost language of the folk. These are all poems which 'are suffused within by that purity which makes children seem so marvellous to us' (Grimm 2005, 4). This was how Jacob and Wilhelm Grimm described the folk tales they collected, the first volume of which was published in 1812. For a generation steeped in the legacy of Herder's writing on ballads, and more specifically of Goethe's *Wilhelm Meister* novels, Wordsworth's so-called 'Lucy' poems will have brought the enigmatic Mignon to mind (as will the character of Emily in *The White Doe of Rylstone*). Mignon has been described as 'exotic, lonely, shy, waif-like, restless, alien and profoundly, inscrutably unhappy. Pre-pubescent and androgynous . . .' (Williams 2001, 220). Her identity remains as inscrutable as that of the illusive, tragic, Lucy Gray from *Lyrical Ballads*:

> She dwelt among th'untrodden ways
>   Beside the springs of Dove,
> A Maid whom there were none to praise
>   And very few to love.
>
> A Violet by a mossy stone
>   Half-hidden from the Eye!
> –Fair as a star when only one
>   Is shining in the sky!
>
> She *liv*'d unknown, and few could know
>   When Lucy ceas'd to be;
> But she is in her Grave, and oh!
>   The difference to me.
>
> (Wordsworth 1992, 163)

'Do not bid me speak', sings Mignon, ('Heiss mich nicht reden') 'bid me be silent, for it is my duty to keep my secret. I would like to show you my whole heart, but fate wills otherwise' (Goethe 1981, 86; Williams 2001, 221). 'Say, Spirit! Whither has she fled/To hide her poor afflicted head?' Wordsworth writes of Emily in *The White Doe*: 'What mighty forest in its gloom/Enfolds her?' (Wordsworth 1988, 135), and in 1820 Jacobsen endorsed this reading of Wordsworth by ending his account with another 'Lucy' poem, 'She was a Phantom of delight'.

Wordsworth's 'The Thorn', with its theme of infanticide, and 'The Female Vagrant', both reflect *Sturm und Drang* preoccupations; H. L. Wagner's *Die Kindermöderin* and Goethe's *Urfaust* are specific examples. Goethe's ballad of 1776 *Vor Gericht* ('Before the Court'), like 'The Thorn', was at least in part inspired by a historical case of a tragedy involving an abandoned, unmarried mother; in Goethe's case, one faced with rejection from society and persecution through the courts. In her book on Henry Crabb Robinson, Hertha Marquardt notes that Clemens Brentano was among the poets who attempted a translation of 'The Thorn' shortly after *Lyrical Ballads* was published (Marquardt 1964, 60).

Friedrich Schiller became Professor of History at Jena University in 1789 on the strength of his *Geschichte des Abfalls der vereinigten Niederlande von der spanischen*

Regierung. It was indeed an appropriate year to produce a History of the Revolt of the Netherlands, but by 1791 his health was suffering from over-work. With financial help from two patrons, he turned to a study of Kant in 1793 and a year later began to build his friendship with Goethe. It is the series of philosophical writings he produced during this period of his life, beginning with *Über Anmut und Würde* (1793), that are often brought together under the generic title of the *Äesthetische Briefe*. They provide us with a seminal response of German Romanticism to the religious crisis and the socio-political dilemmas attendant on the French Revolution and its outcome, and with a measure of why, though changed since the 1770s, British writing continued to draw German readers to it as relevant to their preoccupations.

Lesley Sharpe has summarized Schiller's intentions in the *Äesthetische Briefe* as an exploration of the status and function of the aesthetic in human experience, its relation to our freedom as morally autonomous beings, and the proposal that art and aesthetics are fundamental to what it is to be human (Sharpe 1995, 1). The *Briefe* have long been perceived as a touchstone in the history of European Romanticism, responding to the tensions between a Europe in political turmoil and the functions of art, and between the binary forces of reason and imagination so melodramatically expressed in *Werther*. The *Briefe* constitute a text that Abrams has juxtaposed specifically to English Romanticism as it finds expression in the poetry and prose of Wordsworth, despite Wordsworth's avowed distaste for German metaphysics (Abrams 1971, 278).

In the *Briefe*, Schiller was primarily concerned to explore both the nature of freedom in the broadest terms possible and the way in which freedom might be exercised. Defining the Beautiful was for him a primary concern in this respect; he characterized it as 'freedom in appearance', or 'freedom in visible form' ('Freiheit in der Erscheinung') and as such he pronounced it autonomous (Sharpe 1995, 2). Beauty had then to be incorporated into an inclusive system that linked the aesthetic to morality. 'Grace', he suggested, was beauty in spontaneous movement, while 'moral grace' was the consequence of harmony between the sensuous impulse and moral precept. 'Moral Grace' was manifest in what he called the 'beautiful soul' ('Schöne Seele'); the 'Schöne Seele' was the consequence of a balance established between the natural impulse and duty (Ibid., 3). Schiller's commitment to freedom, and his recognition at the same time of the need for a controlling quality he sought to define through Moral Grace and Dignity, meant that his theory of beauty was endemically contradictory. Reading the debacle of the French Revolution as a process of cultural and political fragmentation, Schiller was interpreting the event in essentially the same way Wordsworth did in Book IV of *The Excursion*: the Revolutionaries had embraced an overly rational, mechanistic theory of human progress (Wordsworth 2007, 137–9).

Schiller proposes that wholeness may be re-established through the process of aesthetic education. Art, uniquely, offers us the ability to 'play' ('Spieltrieb'), a form of irresponsible, unfettered activity, where art is entirely self-indulgent (Sharpe 1995, 4). This, Schiller argues, is a healing process, a notion reflected to a degree in Coleridge's Kantian description in his *Biographia Literaria* of what he calls the 'secondary' imagination: that which 'dissolves, diffuses, dissipates, in order to recreate . . . it struggles to idealize and to unify' (Coleridge 1997, 175). Schiller argues that the way forward for a fragmented civilization is to build the foundations for regeneration on the basis of its fragmentation. Culture is the outcome of man's 'all-dividing intellect'. M. H. Abrams summarizes Schiller's perception of the process of civilization and culture as 'a painful journey into self-division and inner conflict'. The way out of this condition for Schiller is through three stages:'from the natural through the aesthetic to a third ... moral state that will preserve the values of both nature and aesthetics' (Abrams 1971, 214). The Revolution is perceived as constituting a necessary step towards a redeemed and unified existence that will arise not from the political ideas of the Revolution, but from a painfully won renewed and more profound sense of art that will have been created in the course of the upheaval. 'It must be open to us,' Schiller writes, 'to restore by means of a higher Art the totality of our nature which the arts themselves have destroyed' (Ibid., 212). Growing into an aware-ness of this is the process already identified as *Bildung*, a notion of education that Keats described as 'soul-making' in his letter to George and Georgiana Keats of April 1819, that Schiller described as leading us 'onward to our coming of age', and which Wordsworth described in his Ode *Intimations of Immortality* (1807) as a power for good which:

> ... neither listlessness, nor mad endeavour,
> Nor Man nor Boy,
> Nor all that is at enmity with joy,
> Can utterly abolish or destroy.
> (Wordsworth 1983, 276)

It is the poet, not the politician, who must perform this task of education. 'Let him set himself the task of an idyll', Schiller writes, 'which will lead man-kind, for whom the way back to Arcadia is closed forever, onward to Elysium' (Abrams 1971, 215). Abrams emphasizes the common ground here between Schiller's belief in the power of the imagination (effectively taking on the role of the deity) and Wordsworth's claims for the role of the poetic imagination: 'In ... The Prelude, the "glory" of the human soul is that "our home/Is with infinity", and therefore with "something evermore about to be"' (Ibid., 216). German readers did not have to wait for the appearance of The Prelude in 1850 to encounter poems by Wordsworth that seemed to echo the Schillerian notion of the 'Schöne Seele'.

In *Über naive und sentimentalische Dichtung* (1795) Schiller explores the rela-tive merits of ancient and modern poetry through the idea that poetry might be defined as 'sentimental' or 'naïve' in origin. In the process he stresses the importance of learning from the spontaneity of the child's perceptions; the sig-nificance of this in the broader context of *Bildung* and Wordsworth's poetry has already been noted. The sentimental poet (like himself) was the poet who engaged personally with his work. Everything about such a poet, his life, his emotions, the times in which he lived, was there to be incorporated in his writ-ing. The naïve poet, by contrast, does not impose him or herself on the poetry and Goethe, Schiller suggests, epitomizes the naïve poet. Reminiscing about this much later, Goethe is noted by Johann Peter Eckermann as having said:

> The concept of classical and romantic poetry, which is now spreading all over the world and causing so much conflict and division . . . originated with me and Schiller. In poetry I was guided by principles of objectivity and wanted to recog-nise this method only. Schiller, however, whose method was wholly subjective, maintained his way was the right one, and in order to defend himself against me he wrote the essay about naïve and sentimental poetry. (Sharpe 1995, 10)

Goethe probably had in mind here a project he undertook with Schiller which offers an intriguing parallel with Wordsworth and Coleridge. In 1797, the year which saw the beginning of the collaboration that would produce Wordsworth's and Coleridge's *Lyrical Ballads*, Schiller and Goethe embarked on what became known as their 'Balladejahr'. In his *Biographia Literaria*, Coleridge explained that the 'incidents and agents' of his poetry 'were to be, in part at least, supernatural'. Wordsworth's subjects, on the other hand, 'were to be chosen from ordinary life'; he would 'give the charm of novelty to things of every day' (Coleridge 1997, 179–80).

John R. Williams summarizes the nature of the two German poets' collaboration in the following way:

> The differences between the two poets, however, are still discernible in their ballads: Schiller's, for all their romantic or legendary settings, remain largely within the human sphere of ethical or moral choice, while Goethe's draw more on the supernatural traditions of apparitions, magic, and popular belief. (Williams 2001, 107)

Goethe appears closest to the Coleridgean role. Schiller (who may temperamentally remind us of Coleridge) appears to adopt the Wordsworthian voice. What is particularly intriguing is the way both pairs of poets arrived at a similar division of labour when contemplating a ballad anthology not of earlier work, but of their own making. At the very least it suggests that a significant degree of common ground existed between the two countries with respect to theories of imagination, a common ground that had been established over decades of literary exchanges and in Germany given specific focus in the writings of Herder.

A comparison between *Lyrical Ballads* and the poetry of the 'Balladejahr' prompts a comparison between the ways these men attempted to address a post Enlightenment crisis of confidence. Compare, for example, the child in Goethe's *Erlkönig* ballad with the child in Wordsworth's 'Anecdote for Fathers'. The father in Goethe's poem holds his son snug and warm in his arms and reassures the terrified child that the Erlking it sees 'is a wisp of cloud', 'ein Nebelstreif' (Forster 1957, 214–15). At the end of the ride the father's confidence in his rational explanation is proved wanting: his child is dead. In 'Anecdote for Fathers' the father, attempting to impose his adult wisdom on the child, concludes:

> Oh dearest, dearest boy! My heart
> For better lore would seldom yearn,
> Could I but teach the hundredth part
> Of what from thee I learn.
>
> (Wordsworth 1992, 73)

In *Natural Supernaturalism* Abrams describes Schiller's *Ästhetische Briefe* as a 'history of culture as the educational process of mankind' (Abrams 1971, 209). Prompted by the degeneration of the French Revolution from a time of great optimism in 1789 to the onset of the terror in 1792, Abrams describes Schiller as diagnosing the ills of the modern world as a consequence of the separation of civilization from Nature, a debilitating fragmentation that has come about through an unhealthy reliance on reason and the intellect ever since the decline of Classical Greece. He understands Schiller to be proposing that it will nevertheless be through the exercise of reason that a return to Nature and 'wholeness' will be achieved and this will require the insights provided by the new 'senti-mental' poetry: 'our culture shall lead us, by the road of reason and freedom, back to nature again' (Ibid., 213).

Besides citing Rousseau, Kant and Herder as key sources for Schiller's thesis, Abrams notes the abundant scholarship that cites Adam Ferguson's *Essay on the History of Civil Society* of 1767 (translated into German in 1768) as a major influence:

> Ferguson pointed out the price that civilized man and society must pay – in division, isolation, conflict, and psychological distortion – for the efficiency and affluence made possible by the operation of the profit motive and by the ever increasing division of labour and specialization of function in a manufacturing and commercial economy. (Ibid., 210, 508)

Ferguson's critique of a society increasingly beset by class divisions resonates through late eighteenth-century English literature, and Alan Bewell has drawn attention to the way Ferguson's work played its part in influencing Words-worth's analysis of the consequences for society of the new industrial age (Bewell 1989, 60). Wordsworth's poetry of the mid-1790s, culminating in the first edition of *Lyrical Ballads*, may be described as recounting his rediscovery of 'Nature' as a bastion against aspects of a modern society that he, like Ferguson, saw as increasingly dysfunctional. This is not the nature he had known as a child; it is a nature exalted by profound reflection, refined by the process of memory to the point where it sings 'The still, sad music of humanity' (Wordsworth 1992, 118). It was above all Wordsworth's references to nature in this guise that drew later nineteenth-century German writers like Ferdinand Freiligrath (respond-ing to the political implications embedded in the language and imagery), Luise von Ploennies (1803–72), Marie Gothein and Andreas Baumgartner to Words-worth, not least because German aesthetics had evolved (as may be appreciated from the *Ästhetische Briefe*) from very similar concerns embedded in the tension between Enlightenment and Romanticism, Reason and Imagination and between Classical and Romantic aesthetic values, and how engaging with those issues related to the political, religious and social crises of the modern world.

Schiller's theory of beauty forms the basis of his critique of the French Revolution, but the *Ästhetische Briefe* do not signal an escape into philosophy from politics, they remain a profoundly political statement. Art, inspiration and imagination are to be revived to replace a revolutionary credo dominated by intellectual powers that exist at the expense of the sensual and imaginative qualities of human nature. This, of course, mirrors Wordsworth's emphasis in *Lyrical Ballads* on the need for the revolutionary cause (explicitly the new poetry in lyrical ballad form, implicitly the new politics of social and political reform) to embrace 'the hour of feeling':

> One impulse from a vernal wood
> May teach you more of man;
> Of moral evil and of good,
> Than all the sages can.
>
> (Wordsworth 1992, 64)

Wordsworth's Preface for the second edition of *Lyrical Ballads* has frequently been cited as the first manifesto of British Romanticism. Schiller's *Ästhetische Briefe* have earned the same status for German Romanticism, while Schiller's

Journal, *Die Horen*, which published the *Briefe* between 1795 and 1797, has been described as 'the first vehicle for the project of aesthetic humanism . . . the age's most influential organ' (Saul 2000, 207). Schiller was understandably seen by some as avoiding a direct engagement with the pressing political issues of the day, in much the same way that Wordsworth was taken to task for his apostasy where the cause of British political radicalism was concerned. Schiller's *Ästhetische Briefe*, Heine claimed, ushered in a 'Kunstperiode' that condoned 'the hermetic isolation of literature from its environment, as in an ivory tower of sovereign disdain for prosaic reality' (Ibid., 207). We may compare Heine's bitterness with Browning's famous lines from his poem 'The Lost Leader' (1842), 'Just for a handful of silver he left us,/Just for a riband to stick in his coat', in which he attacked Wordsworth's political change of heart. Abrams' account of the *Briefe* emphasizes their aesthetic implications, without employing Heine's acerbic note of disapproval, and Geoffrey Hartman also favours this interpretation, '[Schiller] seems to be talking . . . about the emergence of a cultural rather than political nation, or about the passage from nature to freedom via the indefinitely extended and self-creative process of *Bildung*' (Hartman 1997, 124–5). For Saul, on the other hand, the *Briefe* cannot properly be understood without appreciating their essentially political content, a political content only too apparent in the literary salons of Berlin, 'the court circles at Weimar, and the Bohemian groupings of the Jena Romantics'; all these would 'seek to translate this aesthetic vision into social fact.' (Ibid., 207)

Three Ambassadors: Henry Crabb Robinson, Jeremias Reuss and Samuel Taylor Coleridge

'. . . almost every Newspaper commences with "Schreiben aus London".'
                                                            Coleridge 1956 I, 446

Throughout the war the commerce of literature between England and Germany continued. Indicative of the constant movement between countries is the fact that, while de Staël was in Germany in 1803 complaining that writers like Goethe and Schiller had, in her view, become shallow and provincial, she also met the young English student, Henry Crabb Robinson. More often than not a situation such as this, where a talkative young Englishman appears in a German cultural gathering, is to be explained by the way cultural exchanges invariably followed the broad highways and tortuously winding lanes laid down by the extensive web of trading interests that criss-crossed Europe and that wars only ever briefly seemed to inhibit. We have already noted Wordsworth's brief personal appearance in Hamburg (from whence he travelled to Goslar) in 1798–9. It was in the year after Wordsworth's return to England that Robinson arrived at Jena carrying with him at least one copy of *Lyrical Ballads*.

Crabb Robinson (1775–1867) has always enjoyed an ambivalent place in English literary history. F. W. Stokoe saw Robinson as important, while René Wellek dismissed him out of hand as an insignificant contributor to Anglo-German cultural exchanges, suggesting that Eudo C. Mason's claims for him in this respect were 'extravagant' (Stokoe 1926, 53, 114; Wellek 1965, 8). Any attempt to reassess Robinson's role must begin by distinguishing between the traveller in his twenties and the middle-aged socialite who loved to entertain the great and the good at his London breakfast parties. Defying the fashionable dictates of early nineteenth-century English literary taste, he spent five years at Jena University, matriculating in 1805. Two years later he became foreign editor on *The Times* and, on his own initiative, its first war correspondent, travelling to Spain to cover the Peninsular War of 1808–9. Liberal in politics and a religious dissenter, he worked on behalf of the anti-slavery campaign, was a founder of University College, London, and also of the Athenaeum Club.

In Germany he swiftly became a devotee of German literature, and made it his business to meet as many of the major figures as he could with a view also to promoting the merits of his own country's literary genius. As an enthusiast of Wordsworth's poetry from the first appearance of *Lyrical Ballads*, therefore, it is possible that Robinson was the first to carry Wordsworth's name and, more importantly, to place Wordsworth's poetry in textual form, before a German readership. 'A few days since,' he wrote from Frankfurt in June 1802:

> I had the pleasure of conversing with F. Schlegel, one of the first living poets, and a great Æsthetiker; he is the brother of the translator of Shakespeare. He seemed much pleased with one or two pieces by Wordsworth. We talked of our English poets . . . (Robinson 1967, 122–3)

Robinson's diaries are a rich source of material but of course they only ever provide a glimpse of what he was doing. It is safe to assume that the account of his meeting with Schlegel was replicated many times with less eminent people of a similar type who did not in consequence merit an entry. Some idea of the extent of Robinson's circle of acquaintances can be had from Hertha Marquardt's book, *Henry Crabb Robinson and His German Friends* (1964); her pages are full of the writers, academics, literati and businessmen Robinson mingled with, but even as the list lengthens, we realize how many more there must have been who failed to be mentioned in the course of his hectic schedule. In 1803, he describes his meeting with Herder:

> What I had previously seen of him made me feel that in spite of his eminence there were many points of agreement in matters of taste and sentiment, and caused me to approach him with affection as well as fear. I lent him Wordsworth's "Lyrical Ballads", my love for which was in no respect diminished by my attachment to the German school of poetry. I found that Herder agreed with Wordsworth as to poetical language. Indeed Wordsworth's notions on that subject are quite German. There was also general sympathy between the two in matters of morality and religion. (Ibid., 154)

This account provides strong evidence that it was the second, 1800, edition of *Lyrical Ballads* that Robinson carried with him and that he discussed the Preface (added since the 1798 edition) with Herder. The entry then explores Herder's religious views, stressing a toleration on his part that seems to have been hard won. This explains, he suggests, 'His repugnance to some of Goethe's writings' (Ibid., 155). Wordsworth's treatment of religious themes clearly appealed to Robinson from the first, and this no doubt explains why, on a later visit to Germany in 1829, he confesses that though he spent five evenings with Goethe, he decided not to try to persuade him of Wordsworth's merits: 'He was not aware that I had not the courage to name the poet to whom I was and am most attached – Wordsworth' (Ibid., 439). Robinson's loss of nerve with Goethe appears to have been an exception, however, and he records his attempts to convince Ottilie, Goethe's daughter-in-law, and the poet Karl Knebel of Wordsworth's merits, though in both cases he seems to have met with little success (Ibid., 428).

De Staël met Robinson very soon after her arrival in Germany in 1803 and she was grateful for his offer of help, though disdainful of his suggestion that he might assist her to understand the complexities of German philosophy (Fairweather 2005, 304). Without a doubt, while discoursing on the inadequacies of the British political system, he will have introduced the British poets into his conversation and Wordsworth cannot fail to have been among them. When they met again in 1813 in England, Robinson was frustrated by de Staël's determination to see the British Nation as a paragon of political virtue; he describes her as 'a bigoted admirer of our government which she considers perfect' (Ibid., 420). Her account of England in *De l'Allemagne* has little to say of its literature beyond noting the popularity of stories of chivalry and romance, and the fact that the English 'describe nature with enthusiasm, but it no longer acts as a formidable power which incloses phantoms and presages within its breast' (Staël 1871, 225). Of the literary figures she met, it was primarily Byron who most intrigued her, and who seems to have prompted the few pronouncements she chose to make on English literature in the book. A meeting between Wordsworth and the effusive *émigré* would have been well worth witnessing, but Wordsworth was touring Scotland in 1813 and so could hardly have been further from the social maelstrom of London and from the likelihood of being mentioned in *De l'Allemagne*. Robinson and de Staël do, however, share the role of being active and influential intermediaries between England and Germany during these crucial war years, helping to maintain an active and lively sense of curiosity in Germany about English writing. What Lilian R. Furst suggests with regard to de Staël and *De l'Allemagne* was true also of Robinson's conduct: 'they were a mediator between Germany and England', and 'a manifesto of the new cosmopolitanism' (Furst 1969, 41, 43). But it should always be appreciated that these two people are representative of what was happening far more widely at this time, though for the most part it was happening out of sight, or at best it was occurring on the fringes of surviving written accounts.

Robinson, who would not meet Wordsworth face to face until 1808, played an important part in bringing the poet to the attention of German readers after 1800, but there can be no substitute for the printed word when it comes to establishing Wordsworth as a presence in early nineteenth-century Germany. What currently offers itself as the first published reference to Wordsworth in Germany confirms the fact that Robinson was not alone in passing on Wordsworth's name as a rising star among the new poets of England. By 1804, Wordsworth had just four published books of poetry to his name: *An Evening Walk, Descriptive Sketches*, and two volumes of *Lyrical Ballads*. These were noted in Jeremias Reuss's two volume *Catalogue of Books Published in England, Ireland, and North America for the years 1790–1803*, published in 1804. Reuss's 'biographical/bibliographical compendium' is noted for its Coleridge entry in *The Reception of S. T. Coleridge in Europe*, where Bernard Fabian's discussion of it as 'the first such bibliography of English Literature' is also noted (Burwick 2007, 89). This is, however, the first time that the significance of Wordsworth's presence in Reuss has been discussed.

Reuss's book belongs within the Enlightenment tradition of dictionaries and reference books that amass exhaustive and frequently opinionated lists of factual details; Diderot and D'Alembert's 35-volume *Encyclopédie* (1751–76) is the model for this kind of project. In Germany, one of the most formidable examples of the encyclopaedic habit is J. S. Ersch's and J. G. Gruber's *Allgemeine Encyclopädie der Wissenschaften und Künste* which devotes its first six weighty volumes (1818) to the letter 'A'. The English were no less susceptible to the genre. In 1799 the Revd David Rivers started publishing a revised edition of his *Literary Memoirs of Living Authors of Great Britain*. Rivers was a fiercely loyalist Church of England clergyman who had briefly welcomed the Revolution in France in 1789 but rapidly recanted and from his parish in Highgate (and from a variety of other London pulpits) preached and published inexhaustibly against any kind of reform, urging everyone to play their part in opposing the French aggressor.

> Those who are unable to bear the fatigue of military duty, let them exert them-selves, by exciting everywhere a spirit of heroism: let the man of literature devote his pen to the same service: let the clergy be unwearied in enforcing the necessity of active resistance to the invading foe. (Rivers 1804, 19–20)

His *Literary Memoirs* were part of his war effort, as his entry on John Thelwall makes clear:

> Here (Beaufort Buildings in the Strand) evening after evening, he thundered out philipics against the constitution of his country, with the vehemence of an impas-sioned demagogue, to the admiration of the vilest refuse of the metropolis. (Rivers 1798, 302)

In his Preface to the *Memoirs* Rivers notes that his is the 'fifth work of the kind in the author's recollection', that is, on British authors. He notes that while Germany, with authors such as Meusel and Hamberger, has led the way in the production of literary catalogues, Reuss's 1791 publication on British, Irish and North American authors is particularly impressive, though he is guilty of inac-curacies. He intended his own 1799 catalogue to run to six volumes.

Reuss worked in an excellent place to develop his knowledge of English literature, Hilary Brown notes that Göttingen had 'amassed the best collection of English books on the Continent in the eighteenth century' (Brown 2005, 12). Reuss was born in 1750 and studied theology at Tübingen. In 1785 he moved to Göttingen where he became Professor of Philosophy and, in 1789, he was appointed second-in-command to Heyne at the University Library (the fact that he was Heyne's son-in-law was no doubt an advantage) (Brandl 1886, 241). There will have been plenty of support at Göttingen for his project on British Literature, not least among the visiting English students; and not least among them would have been Samuel Taylor Coleridge. If Heine is to be believed, Coleridge would have found a town with a 'grey, precocious look . . . fully furnished with quaint tales, poodles, dis-sertations, tea-*dansants*, laundresses, compendiums, roasted pigeons, Guelphic orders, carriages for degree-candidates, pipe bowls, Court Counsellors, law counsellors and counsellors to the dean: the prefects and the defects.' 'Strange!' he wrote in 'The Emperor and the Drummer', 'a frightful fate has already overtaken the Emperor's three greatest adversaries: Londonderry cut his throat, Louis XVIII rotted to death on his throne and Professor Saalfield is still professor at Göttingen' (Heine 1943, 36, 236).

Unlike Rivers, Reuss provides no commentary on the publications he lists; his is a more severely factual account, following a regular pattern for the entry format in both the 1799 and the 1804 editions of the book. On numerous occasions he cites his sources, which include *The Columbian Magazine*, the *The Gentleman's Magazine* for 1790–1803, *The Massachusetts Magazine*, *The Monthly Magazine* for 1796–1803, *Nicholson's Journal*, *Tilloch's Philosophical Magazine* and a series of publications referred to as *Public Characters* for 1798–99, 1801 and 1799–1803 compiled by Alexander Stephens (Burwick 2007, 89). This list in itself is an indication of the considerable extent to which English language texts were circulating in early nineteenth-century Germany.

Wordsworth's entry is as follows:

★WORDSWORTH, [W....] *B.A. of St. John's College at Cambridge.*

An evening walk; an epistle, in verse, addressed to a young lady from the lakes of the North of England. 1793. 4.(2sh.) Descriptive sketches in verse; taken during a pedestrian tour in the Italian, Grison, Swiss and Savoyard Alps. 1793.4. (3sh.) ★Lyrical ballads, with a few other poems. Vol. I. 1798. 12. (5sh.) Vol. 2. 1801. 8.(5sh.) ★Six letters a *Granville Sharp*, Esq. respecting his remarks on the uses of the definitive article in the greek text of the N.T. 1802. (4sh. 6d.)

The details of the price of the publications suggest that this has been copied directly from a sales catalogue, including the number of copies available. The error regarding Granville Sharp's 'Six Letters' invites further speculation, however. Incidentally, 'a *Granville Sharp*' is a correct transcription and suggests a possible French source.

First we should note that here (as is the case elsewhere), when we most would like him to, Reuss gives no source for his information. When Coleridge arrived at Göttingen in 1799 he had letters of introduction to von Brandes, whom he described to his wife as the 'Secretary of State of the Göttingen University', and Heyne, the Chief Librarian, described in the same letter as 'in truth, the real *Governor* of Göttingen' (Coleridge 1956 I, 472). Nowhere in any of Coleridge's correspondence is there a reference to Jeremias Reuss but it is difficult not to believe that, faced with Coleridge's ceaseless conversation, Heyne propelled the young Englishman in the direction of his son-in-law. Once apprised of Reuss's project, Coleridge would have been only too willing to have offered suggestions and would certainly have made sure that both himself and Wordsworth had a place in Reuss's book. This was the kind of thing they had come for.

Coleridge, however, had left Göttingen by the time both Volume Two of *Lyrical Ballads* appeared and the letters to Sharp were published. This is information that must have been culled from catalogues, journals and private correspondence finding its way from England into Germany; although it is worth remembering that Robinson had also been a visitor to Göttingen. It must surely be as a result of reading British papers and reviews that Reuss made the error of assuming that it was William Wordsworth who wrote the 'Six Letters' in response to Granville Sharp. Sharp had written a controversial pamphlet on a biblical controversy and the 'Letters' were written by Wordsworth's younger brother, Christopher, who was then an aspiring undergraduate at Cambridge. Though this was known to Christopher Wordsworth's duly impressed mentors at Cambridge, the 'Letters' were originally published anonymously. Reuss therefore must have had some prompting from an English source that 'Wordsworth' was the author and assumed that the author must in consequence be 'William Wordsworth'.

At a time when there was much printed matter circulating to help sustain the interest of German readers, Coleridge and Robinson were influential ambassadors for British poetry in Germany. German magazines and journals such as the *Jenaische Allgemeine Literatur Zeitung* (which enthusiastically reviewed Reuss's work in nos. 22 and 23, 1805) carried regular reports of English publications, though many of these tended to prioritize theological, commercial, medical, historical and legal subject matter. It remains very difficult to be sure of the extent to which hard copies of the texts in question managed to find their way into Germany, though by 1820, on the evidence of Jacobsen's work, Wordsworth was among the poets whose publications were in German hands. Robinson, Coleridge, Holcroft (and Wordsworth himself), are indicative of the steady stream of British travellers, some settling for considerable periods of time, others migratory, who were a familiar feature of German life throughout this time, as they had been for much of the previous century. They brought books with them, they ordered up books to keep them in touch with all aspects of life at home; and these books circulated.

Once brought to the attention of the reading public in compendiums such as those of Reuss, Wordsworth, along with his contemporaries, was on his way to becoming a British poet of sufficient consequence to merit the relatively generous coverage he was to receive in Jacobsen's *Briefe* 16 years later.

3 Letters to a German Noblewoman on the New English Poetry: Friedrich Jacobsen and William Wordsworth

The Contents: Who Were the 'new poets'?

> 'What wits, what poets dost thou daily raise!'
> English Bards and Scotch Reviewers, in Byron 1970, 113

Friedrich Johann Jacobsen was born on 29 June 1774; he died in 1822. His career was in the law, but his passion was German culture, and this was accompanied by an enthusiasm for British literature, particularly poetry. According to the Scottish Germanist Robert Pearce Gillies (1788–1858), he was a man with an expansive and voluble character (Gillies 1851, 270). Most of his publications were on legal issues, but in 1820 he produced a book that reflected his enthusiasm for British poetry. The *Briefe an eine deutsche Edelfrau, über die neuesten englischen Dichter* (*Letters to a German Noblewoman on the New English Poetry*) lists nine women dedicatees, including Jacobsen's wife, Maria, and the chief recipient, Elise von Hohenhausen. Hohenhausen's book on Rousseau, Goethe and Byron (1847) informs us that the writers are to be discussed from an 'ethical and Christian standpoint' (*ethisch-christlichen Standpunkte*) and in this respect, as well as in her means of endorsing the stature of her subjects, she typifies the attitude of many of her contemporaries, influenced by the post-war generation that included Jacobsen.

Byron plays a dominant role in Jacobsen's *Letters*. He serves as a measure of greatness for all the new English poets; but for a literary culture firmly committed to Christian ideals, Byron – like Goethe and Rousseau – might on occasion be found wanting. As an avid reader of British journals, Jacobsen may well have noted verses on Byron that appeared in *The Gentleman's Magazine* in July 1818 (volume 88, part 2, p. 137): 'Rich were thy talents, but thy morals poor!' (Prawer 1961, 62). Hohenhausen argues that the work of a true genius is for all time, exhibiting a universality that exceeds such moral restrictions. These are writers who belong on the stage of 'World Literature', and their work should not therefore be judged against the standards required of lesser mortals whose lives and works are more properly carried on in accordance with the ethical and Christian demands peculiar to their time. Goethe is usually given the credit for establishing the notion of World Literature in the German mind: 'the epoch of world literature is at hand', he told Eckermann in 1827, 'and everyone must strive to hasten its approach' (Weissbort 2006, 204). Jacobsen's *Letters*, however, reveal that this concept was influential well before this. Of the British writers being read in the German states through the eighteenth and into the nineteenth century, Shakespeare had attained the distinction of being considered a universal genius; by 1820 Byron was generally considered to belong in the same category. What we learn from Jacobsen is that in this immediate post-war era, an eloquent case was being made for Wordsworth as a poet of equal genius. Though Jacobsen's enthusiasm failed to bring about a German reception of Wordsworth on anything like the scale of Byron, Moore or Felicia Hemans, it most certainly did much to establish him as a British poet who continued as a presence in nineteenth-century Germany to a level that has not previously been fully appreciated.

In the *Letters*, Jacobsen no sooner begins to reflect on Wordsworth's qualities as a morally upright, pious worshipper of nature, and an unswerving patriot, than he draws Byron into the discussion. He suggests that Wordsworth at his best may remind us of Byron. But, equally, after this predictable opening gesture, Wordsworth's own voice begins increasingly to assert itself, and it does appear that the more Jacobsen read his poetry, and read appraisals of him in the British magazines and reviews, the more he came to admire him, until eventually his meeting with him in London in 1820 confirmed his view that here was one of the most important poets of the age (Jacobsen 1820, 711).

Jacobsen was by no means the only German admirer of Wordsworth to achieve a personal introduction. However, we need to treat his evidence in this respect with care. In the first of his chapters on Wordsworth he refers to 'Herr Kemperhausen', who had written about his visit to Wordsworth at his Rydal Mount home. Eudo C. Mason unquestioningly confirmed 'Kemperhausen' as a German Wordsworthian on the strength of Jacobsen's account (Mason 1959, 126). In fact R. P. Gillies had used the name 'Phillip Kempfherhausen' as a *nom de plume* in his account of his own trip to the Lake District to visit Southey and Wordsworth, published in *Blackwood's Edinburgh Magazine* in 1819 (no. XXIV, 1819, pp. 735–44). John Wilson (under the pseudonym of Christopher North) then used the name (spelling it 'Kemperhausen') as a nickname for Gillies in his series of articles for *Blackwood's*, the 'Noctes Ambrosianae', which began to be published in 1822. The 'Noctes Ambrosianae' are perhaps best summarized as approximating to an Edinburgh-based, alcoholically fuelled prequel to *The Pickwick Papers*; Gillies (as 'Kemperhausen') only appears in the first of them, but one wonders if, when he later visited Jacobsen in Altona in 1821, Jacobsen discovered his mistake. Jacobsen read 'Kempfherhausen's' letters from the Lake District assuming that he was one of the regular flow of German visitors to England eager to meet the major writers of the day. He will have met and talked to many of them as they passed through his native Hamburg and Altona. We do know that in 1813 the 19-year-old Johann Martin Lappenberg arrived in Edinburgh with the intention of seeking out Wordsworth (Gothein 1893, i). Gillies also met Lappenberg soon after his meeting with Jacobsen in Altona. Alan Hill has recently researched the roll-call of Germans – including Jacobsen, Lappenberg, Bunsen and Barthold Georg Niebuhr – who read, and sought out, Wordsworth during this period (Hill 2008; and Young 1871, I, 173–5). Jacobsen's book confirms the ubiquity of British literary texts in Germany; the printed sources he could call on were numerous, and so also was the information to be had by word of mouth from British visitors and Germans passing through Hamburg on their return from Britain. Jacobsen's list of subscribers – to be discussed in a later section of this chapter – provides further evidence of the extent of Anglo-German cultural exchanges at this time. By the 1830s, it has been estimated that half the sea-borne trade of Hamburg was carried in British ships, and many Hamburg firms had branches in London and cultivated British habits. The Bavarian diplomat von Homayer wrote: 'I can find next to nothing that is German in Hamburg, apart from the language ... There can be no question of any German blood here' (Evans 1987, 4). At the end of the century the poet Hermann Claudius (1878–1980) described Hamburg as 'Tor der Welt', 'The proverbial gateway to the world', a city that had always been more familiar with Britain and North and South America than it had been with Germany (Hohendahl 2003, 196).

Jacobsen's *Letters* is 741 pages long. It includes portraits of eight of his poets (Byron, Moore, Montgomery, Wordsworth, Southey, Lady Morgan, Scott and Campbell); it has 39 chapters ('Letters'), and a conclusion. Each chapter tends to focus on a single poet, but there are some that bring several poets together. Some poets, notably Byron and Moore, are mentioned throughout the book; Wordsworth too is reprised towards the end. The first five chapters are devoted to Moore, and he returns to Moore again in chapter 30 (along with a number of others) to discuss the issue of translation. The first chapter begins, however, with a reference to Byron, when we are told that after Byron, Moore is his favourite British poet (his 'Liebling') (Jacobsen 1820, 2). One thing we soon discover about Jacobsen is that he is only truly at ease when he can enthuse about his subject. By the time he has finished describing the lyrical beauties of Moore's poetry, it is hard to imagine any other poet coming anywhere near him. But most of them do; while a few – including Wordsworth – appear to awaken a deeper response triggered by evidence of the poet's religious piety and patriotic commitment.

Jacobsen's book provides a significant endorsement for the theory first posited in the 1920s by Kluckhohn, Wiegand and others that German culture from 1815 to 1848 might be summarized by the term 'Biedermeier', despite the evolution of the politically inspired 'Young Germany' movement. Jacobsen's enthusiasm for Wordsworth, and Wordsworth's subsequent continuing popularity, are in part explained by Virgil Nemoianu's summary of *Biedermeier* characteristics: 'inclination towards morality, a mixture of realism and idealism, peaceful domestic values, idyllic intimacy, lack of passion, cosiness, contentedness, innocent drollery, conservatism, resignation' (Nemoianu 1984, 4). Commenting on the diminished popularity of Caspar David Friedrich's paintings during this period, Beat Wyss suggests that at this time 'the preference was for a cosier style, for more stories, for something more sentimental' (Wyss 2008, 54). There is an uncanny suggestion, indeed, of Wordsworth and Dorothy huddled round their stove during the bitterly cold winter they spent in Goslar in 1798–9, in Heine's ironic sketch of the *Biedermeier* German traveller who, the moment he leaves home, longs to return to his seat 'behind the stove and squat there warmly and read *The German's General Advertiser*' (Heine 1943, 62). In the 1970s Friedrich Sengle developed a comprehensive critique of German literature from 1815 to 1848 based on the ubiquity of a *Biedermeier* sensibility, and Nemoianu's work has extended the idea into a European context.

Poets dealt with individually (in the order they appear) are Moore, Montgomery (one chapter), Wordsworth and Southey (two chapters each), John Wilson (two chapters), Anne Grant of Laggan, Herbert and Bloomfield (one chapter each); Scott and Crabbe come together over three chapters, Samuel Rogers has two chapters, Campbell and James Grahame have one chapter each. Byron has four chapters to himself towards the end of the book. Otherwise, poets grouped together are Eaton Stannard Barrett and Felicia Hemans; Coleridge and Lamb; Lady Morgan and Maria Edgeworth; Anna Seward, William Tennant, and James Hogg; William Hone and William Combe (whose name he misspells); Lord Lyttleton, Edward Young, James Beattie, Goldsmith, and Blair; Henry Milman, Eleanor Porden (whom he spells 'Pordens') and Thomas Browne; Joseph Mellish, Payne, and Sharon Turner. John Clare is referred to in the Conclusion. These are the basic ingredients; the final roll-call of poets exceeds 50, a reminder that the process of canonization for British poets of the period was still in its infancy. Constant point of reference as Byron is throughout the book, the 74 pages of his four chapters are topped by Moore's 81, while Coleridge is given only six pages against Lamb, who gets the lion's share in chapter 12. Three of Coleridge's pages are taken up with quotations from the one poem on offer, *Christabel*. Wordsworth's two chapters (8 and 9) give him 49 pages; he is introduced in the context of the British Lake Poets and followed by Robert Southey (chapters 10–11). Bringing in Coleridge as quite such an afterthought reflects the influence on Jacobsen of *Blackwood's* when it came to assessing this group. He has read of Coleridge falling out with his fellow Lakers, and laments it as a failing on Coleridge's part. He has nothing to say at all about *The Ancient Mariner*, a poem that was soon to gain considerable admiration across Germany in Ferdinand Freiligrath's translation.

Blackwood's was evidently very much to Jacobsen's taste; its 'Horae Germanicae' series enthusiastically introduced German writing to its readers over several years, and these articles included substantial extracts in translation. But this was one of only several sources of British critical opinion he used; another was Francis Jeffrey's consistently anti-German *Edinburgh Review*. For a reader with Jacobsen's positive turn of mind, it would be intriguing to know exactly what he made of Jeffrey's damning indictment of Wordsworth's *The Excursion*, published in 1814. From *Blackwood's* he knew this work as the poet's major opus, containing passages of great beauty. With the rest of his output, up to and including the *River Duddon* volume of 1820, this was poetry that gave evidence of Wordsworth's originality and single-minded commitment to poetry. The relentless strictures that came from Jeffrey's pen must have shocked him, and he refers to them in the *Letters*; but it took more than this to dampen Jacobsen's growing admiration for *The Excursion* and its author. We may safely assume that in November 1814 he had read *Blackwood's* scornful rebuttal of an article by Jeffrey on the subject of Goethe's life: 'It is probable that the ingenuous editor of the *Edinburgh Review* is himself quite ignorant of German literature . . .' (no. XX vol. 4, 212).

While we need to remember that literary criticism was set to evolve from what it was at the turn of the eighteenth century into something very different by the end of the nineteenth, we also need to appreciate the different context for criticism that existed in Germany and England at the time Jacobsen was writing. Jacobsen will have had only a limited understanding of the circumstances that inspired Jeffrey's implacable hatred of what he understood to be the subversive, Jacobinical agenda of the Lake Poets. How much, I wonder, did he fully appreciate the extent of anti-German prejudice in England at the time that he was enjoying the hospitality of his British friends in 1820? This was evident not only in Jeffrey's *Edinburgh Review*, but also in Wordsworth's own Preface to *Lyrical Ballads*, and in Sharon Turner's *Prolusions on the Present Greatness of Britain* (1819), a text Jacobsen knew well and valued highly, as his use of it in the *Letters* shows. This brings us back to a debate that inevitably recurs throughout any discussion of the evolution of German national identity through the nineteenth century, the phenomenon that Wolf Lepinies sums up in his phrase, 'a strange indifference to politics': the belief that Germans developed a peculiar ability to separate culture and metaphysics from the realm of political action. Lepinies cites John Dewey's view that this way of thinking was implanted in the German mind by Kant. Quoting from Dewey's *German Philosophy and Politics* (1915), he notes:

> . . . a 'supreme regard for the inner meaning of things . . . in disregard of external consequences of advantage and disadvantage' distinguishes the German spirit from the worldliness of the Latin mind-set or the utilitarianism of the Anglo-Saxon nations. Even German authors ridiculed the 'German spirit.' In 1933, the year the Nazis came to power, Oswald Spengler described the Germans as a people poor and pitiful who dreamed of an empire in the clouds and called it German idealism. The land of poets and thinkers was in danger of becoming a province of babblers and demagogues. (Lepenies 2006, 11–12)

Scorn for the metaphysical turn of the German mind is commonplace in early nineteenth-century Britain, from the *Anti Jacobin* to Thomas Love Peacock (satirizing Coleridge's enthusiasm for Kantian metaphysics in *Crochet Castle* 1831), through Francis Jeffrey in the *Edinburgh Review* to Sharon Turner's *Prolusions*. Jacobsen emerges from the pages of the *Letters* as an enthusiast for an exalted, other-worldly ideal of culture, who dreams at the same time of a great and powerful German nation. While he urges German poets to compose nationalistic works, he strives to maintain a lofty indifference to matters of immediate, practical political import; and in this he believes he has found a kindred spirit in Wordsworth.

Though there is an evaluative element running through the *Letters*, they remain a near relation to the cataloguing genre in which Reuss worked. One of Jacobsen's major aims is to list the poets publishing in Britain in the early decades of the century; he gives his readers biographical sketches, and wants them to appreciate the range of subject matter and style partly through his own descriptive (rather than analytical) passages, and also through a generous helping of quotation; he quotes in English and provides prose translations in footnotes. The impression given is that he does not wish to appropriate the poetry in any other way than to give a precise equivalent ('word for word') German translation; this decision will have been influenced by the fact that he himself had no pretensions as a poet. Appearances, however, may be deceptive.

His trawl for publishing poets brings names to the surface that in some cases barely survived the century. Joseph Charles Mellish was the *chargé d'affaires* in Hamburg, was a friend of Gillies and wrote German verse; but despite Gillies' approval of him, he was clearly a minor figure even at this time. The case of Eleanor Anne Porden is rather different. Before she became the wife of Sir William Franklin, the arctic explorer, she published a long poem, *The Veils; or, the Triumph of Constancy* (1815) that swiftly became popular. It impressed Jacobsen, and was well reviewed in *The Gentleman's Magazine* (January 1816, 45–9). *The Arctic Expedition* (1818) and *Coeur de Lion* (1822) also enjoyed considerable, if relatively brief, popularity.

Some of Jacobsen's other less familiar names suggest another factor at work when a German author of this period turned to Britain to select poetry by writers of the modern age. Thomas Browne, who published *The Paradise of Coquettes* in 1814, was Professor of Moral Philosophy at Edinburgh; Anne Grant of Laggan (1755–1838) published *The Highlanders and other Poems* in 1808; James Grahame (1765–1811), James Montgomery (1771–1854), and William Tennant (1784–1848) were likewise Scottish, as was John Wilson of *Blackwood's* (1785–1854). A love of the land of mountains, lakes and forests, the cradle of Ossian, undoubtedly influences the reception of British poetry in nineteenth-century Germany. Wordsworth, as a native of the Lake District, seemed to offer poetry and religion that sprang from a landscape and a society that might equally be aligned to the Germania dreamt of by patriots like Jacobsen. Words-worth's 'To a Highland Girl' features prominently in the poetry he quotes in chapter 8, while not many years after this Freiligrath was to produce a transla-tion of 'The Solitary Reaper' (set in Scotland) that remained popular with German anthologists for the rest of the century.

By no means all of what we would now regard as Jacobsen's choice of minor poets were Scottish, however. Henry Milman (1791–1868), Dean of St. Paul's, pub-lished a poem in 1820 that was considered a major work, *The Fall of Jerusalem*. The reviewer in the *Quarterly* verbosely described it as 'a poem to which, without extravagant encomium it is not unsafe to promise whatever immortality the English language can bestow', predicting for Milman a place alongside Milton 'in our poeti-cal Pantheon' (May 1820, 225). Lady Morgan's *Helga: A Poem in Seven Cantos* was likewise considered to be a work that would stand the test of time. Sharon Turner, lawyer, historian, and poet in retirement, is a different case entirely. His *Prolusions on the Present Greatness of Britain* provided Jacobsen with a versified source of pietistic commentary on contemporary British poets which he refers to several times throughout his book. The passage of 118 lines which he quotes in the final chapter encapsulates Jacobsen's beliefs, not only with regard to a vision of a world trans-formed by the triumph of Christianity, but also in respect of the merits of a constitutional monarchy:

> Of all the good from monarchy that flows –
> That polish'd monarchy which Europe knows;
> How grateful to the time-comparing mind,
> Its tendency to humanize mankind!
> To soften manners; throw on life a grace,
> And give society a courteous face!
> The rude, fierce baron, thus became the knight;
> The love-crowned knight, the nobleman polite.
> The forms of cultur'd life descending down,
> All educated mind form'd like the crown.
> Thus, as the mild humanities expand,
> Our sovereigns live the teachers of their land.
>   (Turner 1819, in Jacobsen 1820, 718)

Jacobsen admired the way Turner's critical opinions were founded on his reli-gious and political principals. Turner was prepared to sign up as a subscriber to Jacobsen's book.

The *Letters* is evidence of a volatile book market flourishing within the context of expanding, buoyant trade exchanges between Germany and Britain; and Hamburg lay at the heart of this economic activity. Along with the other two Hanseatic cities, Lübeck and Bremen, Hamburg holds a unique place in relation to the evolution of the German nation. Jacobsen's fervent nationalism is contextualized by the distinctly non-Prussian cosmopolitan history of where he lived. As Richard J. Evans has explained, Germany's second-largest city after Berlin was perceived as 'a "foreign body" in the German Empire, an "English" town in a continental setting' (Evans 1987, viii). Hamburg was an autonomous state within the German Confederation, and continued as such within the German Empire after 1870. A federal state in its own right, it was ruled primarily by liberal, middle-class merchants. Prior to 1815, when it came within the orbit of Prussian power, it had been occupied by Danes in 1801 and by the French in 1806; in 1807–8 15,000 Spanish troops moved in; in 1810, when Napoleon annexed the North German coast, it was incorporated into France, and ceased to operate as a free Hanseatic city. The French withdrew in 1813, reoccupied, then finally withdrew in 1814, when the Constitution of 1712 was restored. Until 1860 the Constitution gave power to the wealthiest of the citizenry, and these included lawyers (like Jacobsen) as much as merchants; a parliamentary element was not introduced until 1860. The war had never completely closed down trade between Britain and Europe and it has been estimated that Germany was absorbing a third of Britain's entire European exports, primarily in textiles, with Hamburg, Bremen, and Frankfurt most heavily involved. With trade came an exchange of personnel, German firms frequently employing British clerks and salesmen. With trade came also a momentum for cultural exchange.

In 'The British Merchant' (1729) Edward Young described the way in which trade was seen to 'gild the world with Learning's brighter sun'. Young's use of the words 'rich' and 'gild' is anything but ingenuous:

> COMMERCE gives Arts, as well as gain
> By Commerce wafted o'er the main,
> They barbarous climes enlighten as they run.
> Arts, the rich traffic of the soul,
> May travel thus from pole to pole,
> And gild the world with Learning's brighter sun.
>
> (Shields 1990, 23)

Paul M. Kennedy has emphasized the importance in this respect of the strong sense of a shared Protestant heritage that existed between the two countries in Jacobsen's time. Cultural ties developed as 'an extension of the commercial relationships', and were endorsed by the sense of a common Christian heritage (Kennedy 1980, 109). The significance of a sense of religious empathy becomes very marked in the course of Jacobsen's book, and it is one reason why Wordsworth in particular came to mean so much to him.

Translating a Poet of Nature, Religion and Nation into German

> 'Never be it ours
> *To see the Sun how brightly it will shine,*
> *And know that noble Feelings, manly Powers,*

Instead of gathering strength must droop and pine,
And Earth with all her pleasant fruits and flowers
Fade, and participate in Man's decline.'
                    'There is a bondage', in Wordsworth 1983, 168–9

The *Letters* should be read with very careful attention to their political, social, and religious European, post-war context. Jacobsen does not read the *Edinburgh Review*, *Blackwood's*, *The Quarterly*, or the *Gentleman's Magazine* primarily for an insight into the issues that dominated the British party-political scene, issues that coloured so much of how the reviewers went about their tasks. As a German recently liberated from the Napoleonic yoke, he celebrates his freedom to be 'German', to travel and to indulge his passion for British poetry. A political agenda is very much in evidence throughout the book, but Jacobsen's politics are contextualized by the European politics of post-war reconstruction under Metternich, where the nationalism of a native of Hamburg is potentially a radical response to Metternich's conservatism. He celebrates the opportunity to read as widely as he pleases from the plethora of texts before him, and this being the case, he is in no mood to administer adverse criticism to any of them.

Eudo C. Mason concluded his book *German and English Romanticism* with a short chapter on Jacobsen's *Letters*, in which he comments on the care Jacobsen took to avoid giving offence to Byron enthusiasts despite the fact that he clearly found himself drawn to Wordsworth. He quotes from the end of the final Wordsworth chapter, 'I am reluctant to part company from Wordsworth, as he strikes so many chords in my mind . . . ' ('Ich trenne mich ungern von Wordsworth, er berührt so viele Sayten meines Gemüths . . . '), adding that it is the poet's moral integrity that inspired him, while he found Byron's lack of seriousness in this respect, notably the immoral parts in *Don Juan*, disturbing ('unheimlich') (Mason 1959, 125).

Mason goes on to suggest that as Jacobsen was in the process of completing his book, a meeting he had with Wordsworth in London in June 1820 gave him further reason to doubt his earlier assertion that Moore and Byron were the greatest English poets. Could it be that after all, as Samuel Rogers told him, Wordsworth was the greatest living poet? (Mason 1959, 125; Jacobsen 1820, 711). Mason describes how Wordsworth and Jacobsen met at Rogers' house shortly before the poet set off with Mary and Dorothy on a tour through Switzerland to the Italian lakes (July–November 1820). Jacobsen was won over, it seems, by Wordsworth's devout Christianity, 'der christlichen Religion und der Moralgestze' (Mason 1959, 125). Given what he had already written at the end of his second Wordsworth chapter, he was ready to be impressed. John Moultrie met Wordsworth shortly after his return from the continent in 1820, and his impression – expressed in verse – helps to explain why Jacobsen responded in the way he did:

> He then had turned his fiftieth year
> > Older in aspect than in age;
> > And less of poet than of sage
> Methought did in his looks appear . . .
> His face and form were thin and spare
> > As of ascetic anchorite,
> > Yet with us boys in converse light
> He joined with free and genial air.
>   (Moorman 1968, II, 327)

Mason's argument does not seem altogether consistent. He states that Jacobsen's book was popular, and also suggests that his work reflects a wider debate going on among his countrymen on the relative merits of Wordsworth and Byron. Later chapters in this book will show that there is evidence for the continuing influence of the *Letters* through into the early twentieth century. Yet Mason's reference to Jacobsen's 'timid eclecticism' ('furchtsamen Eklektizismus') leads him to assert that Jacobsen's book did little to encourage Germans to read Wordsworth. Not even Freiligrath in the next generation, he claims, was able to achieve that (Mason 1959, 125). Mason's treatment of Jacobsen is probably influenced by his enthusiasm for Goethe, and Goethe had made it very clear that he had little time for Wordsworth (and probably even less for Hamburg and its cultural coteries).

In his chapters on Thomas Moore Jacobsen quotes the poet's descriptions of landscape at length. Poetry which transports the reader out of a world of cares and into the realm of sheltering sentimentality appeals to him:

> When tired of life and misery,
> I wish to sigh my latest breath,
> Oh, Emma! I will fly to thee,
> And thou shalt sing me unto death!
> ('To a Lady, On Her Singing' in Jacobsen 1820, 58)

In Wordsworth's case, he quotes lines from Sharon Turner's *Prolusions* to help make the case for the esteem in which he holds him:

> 'Tis rapture to behold true genius soar,
> When guardian judgment dignifies its store.
> Judgment! The kindest Friend that Feeling knows;
> And by whose aid her deathless beauty glows.
> Wordsworth!
> I love thy energies; thy soul; thy views;
> Thy sympathies; the harmonies thy muse
> With such a careless elegance oft breathes.
> Strike her superior lyre and claim her nobler wreaths.
> Thy mind is mightier than thy themes, and gives
> Thy voice, not theirs, to all that round thee lives.
> (Turner 1819, in Jacobsen 1820, 119–20)

Jacobsen has edited out a ten line detour in this passage on Horace, and inserts in its place 'Wordsworth!'. From the final two lines it is clear that Turner feels constrained to complain about Wordsworth's choice of subject matter. Many believed him perverse in the way he sought to express his profoundest reflections on the human condition. Earlier in the poem Turner wrote (and Jacobsen will have read):

> Why give material nature feeling – thought –
> Meaning and voice, – by your emotions sought,
> But to brute matter absent and unknown,
> As the dell's echoes or the forest groan?
> The druid thus rever'd his mistletoe;
> India her cow; and Rome, the wandering crow.
> (Turner 1819, 116)

There is more than a suggestion here of Jeffrey's claim that Wordsworth writes like a superstitious pagan, not a sophisticated, civilized Christian in receipt of revealed religion. It is equally interesting to reflect on what Jacobsen made of the *Prolusions* when he reached the passage in which Turner became even more specific about Wordsworth's failings:

> Too much that German spirit here appears,
> Which loves to mystify our hopes and fears:
> Which, if it gaze upon a portrait, sees
> A moving eye, or hears a moaning breeze:
> Which hunts the supernatural thro' life,
> And courts a fever'd mind, and wild'ring strife.
>
> (Ibid., 117–18)

Though well aware that Wordsworth was frequently subject to fierce criticism in England, Jacobsen stood his ground, enthusiastic about how Wordsworth combines his love of nature with his philosophical and religious reflections, and his patriotism.

The *Letters* is crucially a work of cultural exchange defined by the 1820s, at the centre of which lie the complex processes of translation. Dominico Jervolino has written that 'To speak is already to translate (even when one is speaking one's own native language . . .)' (Ricoeur 2006, xv). Richard Kearny responds to Jervolino by reflecting that 'As soon as there is language there is interpretation, that is translation'. Kearney is discussing Paul Ricoeur's inclusive definition of translation which incorporates a sensitivity not only to the relationship between words and meanings 'within language or between language', but also to 'how translation occurs between one human self and another' (Ricoeur 2006, xii). The 'predicament' of translation, Ricoeur writes, 'is that of a correspondence without complete adhesion. This is a fragile condition, which admits of no verification other than a new translation . . .' (Ricoeur 2006, xvii).

Jacobsen's *Letters* must be considered as a work of translation in every respect. Translation denotes a condition of irresolvable difference; from this difference Jacobsen seeks to enrich his readers' cultural life, to explore and confirm a sense of his own identity as a German, and to propose the possibility of a situation where linguistic and national difference might be transcended. Men like Lappenberg, Gillies, Taylor and Turner wrote of both the differences and the cultural and historical affinities of the two nations; Gillies tended to stress the differences that a nineteenth-century traveller notices 'in regard to language and moods of mind', yet argues that this is a relatively recent phenomenon (Gillies 1826, x). Like Lappenberg and Turner, he sees the differences (including the linguistic divide) becoming significantly marked in the course of the eighteenth century. Gillies' description of his engagement with German culture in his *Memoirs* suggests an attitude not dissimilar to Jacobsen when he made his way into the crowd of British poets that he found so enticing. Gillies describes himself entering a 'stupendous cavern':

> . . .with its glittering stalactites, and its various treasures guarded by Teutonic genii, who would be propitiated by one who came before them humbly, but courageously. (Gillies 1851, 265)

A major preoccupation for Jacobsen becomes very apparent towards the end of the book in chapter 30. Here he writes again about Moore, drawing attention to his feeling for his native country, before launching into a section that outlines the difficulties of finding a worthy national song for Germany, claiming that he knows of no country that has yet produced a form of writing fully worthy of the task, 'No *Volk* possesses a national song which would live up to my ideal' (Jacobsen 1820, 541–2). The National Anthem he craves should be the highest expression of a national literature rooted in earlier, primitive folk song. As he reads through the literature of other nations, specifically the British poets, he is struck by the power of the words and music of 'Rule Britannia', and in France by the appeal of the 'Marseillaise' (ibid., 513). As he sketches a route towards the creation of a German Anthem, we can see him looking beyond that to the aim of establishing a new German style, and beyond that to an idea of 'song' that ultimately transcends national boundaries. Embedded in this process lies the contradiction already noted in the German concept of 'World litera-ture': it belongs in a very German world. There is an act of translation taking place; the 'foreign' is observed, then appropriated, and reassembled in an altered form that is in this context implicitly an act of colonization and Germanization. There is no overt hostility to other nations in Jacobsen's discussion (though the French model is held to be inferior to the British one); later generations are left to reflect on the implications of what Jacobsen proposes. Mary Anne Perkins has discussed the complexity of Romantic Period ideas of nationalism in rela-tion to translation, 'the insistence of the Romantics on the particularity and uniqueness of nationhood', she writes, 'can no longer automatically be associ-ated with exclusivity and chauvinism. It must rather be seen as *one* aspect of a struggle to realize both nationhood and a cosmopolitan, humanitarian ideal' (Perkins 2001, 195). With Jacobsen in mind it is important to note again the significance of Hamburg's place within the history of the evolution of German nationalism. In the late 1760s Hamburg was chosen as the site of a National theatre, a project initiated by Johann Heinrich Löwen, who appointed Lessing 'house critic' of the theatre in 1767. The reason for choosing Hamburg seems to have had more to do with funding than with the commitment of the citizens to the arts, but it was fostered also by the idea that Hamburg was a city open to new ideas, and to the notion of the centrality of the arts to a vision of the Ger-man nation as a whole. Peter Uwe Hohendahl has described Klopstock (who settled in Hamburg in 1770) as a new kind of poet who represented 'the private commitment of the artist to the spirit of the republic. In its public performance his poetry celebrated not the narrow interests of the city-state but the idea of a free political community.' (Hohendahl 2003, 13). The unresolved contradictions for an open city like Hamburg when it embraces nationalism are summed up by Perkins as a tension within Romantic Period nationalism as a whole: 'the idea of nationhood, expressed in a particular nation, must involve the apparent contradictions of the universal (represented by the cosmopolitan ideal), and the particular (represented by the ideal of patriotism)' (Perkins 2001, 195). The vol-atility of the post-war situation is reflected in the long extract from Turner's *Prolusions* Jacobsen quoted in the final chapter of *Letters*:

> 'Tis not the hour to hesitate or pause.
> Kingdoms, like nature, feel the potent laws,
> For ever acting in our double frames.
> Body once rul'd, the spirit now inflames.
> The world, its day of sloth, will know no more.

All nations are in movement. Some to soar;
And some are gliding downward to their fates,
And melt to provinces of mightier states.
One rising, others to maintain their place,
Must mount proportion'd, or endure disgrace,
The lingerers in improvement sink below,
An easy conquest to a wiser foe.
Progress gives strength superior; and its course
All must partake, or bend before its force.

(Jacobsen 1820, 720–1)

This bland, disturbing blueprint for social Darwinism should be born in mind while considering Jacobsen's section on establishing a National Anthem. His thinking is manifestly in tune with Turner, and as we shall see in the next chapter, when he reads Wordsworth's *The Excursion*, he encounters sentiments of a very similar nature that go on to develop a vision of Britain as the mightiest of the 'mightier states' destined to dominate Europe, if not the entire world.

The first point Jacobsen makes about how the National song should be written reminds us of his enthusiasm for Wordsworth. We should listen to the voice of Nature and follow its promptings: 'Man müsste die Natur belauschen, um auf die rechte Spur desselben zu kommen.' He next makes a point which has already been broached in this chapter through reference to Wolf Lepenies' book: 'Ein Nationalgesang müsste auf Jahrhunderte Interesse behalten, folglich ohne alle temporäre Beziehungen seyn.' This will be a song that will remain relevant for many hundreds of years. There can therefore be no reference in it to immediate, current political events (this was the weakness of the *Marseillaise*). Thirdly (and again, Jacobsen's admiration of Wordsworth's poetry comes to mind here) the National song should endorse the view that God actively intervenes to protect his people, 'so müsste der Nationalgesang jedem Gemüthe den Glauben an den speciellen Schutz der Gottheit einimpfen . . .' (ibid., 542–3).

With these ingredients, the song would move on to celebrate the blessings of a Nation's way of life, and urge people to do their best for their country in times of peace and war. It would be taught in all schools and sustain the individual through life and, indeed, help transport the patriot into the next world. Just as Freemasons have a universal identity, he suggests, so Germans would know each other in the afterlife by their singing; there would be a German 'zone':

Wie die Gesetze der Freimaurer müsste der Ton des Liedes in jeder Zone Deutsche an Deutsche ketten. Ganz müsste es durch dasselbe wahr werden, was Schiller sang:
> *Er tritt heilige Gewalt,*
> *Ihm darf nichts Irdisches sich nähern.*
> (He acquires divine power,
> Nothing earthly may approach him.)

(Ibid., 543)

The National Anthem should be supported by other ballads celebrating Germany's greatest moments in history. To bring the project to fruition, Jacobsen proposes that all German poets and musicians should enter a competition to produce the best Anthem, and that the rich of the Nation should provide the prize money. Jacobsen's aspirations will have been in part inspired by Ernst Moritz Arndt's popular poem of 1813, 'Des Deutchen Vaterland'. Patricia Anne Simpson draws attention to Arndt's religious agenda:

Arndt includes God in the imaginary linguistic community: God, who presumably understands the language perfectly, given his purported fondness for singing
Lieder in heaven. With this inclusion, Arndt establishes an alliance between divine
authority and the power of an organic, national realm. (Simpson 2007, 145)

Despite what to us might seem the all too obvious likelihood that (in the
manner of Arndt) Jacobsen's scheme invites aggressive rivalry between nations,
we should again remember the context in which it is being promoted to a post-
war German readership. Jacobsen's optimistic dream of strong nations living
peaceably side by side now that France has been put firmly in its place may
seem naïve in the extreme, but I suspect he truly did envisage that, just as Britain and Germany had fought together and won, in the future they would
continue to trade together and flourish – and in consequence become as one.

Wherever he discerns a National voice in the British poetry he reads, he
notes it with approval; this is the case when he reads Wordsworth's sonnets.
Where Theodor Körner had written a 'beautiful' sonnet in praise of Andreas
Hofer, likening him to William Tell, thereby projecting the war that was to cost
both men their lives onto a larger canvas, Wordsworth wrote not only of Hofer
in his sonnet of 1809, 'Of mortal parents is the Hero born' (Selincourt 1969,
250; Jacobsen 1820, 134), but in 'There is a bondage' he wrote also of tyranny
('Despotismus') rather than a specific tyrant, and thus offers a broader reflection
on the moral and spiritual state of man should he become complacent, cow-
ardly, and selfish once he has secured his freedom:

> There is a bondage which is worse to bear
> Than his who breathes, by roof, and floor, and wall,
> Pent in, a Tyrant's solitary Thrall:
> 'Tis his who walks about in the open air,
> One of a Nation who, henceforth, must wear
> Their fetters in their Souls. For who could be,
> Who, even the best, in such condition, free
> From self-reproach, reproach which he must share
> With Human Nature? Never be it ours
> To see the Sun how brightly it will shine,
> And know that noble Feelings, manly Powers,
> Instead of gathering strength must droop and pine,
> And Earth with all her pleasant fruits and flowers
> Fade, and participate in Man's decline.
>   (Wordsworth 1983, 168–9; Jacobsen 1820, 133–4)

The Subscribers

'. . . *of good poetry, the individual, as well as the species, survives. And how does it
survive but through the People?'*
        Wordsworth, Essay Supplementary to the Preface in Owen 1974, III, 84

Jacobsen's *Letters* provides a snapshot of the way in which Anglo-German cultural exchange functioned; and this is particularly so when we turn to the pages
that list the subscribers to the *Briefe an eine deutsche Edelfrau*. His list of 147 subscribers begins with four impressive German entries, one duchess and three of

the local aristocracy (Jacobsen 1820, vii). The majority of his subscribers are Germans living in Germany. The sixth name on the list, however, is Rudolph Ackermann, listed as 'Buchhändler in London'. Ackermann was born in 1764 in Saxony, and came to London in 1786 after having lived in Paris for several years. Initially he designed coaches. In 1795 he married an English woman and set up a print shop at 101, the Strand. For a few years he combined the print shop business with running a drawing school. His trade in books and fine arts flourished to the point where he closed the school. He became involved in various innovative schemes, including developing a process for waterproofing paper and cloth, carried out at a factory he set up in Chelsea. He was among the first to introduce gas lighting into his premises, and his continued work on carriage design led to a commission to build the carriage for Nelson's funeral procession in 1805. Ackermann's business interests extended not only to Germany, but to South America. His successful journal, the *Repository of Arts, Literature, Fashions, Manufactures, etc.*, included many contributions from William Combe and Thomas Rowlandson. It first appeared in 1809 and had 3,000 subscribers before the end of its first year. Combe's *Dr. Syntax's Tour in Search of the Picturesque* first appeared in Ackermann's *Poetical Magazine*, which ran from 1809 to 1811. He was responsible for introducing the genre of the Illustrated Magazine into England, the first of which was *The Microcosm of London* (1808–10). Equally successful was the *Forget-me-not*, first published in 1825. There can be no more impressive evidence of Ackermann's adoption by the British Establishment than the award of an entry into the Oxford University Press's *Dictionary of National Biography* which describes him as a 'noteworthy inhabitant of the British Isles'. It would be hard to find a German businessman at this time more thoroughly integrated into British Society and considered a pillar of the Establishment. This is reflected in the response to his campaign on behalf of widows and orphans of the allied troops killed in the Battle of Leipzig in 1813. The British Parliament made a donation of £100,000, which more than doubled the amount raised.

Although there is no record of Jacobsen attending one of Ackermann's popular literary gatherings while he was in London, given that he went to at least one of Samuel Rogers' similar functions, it is very likely that he did. As a Lutheran, Ackermann's 'strictly moral view of art and business' will have endeared him to Jacobsen (Hill 2007, 36). Ackermann put himself down for ten copies of the *Letters*.

Also prepared to take ten copies of the *Letters* were the London publishers John Murray and Henry Colburn. Murray, Colburn and Ackermann epitomize a particular breed of entrepreneur who possessed a combination of business acumen and an instinct for literary taste and discrimination that their authors frequently lacked. Jacobsen's list, however, is dominated not by individuals with a direct interest in the book trade, but by businessmen and bankers of various sorts, and with academics and clergymen. One is reminded of Edward Young's perception that cultural dissemination was the handmaid of trade. Jacobsen's two brothers are both included, one of whom was living in Altona while the other is noted as living in London. Of the British subscribers abroad, the contingent in Germany are Coleman MacGregor, the British Consul in Bremen, Hugh Mackey, a 'reformist preacher' based in Emden, and Robert Miles Sloman, a shipmaker of Hamburg. Further afield are Robert King, Alex Renny, E. M. Brodie and Patrick Cumming, businessmen based in Riga. The Danish Consul in Riga, Nicolaus Kriegsmann, put himself down for three copies.

Apart from one more Englishman, Sharon Turner, the remaining subscribers are primarily German, and they are for the most part described as businessmen or lawyers of some description; there are a few doctors among them. These were dilettante enthusiasts like Jacobsen himself, either dabbling to a degree in composition alongside a more sedate career or, like Samuel Rogers, men fortunate enough to have inherited money, whose job it is to invest and spend it. These were the people who were creating libraries, hosting the literary gatherings, lionizing the writers and artists, making sure they had the latest journals on their desks, and above all, moving the texts around. They were responsible for a network that encompassed Europe and beyond. The Scottish poet Thomas Campbell, for example, travelled across Germany in 1819–20, regularly reporting his literary news to Rogers in a series of letters.

Sharon Turner (1768–1847) practised as an attorney in London, but reading Percy's *Reliques of Ancient English Poetry* (1765) as a child left him with a lifelong fascination for Icelandic and Anglo-Saxon language and culture. He read widely in the area and began to write history. In 1799, after much original research into the Anglo-Saxon manuscripts in the Cottonian Library at the British Museum, he published the first part of his *History of England from the Earliest Period to the Norman Conquest.* The fourth and final volume appeared in 1805. Turner's originality was soon recognized, and he continued with a further series of histories, which appealed also to German readers. A version of his *History of England* was translated into German and published in Hamburg in 1828. In 1829 Turner retired from the law due to ill health, and his work now began to reflect increasingly dogmatic, fundamentalist religious views, as well as the scepticism for German philosophy already noted. One target of his various attacks on modern theology was the poet already noted as included in the *Letters*, Henry Milman, the Dean of St. Paul's. Turner's poetry was confined to two main projects, the *Prolusions* of 1819 which so interested Jacobsen, and a lengthy apologia for Richard III, which he worked on between 1792 and 1838. He belongs to a group of largely forgotten historians who began to study early history in a way that revolutionized the use of sources and established the basis of modern historiography; they include Benjamin Thorpe and Johann Lappenberg, a forerunner of Ranke and friend of Jacobsen (discussed in Chapter 2), Sir Francis Palgrave (1788–1861) and the Germanist John Mitchell Kemble (1807–57).

Jacobsen concludes his final, thirty-ninth chapter of the *Letters* with a quotation from Turner's *Prolusions* that encapsulates a fervent belief of his own, 'Ist es nicht von Gott, so kann es nicht bestehen':

> This maxim governs every land,
> – 'If this be not from God it cannot stand.'
> Reason and truth are earth's enduring rocks,
> Which scorn the waves of time, and dare their fruitless shocks.
> (Jacobsen 1820, 729)

As the *Prolusions* show, Turner followed the British literary scene with great interest. He advised John Murray on legal matters over many years and gave legal advice to the *Quarterly*, occasionally writing for it himself. He met Wordsworth in 1808 in London in the company of Coleridge, Longman (the host) and Mr Hill, the 'proprietor' of a journal. It is perhaps predictable that Wordsworth declared himself less than impressed with Turner, and referred to him as one of a number of 'curious fishes' that were present that evening (Moorman 1965, II, 118). At the time when he met Jacobsen 12 years later in 1820, however, Wordsworth was working on his sonnet sequence *Ecclesiastical Sketches* and using Turner's *History of the Anglo-Saxons* as a major source, alongside Bede, Hanmer and Stillingfleet. It would no doubt have pleased Jacobsen had he heard Wordsworth express his debt to Turner at their meeting.

By far the most generous subscriber to the *Letters* was a neighbour and long-standing friend of Jacobsen, Friedrich Perthes (1772–1843), the publicist and book-merchant of Hamburg already mentioned in Chapter 2 in connection with Joseph Görres. Perthes put himself down for 50 copies. He was committed to the Nationalist movement, and had struggled under the censorship that followed Napoleon's annexation of Hamburg in 1811. He shared Jacobsen's enthusiasm for the freedom of cultural exchange that Hamburg had come to epitomize as a Hanseatic city. Perthes is representative of those Germans who looked back to much earlier times to discover the roots of German identity, and no doubt he would have understood Jacobsen's decision to quote at length from Wordsworth's *The White Doe of Rylstone*. This poem (published in 1815), is set in the 16th century, a time when England, under Queen Elizabeth I, was forging its National identity in the context of bitter friction between Protestants and Roman Catholics. Jacobsen recognizes Wordsworth's preoccupation in *The White Doe* as being with those who strive to rise above the immediate demands of political faction in pursuit of greater spiritual truth, in the process endorsing many of the ideals shared by Perthes, Görres and their circle. By 1820 these men had largely retired from active political engagement, and so the fate of Emily, the heroine of *The White Doe*, left to mourn the loss of her family after the abortive Catholic 'Rising of the North' in 1569, will have struck a particular chord:

> Her sanction inwardly she bore,
> And stood apart from human cares:
> But to the world returned no more,
> Although with no unwilling mind
> Help did she give at need, and joined
> The Wharfdale Peasants in their prayers.
> At length, thus faintly, faintly tied
> To earth, she was set free, and died.
> Thy soul, exalted Emily,
> Maid of the blasted Family,
> Rose to the God from whom it came!
> – In Rylstone Church her mortal frame
> Was buried by her Mother's side.
> (Wordsworth 1988, 145; Jacobsen 1820, 163)

Beginning with the extract above (line 1,877), Jacobsen goes on to quote the final 52 lines of the poem towards the end of his final chapter on Wordsworth, commenting on the poet's haunting vision of a heroine untouched by worldly matters. A true nation must be rooted in spirituality, and he regrets not having the space to quote similarly uplifting and beautifully written passages from *Peter Bell* and *Benjamin the Waggoner*, assuring us that these poems will soon be available in a third volume of *Lyrical Ballads*. He must content himself, he says, with printing one of Wordsworth's best loved poems, 'She was a phantom of delight'. It is a poem that Jacobsen clearly sees continuing the theme of disembodied, spiritualized beauty epitomized by Emily in *The White Doe*. Although we do not know the beautiful girl Wordsworth dreams of in this poem, he writes, we can imagine her (just as he himself imagines her as he reads the poem):

> *. . . und ich vermag es nicht zu unterlassen, Ihnen das Sonnett abzuschreiben, welches die englische Nation am mehersten von Wordsworth bewundert, wenn Sie auch die schöne Jungfrau kennen, welche dem Dichter so im Schreiben vorgeschwebt haben mag, wie mir im Lesen.* (Jacobsen 1820, 166)

Jacobsen's reference to the 'admiration of the English Nation' suggests that, while he seems to relish the thought of the mysterious girl as an object of human desire, he also translates the phantom as the illusive spirit of Nationhood:

> She was a Phantom of delight
> When first she gleam'd upon my sight;
> A lovely Apparition, sent
> To be a moment's ornament;
> Her eyes as stars of Twilight fair;
> Like Twilight's, too, her dusky hair;
> But all things else about her drawn
> From May-time and the cheerful Dawn;
> A dancing Shape, an Image gay,
> To haunt, to startle, and way-lay.
>
> (Wordsworth 1983, 74; Jacobsen 1820, 166–7)

Biography and Criticism

> '*For twenty years he has lived in this grand country, and there devoted his whole soul to his divine art.*'
>
> *Gillies/Kempferhausen, in Blackwood's March 1819, 741*

Jacobsen's two Wordsworth chapters begin a section in the *Letters* on 'the Lake School poetry', of whom Wordsworth is said to be the most important member, followed by Southey, with Coleridge coming a poor third. On this, he claims (using his edited quotation from Turner's *Prolusions*) both Moore and Sharon Turner agree. Jacobsen then embarks on a biographical sketch of Wordsworth.

The source of the information on Wordsworth for the *Letters* remains a mystery. Reuss's brief account was probably to hand, but here we have a great deal more detail, beginning with the poet's birth at 'Cockesmouth' in April 1770, his schooling at Hawkshead, and his arrival at Cambridge in 1788 (which should be 1787). The walking tour of France, Switzerland and Italy is noted, and the publication in 1793 of *Descriptive Sketches* and *An Evening Walk*. Wordsworth then takes up residence in 'a cottage' at Alfoxden 'near Bridgewater' in Somerset, where he meets Coleridge. *Lyrical Ballads* is published in 1798, and soon after this, he travels to Germany with his sister and Coleridge. There is no mention of where they stayed, simply that the object of the trip was to study. Wordsworth returns to Grasmere, and soon after that moves to Rydal; in 1803 he marries Mary Hutchinson (that should be 1802) and has since had five children.

One daughter has died (which is correct, Catherine died in 1812) and two sons have died (which is incorrect; Thomas died in 1812, John and William lived until 1875 and 1883 respectively). 'Miscellaneous Poems' (by which he means *Poems in Two Volumes*) was published in 1807, and in 1814 a section of his major work, *The Recluse*, was published under the title of *The Excursion*. Mention is made of *The White Doe of Rylstone* as he summarizes Wordsworth as a very English poet who writes from the heart about love and duty as it relates to family responsibilities, and to his beloved country.

Jacobsen will have had access to biographical dictionaries; the best known of these is Alexander Stephens' *Public Characters*, but printed detail on Wordsworth's life was scarce, certainly not running to the kind of information that Jacobsen provides. Whittaker's *New Biographical Dictionary of 3000 Public Characters* (London 1825) notes that the poet was from a respectable family; it does have the correct date for his arrival in Cambridge, but it does not have Jacobsen's misleading reference to Bridgewater (which presumably should have been Bristol). Whittaker's author goes on to note the poet's early enthusiasm as 'a friend of liberty', commenting that for his poetry 'the consequence was rather ludicrous'. Collections of biographies of eminent men were popular at this time, but they contained mainly military and political subjects. Wordsworth was not going to merit anything like this level of interest until at least around the time that Jacobsen published the *Letters*. *The Parnassian Garland, or, Beauties of Modern Poetry*, edited by John Evans in 1807, is indicative. Of the 'Lake School' of poets, Southey merits eight entries, Coleridge six, and Wordsworth just one. That one happens to be the first Wordsworth poem that Ferdinand Freiligrath translated, 'Song for the Wandering Jew'. The German enthusiasm for Wordsworth that took Lappenberg across to Scotland in 1813 will have resulted in his finding out (and no doubt jotting down) details of the poet's life known to the literati of Edinburgh. Lappenberg and Jacobsen were neighbours (as Gillies reports), so here we have a likely source of his less than accurate information. Apart from Lappenberg, there was the regular flow of English and German travellers through Hamburg (Remnant, Holcroft, perhaps Crabb Robinson) all of whom were likely to end up at Jacobsen's table, telling him what they knew – or had heard – of Wordsworth's story.

The biography done, Jacobsen turns to the critical reception of Wordsworth in Britain, summarizing Jeffrey's damning review of *The Excursion* in the *Edinburgh Review* in a way that significantly softens the blows. Jeffrey's famous review (November 1814) beginning 'This will never do' is one of the most famous examples of unrelenting critical invective – bordering at times on hysteria – ever written. It is important to note, therefore, that strained through the joint process of translation and paraphrase, the savage irony of the original takes on a tone more of mild rebuke. Jacobsen's rendering of Jeffrey's charge that Wordsworth's solitude has resulted in a 'tendency to extravagance' and 'puerility' is far less dismissive than its original:

Einsames Nachsinnen zwischen diesen Naturszenen kann sicher die Seele für die Majestät poetischer Anschauung empfänglich machen, (obgleich es bemerkenswerth ist, dass alle grosse Dichter in dem vollen Strom der Gesellschaft lebten oder leben) aber die Collision mit gleichgestimmten Seelen, die Warnung vor verherrschenden Eindrücken scheint nöthig, die Fülle der selben zu hemmen und den Hang zur Uebertreibung und zum Kleinlichen zu unterdrücken. (Jacobsen 1820, 122)

Jacobsen is effectively summarizing Jeffrey's review here, and this helps to account for the stilted style. Square brackets in the following translation of the above are interpolations made in the light of a knowledge of the original:

> Lonely ponderings amidst these scenes of nature always makes the soul receptive to the majesty of the poetic view (although it is worth noting that all great writers lived or live in the full flow of society) but the [consequences of] a coming together of similarly joyful souls [the mingling of the human soul with the spirit of Nature] [carries with it] a warning that overwhelming impressions may hamper self-worth and result in a tendency to exaggeration and punctiliousness [for Jeffrey's 'puerility'?].

The passage from which Jacobsen was working is a great deal longer, but it is important to quote it in order to appreciate how he was – in every sense of the word – translating Wordsworth into the poet he had need of:

> Long habits of seclusion, and an excessive ambition of originality, can alone account for the disproportion which seems to exist between the author's taste and his genius; or for the devotion with which he has sacrificed so many precious gifts at the shrine of those paltry idols which he has set up for himself among his lakes and his mountains. Solitary musings, amidst such scenes, might no doubt be expected to nurse up the mind to the majesty of poetical conception, – (though it is remarkable that all the greater poets lived, or had lived, in the full current of society): – But the collision of equal minds, – the admonitions of prevailing impressions – seems necessary to reduce its redundancies, and repress that tendency to extravagance or puerility, into which the self-indulgence and self-admiration of genius is so apt to be betrayed, when it is allowed to wanton, without awe or restraint, in the triumph and delight of its own intoxication. (Haydon 1971, 41)

The crucial point that Jacobsen misses out is Jeffrey's insistence that it is living in society that provides the necessary checks against the imaginative self-indulgence to which Wordsworth is markedly prone.

Three paragraphs further on, Jacobsen gives a brief account of a long and considered article on Wordsworth that appeared in December 1818 in *Blackwood's*: 'Essays on the Lake School of Poetry. No. II. On the Habits of Thought, inculcated by Wordsworth'. First, however, comes the passage which reports on the travels of 'Herr Philipp Kemperhausen': 'Im Sommer 1818 besuchte Herr Philipp Kemperhausen, ein Deutscher, den Dichter in seinem Wohnorte' (Jacobsen 1820, 122). Gillies'/Kemperhausen's account of Wordsworth is one of unqualified enthusiasm, and it is interesting to see the passage that Jacobsen chooses to include as a direct quotation (unlike his excerpts of poetry, he translates it into German). This is Gillies' original text:

> Other poets, at least all I have ever known, are poets but on occasions – Wordsworth's profession is that of a poet; and therefore when he speaks of poetry, he speaks of the things most familiar, and, at the same time, most holy to his heart. For twenty years has he lived in this grand country, and there devoted his whole soul to his divine art. (*Blackwood's* No. XXIV March 1819, 741)

Jacobsen then goes on to quote a slightly less enthusiastic critic, 'ein anderer Kunstrichter' not named, who praises Wordsworth's 'grandeur of beliefs, delicacy of the heart' and 'warm feeling for the beauty of Nature', but notes also that Wordsworth has been criticized for allowing his enthusiasm in this respect to overrule his common sense, 'Der Critiker wirft ihm dann vor, dass er oft sich anstrengt, mehr als bloss vernünftig zu seyn' (Jacobsen 1820, 124).

The *Blackwood's* article of December 1818 to which he now turns, declares that Wordsworth's style of philosophical poetry is unique among his British contemporaries; he writes as one persistently out of tune with the taste of his day. This is not dismissed as necessarily a bad thing, a point made by way of a side-swipe at Byron's habit of writing about 'the Giaours and Corsairs, etc. of modern days':

> In these pieces, elements of human nature, which are by no means of the highest kind, are represented boiling and foaming with great noise, and their turbidity is falsely taken for the highest kind of nobleness and magnificence. (*Blackwood's* December 1818, 257–8)

The lowly born, philosophic pedlar of *The Excursion* is, by implication, much to be preferred (no doubt partly because Jeffrey had taken such exception to him in the *Edinburgh Review*). As Gillian Hughes has noted, *Blackwood's*, in no small measure through the contributions of Gillies and James Hogg, was associated with a tendency to satirize 'the spurious refinement of literary Edinburgh' (Hughes 2003, 67). Not surprisingly, therefore, the *Blackwood's* reviewer maintains a position of studied impartiality, illustrated by the following extract, a passage that would certainly have attracted the notice of the pietistic Jacobsen:

> ... the reverential awe, and the far extended sympathy with which he looks upon the whole system of existing things, and the silent moral connections which he supposes to exist among them, are visible throughout all his writings. He tunes his mind to nature almost with a feeling of religious obligation; and where others behold only beautiful colours, making their appearance according to optical laws, or feel pleasant physical sensations resulting from a pure atmosphere ... this poet (whether justly or not) thinks he traces something more in the spectacle than the mere reflection of his own feelings, painted upon external objects, by means of the association of ideas; or, at least, seems to consider what we then behold as the instantaneous creation of the mind. (*Blackwood's* December 1818, 260)

Immediately after this passages the writer quotes two passages from Book One of *The Excursion* that he believes epitomize Wordsworth's art (ll.219–30; ll.248–53). Jacobsen follows him almost exactly, even down to including a footnote for the second passage which explains who is being referred to. The first describes the spiritually uplifting experience of the Pedlar as he watches the sunrise and, in a departure from the spirit of *Blackwood's*, Jacobsen exclaims that the passage reminds him of Byron's longing 'to mingle with the universe' (a line from *Childe Harold's Pilgrimage*, Book IV stanza 178):

> O then what soul was his, when on the tops
> Of the high mountains, he beheld the sun
> Rise up, and bathe the world in light! He looked –
> Ocean and earth, the solid frame of earth,
> And ocean's liquid mass, beneath him lay
> In gladness and deep joy. The clouds were touched,
> And in their silent faces did he read
> Unutterable love. Sound needed none,
> Nor any voice of joy. His spirit drank
> The spectacle, sensation, soul, and form,
> All melted into him, they swallowed up
> His animal being.

The following 19 lines are cut in *Blackwood's*, and Jacobsen does the same, resuming with:

> All things there
> Breathed immortality, revolving life
> And greatness still revolving; infinite;
> There littleness was not; the least of things
> Seemed infinite; and there his spirit shaped
> Her prospects, nor did he believe; he saw.
>   (Wordsworth 2007, 54–5; Jacobsen 1820, 124–5)

An indication of the extent to which such a passage, set among the sublimity of British mountains, might be expected to appeal to a German readership, may be had from an unlikely source, an *Interlinear German Reading Book* devised by Franz Thimm. This first appeared in the 1840s and was still being reprinted in the early twentieth century. Among the passages used is Heine's account of climbing the Brocken in the Hartz mountains. Though Heine's feet remain firmly on *terra firma* throughout his expedition, we encounter a very similar sense of the mystical power this terrain can exert on the imagination. In Thimm's primer (edited by Franz Hahn) it appears on the page in the form of parallel lines of English and German text (Hahn 1901, 30–4).

Jacobsen's second passage from *The Excursion* included here comes from the end of Book I, when the Wanderer comforts the poet after telling him the sad story of Margaret's lonely death:

> My friend enough to sorrow you have given;
> The purposes of wisdom ask no more;
> Be wise and chearful; and no longer read
> The forms of things with an unworthy eye . . .
>   (Wordsworth 2007, 75; Jacobsen 1820, 125–6)

This passage (17 lines are quoted) is an important basis for Jacobsen's reading of Wordsworth as a reclusive poet prepared to claim that communion with the beauties of Nature provides a balm for human sorrows that no amount of political action can ever hope to equal. Despite the fact that Margaret's destitution is a consequence of the grinding poverty that has forced her husband to join the British army to fight against the Colonists in the American War of Independence, it is the sight of 'Those weeds, and the high spear-grass on that wall/By mist and silent rain-drops silver'd o'er' that provide the basis for a final, spiritually satisfactory resolution of the tragedy:

> That what we feel of sorrow and despair
> From ruin and from change, and all the grief
> That passing shews of Being leave behind,
> Appeared an idle dream, that could not live
> Where meditation was.
>   (Wordsworth 2007, 75–6; Jacobsen 1820, 125–6)

It is worth noting that there is a passage in the Gillies/Kempferhausen essay that reads like a version of these lines. Standing in the graveyard of Ambleside church at dawn, Gillies describes the beauty of the Lake District scenery in the morning light:

> The old grey and green tomb-stones sunk into the earth by the weight of forgetfulness – with their inscriptions obliterated by moss and lichens – the new made

graves on which the daisies had scarcely had time to wither – and on which the dew-drops lay like the tears of recent grief . . .

and he claims that this sight:

. . . brought to my heart only the salutary conviction, that trouble, though a neces-sary, is but a transient thing, and that there is wisdom in opening the heart to the gracious influences of happiness, even when stealing upon us in the midst of images of sadness and sorrow. (*Blackwood's* No. XXIV March 1819, 736–7)

Jacobsen's case for Wordsworth as one of the most important contemporary British poets is concluded with this second passage from *The Excursion*. He returns to *The Excursion* in his second Wordsworth chapter. At this point he begins to look elsewhere for examples of poetry that display Wordsworth as a deeply spiritual, patriotic lover of his native country, the poet Gillies had described as having 'walked alone through a world almost exclusively his own, and who has cleared out for himself . . . a wide and magnificent path through the solitary forests of the human imagination' (*Blackwood's* No. XXIV March 1819, 740).

4 The Making of a German Wordsworth

Jacobsen's Choice of Poetry

''Twill murmur on a thousand years'
'The Fountain' in Jacobsen 1820, 127

When we look at Jacobsen's choice of Wordsworth's poetry, culled largely from the two-volume Collected *Poems* of 1815 and the 1814 *Excursion*, we can see him becoming increasingly enthusiastic about poetry that resonated with his ideal of what a German National poetry should aspire to. Though his starting point is the *Blackwood's* essay on Wordsworth, it is not long before he begins to make choices based on his own predilections. *Blackwood's* encouraged him to consider Wordsworth's distinctive mystical, metaphysical tendencies. The *Blackwood's* essay on Wordsworth of December 1818 contained a long quotation from Schlegel which, it claimed, helped the reader understand the poet's 'turn of internal thought' (*Blackwood's* December 1818, 259).

After quoting from *The Excursion* ('O then what soul was his . . .') to show Wordsworth 'mingling with the universe' in Byronic fashion, Jacobsen turns to a 'simple' lyric, 'The Fountain' from *Lyrical Ballads* (1800), that expresses the same sentiment. In this Jacobsen is also closely following the *Blackwood's* author. From these lines we learn that the Blackbird and the Lark do not 'wage a foolish strife' with nature; like the water from the fountain, the pattern of their lives follows a natural course:

> The blackbird on the summer trees,
>   The lark upon the hill,
> Let loose their carols when they please,
>   Are quiet when they will.
> With nature never do they wage
>   A foolish strife, they see
> A happy youth, and their old age
>   Is beautiful and free.
> Down to the vale this water steers,
>   How merrily it goes,
> Twill murmur on a thousand years,
>   And flow as now it flows.

(Ibid., 126–7)

A closer look at this extract, however, reveals some interesting anomalies. 'The Fountain' is set in stanzas of four lines; the *Blackwood's* article sets the verse in a single 12-line block, and unless the reader is well acquainted with *Lyrical Ballads*, he or she might well assume that we are looking at a self-contained poem. No title or indication of the source of these lines is given. We notice also an awkward shift of subject in line nine from the blackbird and lark to 'this water'. What the *Blackwood's* author has done is to create a short Wordsworthian lyric of his own, using 'The Fountain' (Wordsworth 1992, 215–16), to suit his own purposes. He has combined verses ten and eleven, and then tacked the sixth verse on the end. Jacobsen, presumably unaware of what is going on, faithfully follows suit. As with the *Blackwood's* article, he does not name the poem, assuming that it is a discrete lyric. We will have cause to return to these lines when discussing Luise von Ploennies' anthology of English poetry published in 1863.

Jacobsen continues to follow *Blackwood's* with his next example, the final four stanzas of 'Elegiac Stanzas, suggested by a Picture of Peele Castle' (*Poems in Two Volumes* 1807). From this point on, however, Jacobsen chooses his examples independently. The essay in *Blackwood's* concludes by quoting *Ruth* in full, a poem described in typically cautious terms as one of the poet's 'detached performances, which are masterpieces in their way' (*Blackwood's* December 1818, 261). In Jacobsen's presentation of Wordsworth to his German readers, the nuance of 'in their way' is lost in translation.

There is a Christian gentleness ('. . . christliche Milde') in Wordsworth's poetry that Jacobsen repeatedly comments on, and 'Peele Castle' illustrates the poet's acceptance of God's will in bereavement (in a very similar way to that expressed in the passage already quoted that tells of Margaret's death in *The Excursion*). In *Blackwood's* the phrase used to describe the sentiment is 'Christian tenderness and sorrow' (*Blackwood's* December 1818, 261). The poem shows us Nature in sterner mood than before, there is also an appeal to an ideal of stoicism and defiance, a quality sought for by reference to a past of heroic achievement:

> And this huge castle, standing here sublime,
> I love to see the look with which it braves,
> Cased in the unfeeling armour of old time,
> The lightning, the fierce wind, and trampling waves.
> (Wordsworth 1983, 266–8; Jacobsen 1820, 127)

'Ein Heldenleben' indeed!

The extract from 'Elegiac Stanzas' is followed by 'To a Highland Girl' and 'Written in March'. In a brief paragraph Jacobsen explains that these poems particularly appeal to him because they show how similar Wordsworth can be to the ideal of poetry defined by 'Schmidt von Lübeck'. In 'To a Highland Girl' (quoted in full) the intense spiritual beauty of the natural scene is compared to the beauty of an artless 14-year-old girl. She represents the poet's longing for a relationship with a vision of beauty and with a notion of passion which is otherwordly, 'fashioned' (like the beautiful setting in which he sees her) 'in a dream'. Yet the poet's admiration for the girl is made all the more compelling because it is tinged with a sense of carnal longing which suggests an unintentional element of voyeurism:

> Yet, dream and vision as thou art,
> I bless thee with a human heart . . .
> . . . and I would have
> Some claim upon thee, if I could,
> Though but of common neighbourhood.
> What joy to hear thee, and to see!
> Thy elder brother I would be,
> Thy Father, any thing to thee.
>   (Wordsworth 1983, 192–4; Jacobsen 1820, 128–30)

Jacobsen is here responding to the theme of Romantic longing that seeks to spiritualize human passion in a way that is familiar in Novalis and Eichendorff. In Eichendorff's 'Farewell', the poet addresses Nature as his loved one:

> When the day begins to break, the earth steams and gleams, the birds sing so merrily that your heart sings in answer. Then let dismal earthly sorrows vanish and blow away, you shall rise again in youthful splendour. (Forster 1957, 312)

'Schmidt von Lübeck' was Georg Philipp Schmidt (1766–1849), who believed poetry should be an intense and intimate outpouring of the imagination. This is how Jacobsen reads ('translates') 'To a Highland Girl' and 'Written in March'. Schmidt settled in Altona in 1818 and is in the list of subscribers to the *Letters*. His main claim to fame is his poem 'Der Wanderer' which Schubert set to music, two lines of which are often said to encapsulate the bitter-sweet spirit of German Romanticism so beloved by Jacobsen:

> *Dort, wo du nicht bist,*   [The place where you are not
>
> *Dort ist das Glück.*   Is the place where happiness is]

In 'To a Highland Girl' we read of how memory will supply a vision of beauty experienced in a place where the poet may not stay:

> Nor am I loth, though pleased at heart,
> Sweet Highland Girl! from Thee to part,
> For I, methinks, till I grow old,
> As fair before me shall behold,
> As I do now, the Cabin small,
> The Lake, the Bay, the Waterfall;
> And Thee, the Spirit of them all!
>   (Jacobsen 1820, 130)

Reference to Schmidt serves also as a reminder that Wordsworth's *Excursion* offered the reader a monumental poem built around the figure of ubiquitous significance to European Romanticism, *Der Wanderer*.

The final poem in this chapter, 'There is a bondage', celebrates the patriotic poet Jacobsen so admires. We have already noted his comparison between Körner's and Wordsworth's sonnet on Andreas Hofer in addition to 'There is a bondage'. The poet of nature who rises above the day-to-day turmoil of life to celebrate a philosophic calm and beauty, and who finds a resolution to human suffering and injustice through intense communion with the natural world, is also the poet living through tumultuous times when Napoleon is terrorizing the world:

> Hills, torrents, woods, embodied to bemock
> The Tyrant, and confound his cruelty.
> ('Hofer' in Selincourt 1969, 250)

'There is a bondage' (see above p. 46) was composed in 1802, and may well be a reflection on the brief cessation of hostilities that took place in that year. Wordsworth warns against complacency. If we do stand clear of the oppression that has engulfed mainland Europe while it only threatened Britain during the recent war, we must never forget that a country freed from such a threat (no longer 'Pent in, a Tyrant's solitary Thrall') can still harbour injustice. He appeals to the individual conscience to reflect on the kind of peace-time society that may be about to emerge, suggesting that true freedom is something that can never be compromised; if there are those who walk 'in the open air' while around them (implying elsewhere in Europe) there are those who still suffer oppression, then the supposedly free citizens 'must wear/Their fetters in their souls'. This would certainly be consistent with the way Wordsworth continued to express his dissatisfaction with the conduct of the war in subsequent years. He never once doubted the moral justification of waging war against Napoleon, but on several occasions (most notably in his pamphlet on the Convention of Cintra published in 1809) he complained bitterly that the country's leaders were conducting the war from base, materialistic, opportunistic motives rather than from the high moral obligation placed upon them to rid the world of tyranny.

This sonnet, therefore, understandably attracts Jacobsen because it attaches a note of high moral and spiritual purpose to the subject of political liberty, presenting politics as a matter of the 'soul', rather than the mundane 'roof, and floor, and wall' of the prison cell the tyrant threatens us with; but for all that, its presence at the end of this chapter reinstates a political theme after we have been delighted with Wordsworth's evocations of Nature and Beauty in their most ethereal forms. The tension between idealism and the realities of physical existence, whether manifest in personal hardship or collective political experience, is a central preoccupation throughout Wordsworth's poetry, and it strikes a chord with Jacobsen. His choice of extracts illustrating *The Excursion* in the chapter which follows continues to show that this is the case.

In chapter nine Jacobsen concentrates on two of Wordsworth's long poems, *The Excursion*, and *The White Doe of Rylstone*, ending the chapter by returning to the lyrical 'She was a phantom of delight'. By 1820 *The Excursion* was established as Wordsworth's major work; whatever might be said of his shorter poems, the debate on the poet's reputation turned on how *The Excursion* was received, and Jacobsen's decision to devote so much space to the poem reflects British critical orthodoxy until Matthew Arnold began to turn the tide in the 1870s with his emphasis on the merits of the shorter poems (Bushell 2002, 5–8).

The Excursion began its existence as a blank verse poem (*The Ruined Cottage*) drafted after Wordsworth had gone with Dorothy to live at Racedown in 1795. It tells the story (then set in the West Country) of an industrious couple who are the victims of agricultural depression in the 1770s. The husband joins the army to fight against the American colonists in the War of Independence. He is killed and his wife, Margaret, eventually dies in poverty. This was revised to become Book One of *The Excursion* in 1802, two years after Wordsworth moved to Grasmere. The location of the poem became the Lake District, and a narrative framework for it was created. The narrator is the poet, who is in the company of a Scottish pedlar, known as the Wanderer. There are numerous precedents in eighteenth-century English literature for Wordsworth's choice of a philosophic pedlar as a conduit for profound insights into human nature. Pope's account of the Man of Ross (John Kyrle) in Epistle III of the *Moral Essays*, Gray's melancholy narrator in 'Elegy in a Country Churchyard', and Goldsmith's displaced poet in 'The Deserted Village' help to establish the type; but Wordsworth goes considerably beyond what these examples suggest. The Wanderer's Scottish origins are humble in the extreme, his parents lived 'on a small hereditary Farm,/An unproductive slip of rugged ground' (Wordsworth 2007, 51). His formal schooling is minimal. The wisdom he acquires is evidence of naturally profound habits of thought made all the more intense by his experience of the natural objects around him; this is the context for the passage Jacobsen quotes (guided by *Blackwood's*) of The Wanderer's experience of the sun rise.

For Francis Jeffrey, the idea of such a character providing the intellectual spine of a philosophical poem of epic length was ludicrous in itself, but it also smacked of the persistently subversive Jacobinical trend that he had accused the Lake School poets of 12 years before in the first number of the *Edinburgh Review*. The Wanderer personified in uncompromising terms the principle of 'simplicity' that Wordsworth had invoked in the 1800 Preface to *Lyrical Ballads*. Though the *Blackwood's* article of 1818 never once raises the specific issue of 'simplicity', it approaches the issue circumspectly by suggesting that Wordsworth's unfashionable ideas are reminiscent of those held by people who in our own society might be considered primitive:

> It is remarkable that even the external characteristics of his poetry are similar to what we are told an analogous turn of internal thought anciently produced among the Hindoos. (*Blackwood's* December 1818, 259)

The word 'primitive' is not used; it does not need to be. The *Blackwood's* author has already endorsed the influence of Christianity on the evolution of our poetry, and the combination of 'anciently' and 'Hindoo' completes the inference. But this is not intended as a denial of Wordsworth's credibility. In the context of this discussion, it is particularly interesting to note that it is at this point that the lengthy quote from Schlegel is used, giving credence to the idea that a study of alternative cultures and religions is of great value, and that no one should consider themselves superior in this respect. 'The first things which strike us in the Indian poetry are,' Schlegel is quoted as saying, 'that tender feeling of solitude, and the all-animated world of plants . . . and those charming pictures of female truth and constancy, as well as of the beauty and loveliness of infantine nature . . .' (*Blackwood's* December 1818, 259). The passage throughout suggests parallels with the material that Wordsworth put into *The Excursion*, and also the subjects of many of his other poems. Jeffrey's response to this in the *Edinburgh Review* was not to quote Schlegel, but to pronounce Wordsworth a pagan as well as an unreformed Jacobin.

Blackwood's was certainly not averse to having some fun with the eccentricities of Wordsworth's beliefs; beliefs which, as the article points out, dominate his motives for composition to the point where the poetry may suffer, becoming little more than a vehicle for 'obtrusive argumentation' (*Blackwood's* December 1818, 260). In February 1819, *Blackwood's* published a parody that yoked Wordsworth to Coleridge in *The Rime of the Auncient Waggonere: in Four Parts*. Coleridge's Ancient Mariner and Wordsworth's Benjamin the Waggoner ('this tippsye manne,/The red nosed waggonere') are reconstituted in a single, drunken lout from whom nothing of any value may be learnt:

> Such is the fate of foolish men,
>   The danger all may see,
> Of those, who list to waggoneres,
>   And keep bad companye.
>   (*Blackwood's* No. XXIII, Feb. 1819, 571–4)

To the Poet and the Wanderer of *The Excursion*, Wordsworth added a third character, the Solitary. After a brief period of happy family life, the Solitary attempts to cope with the devastating loss of his wife and children by throwing himself into political radicalism at the outbreak of the French Revolution. The failure of the Revolution drives him to emigrate to America, seeking freedom first among the recently freed white inhabitants, and then among the natives of the outback. Profoundly disillusioned, he returns to live in the Lake District an embittered and cynical man. Telling the tale of Margaret, and then hearing the Solitary's story (interspersed with the observations of the Wanderer), takes Wordsworth to the end of Book IV. The purpose of *The Excursion* is to track the route by which the Solitary may be persuaded to re-engage with the society from which he has become so profoundly alienated. In Book V the three men go to visit a Pastor, and in his company the discussion continues. The content consists for the most part of a series of anecdotes about the lives of people who have lived in the area, their sufferings, their triumphs over adversity, and their prospects in a rapidly changing social and economic environment. Wordsworth manages to find a place for most of the major issues that preoccupied the nation as a whole, including the state of the political establishment, the role of the Church of England, industrialization, rural poverty and the break-down of rural communities, child labour and education. The final Book concludes with an impromptu service of Evensong held on an island in a Lake during which both the Wanderer and the Pastor sum up their hopes for a brighter future (Wordsworth 2007, 296–7). It remains to be seen whether this experience has been sufficient to bring the Solitary back into the World:

> How far those erring notions were reformed;
> And whether aught, of tendency as good
> And pure, from further intercourse ensued;
> This – (if delightful hopes, as heretofor
> Inspire the serious song, and gentle Hearts
> Cherish, and lofty minds approve the past)
> My future labours may leave not untold.
>   (Wordsworth 2007, 296–7)

Jacobsen quotes 15 passages from *The Excursion* in chapter nine, some at length. He selects the quotations from Books I, III, IV, VI, VII, VIII, and IX. He begins by relating the tale of the Solitary, the tragic loss of his family; first the children, then his young wife: 'And, so consumed, She melted from my arms;/And left me, on this earth, disconsolate' (Jacobsen 1820, 138; Wordsworth 2007, 122). Most particularly, he recounts the harmful effect of his ill-chosen political enthusiasm:

> By pain of heart, now checked, and now impelled,
> The Intellectual Power, through words and things,
> Went sounding on, a dim and perilous way.
>   (Jacobsen 1820, 139; Wordsworth 2007, 122)

The 'dim and perilous way' (recalling the narrative of Satan in Milton's *Paradise Lost*) is marked out by the French Revolution:

> Thus was I reconverted to the world,
> Society became my glittering Bride,
> And airy hopes my Children . . .
>
> . . . and in still groves,
> Where mild Enthusiasts tuned a pensive lay
> Of thanks and expectation, in accord
> With their belief, I sang Saturnian Rule
> Returned, – a progeny of golden years
> Permitted to descend, and bless mankind.
>
> (Jacobsen 1820, 139; Wordsworth 2007, 123)

Jacobsen does not pursue this theme into Book IV but moves on to Book VI, by which time the Pastor has appeared and is telling the trio stories about his various parishioners.

Book VI begins with a patriotic celebration of Church and State:

> – Hail to the State of England! And conjoin
> With this a salutation as devout,
> Made to the spiritual fabric of her Church . . .
>
> (Wordsworth 2007, 196)

This is followed by a tale of reconciliation in old age between a Whig and a Jacobite, but Jacobsen passes over this politically explicit material, and moves on to the story the Pastor then relates, concerning the fate of a young woman called Ellen. In marked contrast to the material that has preceded it, there are no politics involved in this story at all, it reinforces the themes of Nature as the great healer, and the sanctity of domestic life. Ellen falls in love, but is abandoned by her lover when she is carrying his child. Her mother supports her, but this is insufficient, and so the girl leaves home to become a foster mother. She is badly treated by her employers, her child dies, and so too eventually does she. The Pastor, however, does not condemn the girl. She knows she has sinned and stoically accepts her consequent fate, believing that due penitence in this life will win forgiveness in the next. Jacobsen explains how Wordsworth movingly describes her visits to her child's grave. The passage he is referring to describes her as 'a rueful Magdalene':

> So call her; for not only she bewailed
> A Mother's loss, but mourned in bitterness
> Her own transgression; penitent sincere
> As ever raised to Heaven a streaming eye.
>
> (Wordsworth 2007, 222)

Jacobsen quotes the passage that describes her eventual death as a moment of triumph, when the evils of this world are finally left behind. He begins with lines 1,057–8, cuts 11 lines, and concludes with lines 1070–3:

> The ghastly face of cold decay put on
> A sun-like beauty, and appeared divine!
> So, through the cloud of death, her Spirit passed
> Into that pure and unknown world of love,
> Where injury cannot come:– and here is laid
> The mortal Body by her Infant's side.
>
> (Jacobsen 1820, 145; Wordsworth 2007, 224)

Ellen, despite her undoubted transgression, maintains an aura of innocence that Wordsworth bestows on the Highland Girl, on Margaret (from Book I of *The*

Excursion), on Emily in *The White Doe of Rylstone*, and on countless other of his female characters. The reader is urged to value penitence and the will to make amends, and to look for a Christian spirit of forgiveness.

From Book VII, Jacobsen takes a story that does have a very specific political agenda. It tells of a country boy who goes to the wars, and returns a hero, but continues to live as he did before among his people. He is that type of simple, patriot countryman who asks no more than to be able to serve his country in its hour of need. Jacobsen quotes the passage in which Wordsworth compares the young man to a mountain ash tree, brightening up the surrounding wood-land with its 'richest blossoms':

> . . . in his native Vale
> Such and so glorious did this Youth appear;
> A sight that kindled pleasure in all hearts
> By his ingenious beauty, by the gleam
> Of his fair eyes, by his capacious brow . . .
> (Jacobsen 1820, 145; Wordsworth 2007, 249)

When, later in this passage, Wordsworth links the young patriotic hero to the idea that here we have a home-grown, 'folk', version of what we read in Classi-cal mythology, we can appreciate why for Jacobsen, steeped in the myths of ancient Germania, it was irresistible:

> As old Bards
> Tell in their idle songs of wandering Gods,
> Pan or Apollo, veiled in human form;
> Yet, like the sweet berated violet of the shade,
> Discovered in their own despite to sense
> Of Mortals, (if such fables without blame
> May find chance-mention on this sacred ground),
> So, through a simple rustic garb's disguise,
> And through the impediment of rural cares,
> In him revealed a Scholar's genius shone;
> And so, not wholly hidden from men's sight,
> In him the spirit of a Hero walked
> Our unpretending valley.
> (Wordsworth 2007, 249–50)

The young soldier, son of a simple farmer, is another version of the central fig-ure of *The Excursion*, the Wanderer. This includes his naturally acquired scholarly gifts.

Turning now to the conclusion of the young man's tale, we should recall the criticism that *Blackwood's* had levelled at Wordsworth: that his poetry suffered more than it might from his over-enthusiastic determination to use it as a vehi-cle for his philosophical beliefs. This habit of 'obtrusive argumentation' designed to establish his 'philosophical opinions' was what Keats, in a letter to John Hamilton Reynolds of February 1818, famously complained of when reading Wordsworth: 'We hate poetry that has a palpable design upon us' (*Blackwood's* December 1818, 260). The young patriot soldier returns from the wars, resumes his rustic duties, and catches a chill so extreme that it kills him:

> This generous Youth, too negligent of self,
> (A natural failing which maturer years
> Would have subdued) took fearlessly – and kept –

His wonted station in the chilling flood,
Among a busy company convened
To wash his father's flock. Convulsions dire
Siezed him, that self-same night; and through the space
Of twelve ensuing days his frame was wrenched,
Till nature rested from her work in death.

(Wordsworth 2007, 253)

Wordsworth revised this passage extensively after 1814, but the problem would not go away. From the moment these lines were published, the banality of them has rarely failed to be the occasion of regret or indeed considerable amusement. Such was Wordsworth's commitment to the teaching behind his story of the patriotic young countryman, that initially he failed to realize how for the majority of his readers, the circumstances of his hero's death would appear as an absurdly inconsequential conclusion to the tale. The youth dies as he had lived, a simple country boy who, regardless of his intellectual merits and bravery as a patriotic soldier, remains unspoilt by the temptations of worldly fame and greatness. To make him an exemplar of this naturalness of spirit (a type Wordsworth praises in his *Poems in Two Volumes* of 1807 in 'Character of the Happy Warrior'), there can be no heroics attached to his untimely death. We can only assume that Jacobsen at least understood what Wordsworth was intending when his young hero succumbed to death by sheep-dip.

Jacobsen's lack of interest in any material that might appear to draw too heavily on issues of immediate political moment is clear. The story of the old Jacobite and his Whig neighbour in Book VI is a case in point, though the reference here is specific to British history in a way that Jacobsen might have judged to be of little interest to a German reader. This, however, is less likely to have been the case with the Wanderer's references in Book VIII – at some length – to the evils of the factory system; but they too were passed over, despite the fact that in the course of them specifics tend to give way to a more general lamentation on the consequences for the natural world and the way of life it sustained. His Wordsworth is the poet who finds in the grand canvas of British history, and in the example of simple lives lived amidst the beauties of nature, an ideal that looks beyond the immediate concerns that matters of day-to-day politics would emphasize. A good many English Victorians were only too ready to read and commend *The Excursion* on precisely these grounds, and such people would have approved of the passage that Jacobsen chose to select for quotation from Book VIII. This describes how 'Men of all lands' will eventually see in Nature itself, rather than in their delusions of power over Nature, the true source of wisdom:

Learning, though late, that all true glory rests,
All praise, all safety, and all happiness,
Upon the Moral law. Egyptian Thebes;
Tyre by the Margin of the sounding waves;
Palmyra, central in the Desert, fell;
And the Arts died by which they had been raised,
– Call Archimedes, from his buried Tomb
Upon the plain of vanished Syracuse,
And feelingly the Sage shall make report
How insecure, how baseless in itself,
Is that Philosophy, whose sway is framed

> For mere material instruments: – How weak
> Those Arts, and high Inventions, if unpropped
> By Virtue.
>
>   (Jacobsen 1820 147; Wordsworth 2007, 264–5)

This is, however, an example of where Jacobsen has tampered significantly with Wordsworth's original text. His decision to indent the first line of the extract is a clear sign to his readers that this is not just the beginning of a new sentence, it is the beginning of a new section. In fact he is picking the extract up in mid-sentence, after a semi-colon. Wordsworth's original sentence is grammatically complex, but its meaning (already outlined above) is unambiguous. The 'sentence' newly created by Jacobsen is grammatically unsatisfactory and confusing. Is 'Learning' ('Innewerdend') a verb in gerund form or a noun? The root of this uncertainty lies in the fact that Jacobsen's sentence has cut Wordsworth's subject. Wordsworth intended us to read the following (ll.210–218), where we do (eventually) find the subject, 'Men of all lands':

> For with the sense of admiration blends
> The animating hope that time may come
> When strengthened, yet not dazzled, by the might
> Of this dominion over Nature gained,
> Men of all lands shall exercise the same
> In due proportion to their Country's need;
> Learning, though late, that all true glory rests,
> All praise, all safety, and all happiness,
> Upon the Moral law.
>
>   (Wordsworth 2007, 264)

It is 'Men' who 'Learn' (belatedly) the authority of the 'Moral law'. Jacobsen's editing may conceivably originate in his failure to grasp Wordsworth's tortuous grammatical gymnastics; even if that is so, it is equally certain that we see his intentions as a translator are to point up qualities in his subject text that he is confident will appeal to his German target text readers. In this instance his main concern is to emphasize Wordsworth's respect for the 'Moral law'. Jacobsen's German translation by no means entirely irons out the problems created by the grammatical shortcomings of the incomplete English sentence. What he has done, however, in keeping with his own priorities, is to enhance the importance of the 'Moral law' by setting it up as the grammatical subject of his sentence:

Innewerdend, ebgleich spät, das aller wahr Ruhm, alles Lob, alle Sicherheit und alles Glück aus dem moralischen Gesetze beruhet. (Jacobsen 1819, 147)

Moving on to the final Book of *The Excursion* (Book IX), Jacobsen's first extract reaffirms the previous Book VIII passage:

> The primal duties shine aloft – like stars;
> The charities that soothe, and heal, and bless,
> Are scattered at the feet of Man – like flowers.
> The generous inclination, the just rule,
> Kind wishes, and good actions, and pure thoughts –
> No mystery is here, no special boon
> For high and not for low, for proudly graced
> And not for meek of heart. The smoke ascends
> To heaven as lightly from the Cottage hearth

> As from the haughty palace.
>
> (Jacobsen 1820, 147–8; Wordsworth 2007, 281–2)

The Excursion contains a good many passages that make it clear that for all the worthy idealism expressed here, the way forward must involve confronting the political realities described elsewhere (but ignored by Jacobsen) in Book VIII. His eye is caught by Wordsworth's reference to 'The primal duties' which set out for us grand, abstract aspirations: generosity, justice, kindness, goodness, purity. All this may be said to be as true for the cottage as the palace, but when Book IX draws to a close and Wordsworth prepares to present his reader with a vision of what Britain – freed from the constraints that twenty-one years of warfare have imposed – might become, he does so in the light of a clear sense of the practical magnitude of the task. With Jacobsen, he clearly believes that the way to a better future lies as much in the realm of a spiritual struggle as it does with identifying and tackling earth-bound political problems, but Jacobsen has manufactured an *Excursion* which emphasizes the spiritual dimension to a greater degree than Wordsworth's original text of 1814.

The last extended passage quoted from Book IX accords entirely with Jacobsen's view of Nationalistic endeavour; he might well have taken what Wordsworth has to say here as a template for the German National anthem he hoped to see written in the near future:

> Look! And behold, from Calpe's sunburnt cliffs
> To the flat margin of the Baltic sea,
> Long-reverenced Titles cast away as weeds;
> Laws overturned, – and Territory split;
> Like fields of ice rent by the polar wind
> And forced to join in less obnoxious shapes,
> Which, ere they gain consistence, by a gust
> Of the same breath are shattered and destroyed.
> Meantime, the Sovereignty of these fair Isles
> Remains entire and indivisible;
> And, if that ignorance were removed, which acts
> Within the compass of their several shores
> To breed commotion and disquietude,
> Each might preserve the beautiful repose
> Of heavenly Bodies shining in their spheres,
> – The discipline of slavery is unknown
> Amongst us, – hence the more do we require
> The discipline of virtue, order else
> Cannot subsist, nor confidence, nor peace.
>
> (Jacobsen 1820, 148–9; Wordsworth 2007, 284)

As he writes, Wordsworth looks out across a Europe devastated by war, hardly daring to believe that the end is in sight, and in fact the war was to drag on for another year after the poem was published. Jacobsen can remember only too well what it had been like. In Wordsworth's description of Britain, 'these fair Isles' where 'Sovereignty . . . Remains entire and indivisible', Jacobsen can recognize the landscape through which the poet walks in Gillies' *Blackwood's* article, though of course he imagines he sees it through the eyes of a fellow German; and perhaps that last fact may have helped him relate to it as the landscape he longed for in his own country, the realization of a united Germany, the rebirth of the fabled forests, mountains, lakes, and pastoral settlements of Germania.

Reading on, however, he will have encountered a powerful expression of British imperialist ambition uttered by the Wanderer. It must certainly have made Jacobsen reflect seriously on how Anglo-German relations were likely to progress in the coming decades, though perhaps by 1820 he may have felt that Wordsworth's thoughts were already rendered obsolete by the course of European history since the overthrow of Napoleon. Wordsworth's assumption is clearly that Europe was destined to be left in a far more divided and vulnerable state at the end of the war than it in fact was. He could hardly have been expected to anticipate Metternich. It is important to quote at some length from this passage in order to appreciate that beyond the undoubted enthusiasm of Jacobsen's engagement with British poetry, he will have been fully aware of other, more difficult political aspects of the relationship between a country that had escaped the worst ravages of the Napoleonic wars, and a Germany beginning to seek its own national identity and, if Jacobsen's chapter 30 is anything to go by, share the ambitions that the Wanderer expresses at this juncture in Book IX of *The Excursion*. Where Sharon Turner's dream of British world domination tends to remain cloaked in the rhetoric of a triumph for 'nature' and the Christian religion, Wordsworth's Wanderer is bluntly explicit. The whole world, he proclaims, will feel the benefit of British civilization:

> Change wide, and deep, and silently performed,
> This Land shall witness; and, as days roll on,
> Earth's universal Frame shall feel the effect
> Even till the smallest habitable Rock,
> Beaten by lonely billows, hear the songs
> Of humanised Society; and bloom
> With civil arts, and send their fragrance forth,
> A grateful tribute to all-ruling Heaven.
> From Culture, universally bestowed
> On Britain's noble Race in freedom born;
> From Education, from that humble source,
> Expect these mighty issues; from the pains
> And quiet care of unambitious Schools
> Instructing simple Childhood's ready ear:
> Thence look for these magnificent results!
>   (Wordsworth 2007, 285–6)

Wordsworth's assumption is that God has spared Britain from the worst excesses of the French Revolution and the subsequent turmoil so that it might lead the Nations into the future as the dominant power. The lines which immediately follow this passage state, 'Vast the circumference of hope – and Ye/Are at its centre, British Lawgivers' (ll. 401–2). As he read what, to any prospective rival for such power, or indeed any European state anxious to retain its independence, must have sounded deeply threatening, Jacobsen may well have reassured himself that things had changed a good deal in 'guilty Europe' during the intervening five years:

>   Your Country must complete
> Her glorious destiny. – Begin even now,
> Now, when Oppression, like the Egyptian plague
> Of darkness, stretched o'er guilty Europe, makes
> The brightness more conspicuous, that invests
> The happy Island where ye think and act;

> Now, when destruction is a prime pursuit,
> Shew to the wretched Nations for what end
> The Powers of civil Polity were given!
>
> (Ibid., 286)

The omission of any reference to these lines or their purport from Jacobsen's account of the poem may be explained in a variety of ways. They would clearly not endear Wordsworth to a German readership, and given that Jacobsen's enthusiasm for him is manifestly genuine, he would wish to avoid that mistake. Jacobsen also no doubt did believe that history had overtaken this part of the poem. We would, however, be wrong to conclude that he intended to avoid any suggestion at all of the worldly political issues that Wordsworth's *Excursion* raises. The passage he chooses to quote before going on to describe how the poem ends deserves close attention precisely because it is far more politically contentious than anything quoted up to that point. We may safely assume that this was a passage he had been saving for this moment, because to this point his account faithfully follows the course of the poem. Now he takes us back to Book V. The context of the passage (which he does not explain) is a discussion between the poet and the Wanderer about the way the Nation has lost its Christian commitment to 'Truth and Justice'. Religion has become too often a meaningless ritual; here the poet passionately argues that the decay of genuine Christian conviction is not so much a problem for any one Nation, it is the whole earth that is sick:

> Earth is sick,
> And Heaven is weary of the hollow words
> Which States and Kingdoms utter when they speak
> Of Truth and Justice.
>
> (Jacobsen 1820, 151; Wordsworth 2007, 178)

It is something of a shock to encounter the mild mannered Jacobsen suddenly confronting us with a side of *The Excursion* that up to this point he has meticulously avoided. It is as though he could not, in the end, resist unleashing a Wordsworth who still harboured a strong sense of bitter disenchantment with the political establishment of his day. Having done so, however, he hastily distances himself from the sentiment expressed in these lines. In a unique moment of intervention, he adds his own gloss to his translation:

> *Die Erde ist krank und der Himmel ist müde der hohlen Worte, welche Staaten und Königreiche von sich geben, wenn sie von Warheit und Gerechtigkeit sprechen. (Die gerechten Könige sind von ihm vergessen!)*

'He forgets about the just kings!' The fact remains that Wordsworth's outburst against the duplicity of those placed in authority over us is Jacobsen's final quotation from *The Excursion*; how different from the passage from Turner quoted in his final chapter: 'Of all the good from monarchy that flows –/That polish'd monarchy which Europe knows' (Jacobsen 1820, 718). We should never lose sight of the fact that Jacobsen is reading Wordsworth's poem as a statement of war weariness from 1814 with which he can readily identify. Equally we may assume that he has been particularly struck by Wordsworth's claim that the world we live in has drifted away from God and Nature; it is therefore a world that has consequently produced corrupt states and kingdoms, although perhaps now we may see that the level of despair expressed by Wordsworth while the war was still going on is no longer appropriate.

It may well be that the final poem by Wordsworth Jacobsen chose to quote in the *Letters* (coming towards the end of the whole book) is partly intended to show us how the poet had revised his opinion. This is Wordsworth's sonnet of 1820, included in the *River Duddon* volume, 'on the Death of his Late Majesty':

> Ward of the Law! – dread Shadow of a King!
> Whose Realm had dwindled to one stately room;
> Whose universe was gloom immers'd in gloom,
> Darkness as thick as Life o'er Life could fling,
> Yet haply cheered with some faint glimmering
> Of Faith and Hope; if thou by nature's doom
> Gently has sunk into the quiet tomb,
> Why should we bend in grief, to sorrow cling,
> When thankfulness were best? – Fresh-flowing tears,
> Or, where tears flow not, sigh succeeding sigh,
> Yield to such after-thought the sole reply
> Which justly it can claim. The Nation hears
> In this deep knell – silent for threescore years,
> An unexampled voice of awful memory!
>   (Jacobsen 1820, 736; Selincourt 1969, 215)

This appears in the concluding, *Anhang*, section. What Jacobsen translates into German is a sentimental farewell to a King whose reign was blighted with sickness through the war years, yet whose life was sustained 'with some faint glimmering/Of Faith and Hope'. It is a solemn tribute to a powerful, but troubled, ruler of his people. A British reader might as easily be struck by a typically levelling Wordsworthian undertone that runs through it. The death of George III leaves the poet reflecting in a far more equivocal way than Jacobsen is prepared to allow on Kingship and the future of the realm under George IV.

In a variety of ways, therefore, we should always be aware of the fact that the *Letters* presents us with Jacobsen's *translation* of Wordsworth. *The Excursion* we read here is very much Jacobsen's *Excursion*, and although his final quotation from it is a passage that seems to challenge the poem we have been reading about up to that point, his account of the way the poem finishes returns us to his favoured emphasis on the way religious conviction should inspire and sustain political motivation. He thus concludes by describing the open-air act of worship that brings the poem to an end, enthusing once more on the spiritual intensity and beauty of Wordsworth's descriptions of nature.

Jacobsen now turns his attention to *The White Doe of Rylstone*, and his enthusiasm for this poem has already been discussed in the previous chapter. In the context of his reading of *The Excursion*, however, it is worth noting again that *The White Doe* is a poem that looks at the consequences of warfare, and in particular at the aftermath of warfare. The cumulative effect of the final 52 lines which Jacobsen quotes is to lift all talk of politics and human strife out of the realm of the actual into a totally abstract, spiritualized existence. This is as much a blessed release from the difficult issues that confront Jacobsen in the post-war world of Metternich's *Realpolitik* as it is for the unfortunate Emily, who spends her last years wandering among the ruins of Bolton Abbey, before finally being released from her grief through death:

> . . . this hoary Pile,
> Subdued by outrage and decay,

> Looks down upon her with a smile,
> A gracious smile, that seems to say,
> 'Thou, thou art not a Child of Time,
> But daughter of the Eternal Prime.'
>
> (Jacobsen 1820, 164; Wordsworth 1988, 146)

The decision to conclude the chapter with 'She was a phantom of delight' (quoted in full) is therefore a perfect way for Jacobsen to sum up his Wordsworth. It is the poem by Wordsworth, he tells us, that the English Nation most admires, 'welches die englische Nation am mehrsten von Wordsworth bewundert'. It returns us to the theme of tension between what is perceived as real, and what is ideal; the interface between reason and imagination, between art and everyday life. This poem engages with that balance in a masterly way (as does 'To A Highland Girl'). The 'phantom of delight' is 'A lovely apparition' seen first from a distance, then 'upon a nearer view/A spirit yet a woman too', and then in the third verse:

> ...I see with eye serene
> The very pulse of the machine;
> A Being, breathing thoughtful breath
> A Traveller betwixt life and death ...
>
> (Jacobsen 1820, 167; Wordsworth 1983, 75)

For Jacobsen, Wordsworth seems to be the British poet who best captures this sense of living a life poised between two states, the worldly and the spiritual. He noted a number of examples in *The Excursion* that were suggestive of this, and quoted a passage from Book IX which describes 'A snow-white Ram' and its reflection in the water with evident relish:

> Thus having reached a bridge, that overarched
> The hasty rivulet where it lay becalmed
> In the deep pool, by happy chance we saw
> A two-fold Image; on a grassy bank
> A snow-white Ram, and in the crystal flood
> Another and the same! Most beautiful,
> On the green turf, with his imperial front
> Shaggy and bold, and wreathed horns superb,
> The breathing Creature stood; as beautiful,
> Beneath him, showed his shaggy Counterpart.
> Each had his glowing mountains, each his sky,
> And each seemed centre of his own fair world:
> Antipodes unconscious of each other,
> Yet, in partition, with their several spheres,
> Blended in perfect stillness, to our sight!
>
> (Jacobsen 1820, 150; Wordsworth 2007, 287)

This was the Wordsworth he hoped to establish in the reading habits of his fellow countrymen, and it would seem that his efforts were by no means wasted.

Jacobsen's *Letters* and the Galignani *Wordsworth*

> '...for the present time I have not laboured in vain ... the products of my industry will endure.'
> Wordsworth, *Essay, Supplementary to the Preface*, in *Owen 1974, III, 80*

Jacobsen's *Letters* played a significant role in establishing a sense of who the British poets of the early nineteenth century were in the minds of many German readers. The list of subscribers alone indicates the likely range of the book's influence. In this section I want to draw attention to just one piece of evidence for how well the *Letters* seemed to survive and travel in the first half of the century.

Galignani's Messenger, a literary magazine produced by Giovanni Antonio Galignani, was first published in Paris in 1814. It swiftly became very popular, and had a wide circulation among English residents in Europe. Galignani's sons, John Anthony and William (who were born in London) carried on the business. They also developed a lucrative trade in publishing pirated editions of popular English books in Paris. In time their activities played a key role in the campaign to reform the laws of copyright initiated by Sergeant Talfourd in 1837, a process that reached the statute book five years later. The 1842 Act then remained in place until it was revised again and became law in 1911.

In 1828 the Galignani brothers published a pirated edition of Wordsworth's 1827 five volume *Poems* in Paris and – as was the custom – it included a Memoir of the poet. It is instructive to compare the Galignani Memoir with Jacobsen's biographical section in the *Letters*. It is safe to assume that the Galignanis had many reviews of Wordsworth to hand, so they too will have had the *Blackwood's* material upon which Jacobsen had relied so heavily. Both books use the Carruthers portrait of Wordsworth. The Galignani Memoir begins in a very similar vein to Jacobsen, although there is a little more information on the poet's life prior to his arrival at Cambridge; unlike Jacobsen, they send him to University in the correct year. The Galignani author knows about Wordsworth's second visit to France, and explains that 'He was driven from the capital by the tremendous horrors of the Reign of Terror' (Galignani 1828, xiv). Alfoxden is now more properly described as 'an ancient Mansion', and is correctly located a few miles from Nether Stowey. Dorothy is mentioned, but in the context of this study it is interesting to note that her name appears in its Germanic form, 'Dorothea'. Wordsworth's engagement with political controversy is also noted with approval (a firm rejection of the anti-Jacobin line taken by Whittaker's); in particular, his 'powerfully written' pamphlet on the Convention of Cintra is mentioned: '... it is scarcely fanciful to suppose, that it might have been one of the causes of the change in the proceedings of Government, which ultimately led to so glorious and happy termination for all Europe' (Galignani 1828, xv). He is also described as a poet who, for all his attachment to his home among the Lakes, loves to travel.

At the beginning of the 'Memoir', however, the writer makes the point that discovering biographical information about Wordsworth is particularly difficult:

> The tranquillity of a life devoted to letters, and the seclusion which is esteemed most favourable to the inspiration of the Muse, afford few materials for the pen of the biographer. (Galignani 1828, xiii)

As with Jacobsen, I have to assume that the Galignani author had to rely on word of mouth accounts of the poet's history to supplement the sparse written sources (one of those being Jacobsen's *Letters*):

> ... the authentic information which is only to be derived from primary sources is not sufficiently copious to gratify the scarcely illegitimate curiosity of the public. (Galignani 1828, xiii)

Based in London, the writer was clearly able to do a somewhat better job for the 'Memoir' than Jacobsen, and a considerable use of Hazlitt's *The Spirit of the Age* suggests that Hazlitt might also have been one of the writer's verbal informants. The Wordsworth we read about, however, remains essentially the reclusive, contemplative poet of nature celebrated in Jacobsen. He is a poet with a highly developed, unique sense of the spiritual truths to be discovered from an intense communion with the mountains and lakes amongst which he lives his retired life.

None of this, of course, suggests that a copy of Jacobsen's book was open on the desk while this biography was being drafted. That cannot even be inferred from the fact that the author of the Galignani Memoir uses the same sunrise passage from *The Excursion* early in his account to illustrate what is most to be admired in Wordsworth's poetry. He, like Jacobsen, was no doubt familiar with the essay in *Blackwood's*. However, given that *Blackwood's* and Jacobsen both use this extract, it is less than convincing when the Galignani author claims that it was 'taken almost at random' (Galignani 1828, xiv). What is most interesting in a comparison between Jacobsen and the Galignani 'Memoir', however, is that on the issue of the relative merits of Wordsworth and Byron, the Galignani text appears to offer a compromise position between what in *Blackwood's* we have seen as an undisguised expression of disapproval ('the Giaours and Corsairs, etc. of modern days ... Are represented boiling and foaming with great noise'), and Jacobsen's attempt to raise Wordsworth's profile without offending his German readers' enthusiasm for Byron. Even more significant is the fact that in taking up this position, the Galignani writer refers to the same stanza from *Childe Harold* that Jacobsen does. Byron expresses his love of nature as being above his love of man, and expresses his longing 'To mingle with the Universe, and feel/ What I can ne'er express, yet cannot all conceal' (Byron 1970, 251). This passage is not referred to at all in the *Blackwood's* essay. Once again, it is hard to believe that this comes about by coincidence ('almost at random'), and that being the case, it strongly implies that Jacobsen is the source. It should still be admitted, however, that this is one of the most frequently quoted passages from Byron's entire output, but the fact that it appears at this particular juncture in the discussion of Wordsworth's merits must certainly suggest that a volume of Jacobsen's *Letters* was to hand. Having quoted the sunrise passage from *The Excursion* Book I, the Galignani author continues:

> It is difficult for those who are acquainted – and who is not? – with the writings of Lord Byron, to read the above magnificent lines [of Wordsworth] without being struck with the almost startling resemblance borne to them by a passage in a poem of the noble Lord's, who, it is evident, from many other parts of his works, had studied our poet with advantage. (Galignani 1828, xiv)

Wordsworth himself had no doubt about Byron's unacknowledged debt to him, commenting in 1820 to Thomas Moore on Byron's 'plagiarisms': 'the whole third canto of "Childe Harold" founded on his [Wordsworth's] style and sentiments' Moore noted in his *Journal*, adding that Wordsworth went on to claim that 'Tintern Abbey' was 'the source of it all', including 'the celebrated passage about solitude' subsequently repeated by Jacobsen, and now alluded to by the Galignani author (Moore 1853 III, 161).

*

It was Friedrich Jacobsen who first established Wordsworth as a British poet of importance in the German mind regardless of how Goethe, and no doubt others who knew what Goethe thought, rated him. The imprint of Jacobsen's Wordsworth chapters in the *Letters* remains visible for much of the remainder of the century as German anthologists and translators picked their way among the British poets. Inevitably he does not remain exactly the same poet; and this is certainly true when Ferdinand Freiligrath begins to read *The Excursion*. Before looking at Wordsworth's appearance in mid-nineteenth-century Germany, however, it will be helpful to take a more comprehensive view of the processes by which the poet was being translated into the minds of his German readership.

5 Translation in Theory and Practice: Friedrich Jacobsen, Ferdinand Freiligrath and Marie Gothein

Translation and Literature in Germany and Britain

'The role of the interpreter or translator . . . can be seen as little more than a technical relay . . . At the other end of the continuum of possibilities lies the translator who operates in a situation where his or her own cultural belonging is a problematic element in the act of translation.'

Palmer in *Salama-Carr* 2007, 14

This chapter considers translation as an evolving area of scholarly debate, and the way that debate contextualizes the major preoccupations of this book. The decision to 'translate' the work of a poet from his or her native tongue into another language creates a space within which we may study cultural, social and historical issues in a particularly revealing light. The ubiquity of translation within literary culture has, until relatively recently, been largely ignored as a significant issue for theoretical debate. Nowhere has this tended to be the case more than in the writing of eighteenth-century English literary history. Here, not surprisingly, the emphasis has tended to be on the emergence of a distinctive 'English' national literature; but England's 'national' literature owed much to the extensive translation of classical texts.

As the quotation at the head of this section indicates, 'translation' is a term indissolubly linked with the matter of interpretation. Translation Studies is located within the wider field of hermeneutics, and it is primarily due to the work of Friedrich Schleiermacher (1768–1834) and Alexander von Humboldt (1769–1859) that this situation came about. The interrelatedness of translation and interpretation are explored in what is now generally recognized as a seminal twentieth-century text for the development of translation theory, George Steiner's *After Babel: Aspects of language and translation*. First published in 1975, the book received a mixed critical reception. It has since been republished, in 1992 and 1998. In his Preface to the Second Edition, Steiner reflected first on the ubiquity of a theoretical literature on translation 'from the time of Seneca to that of Walter Benjamin and W. v. O. Quine', then secondly on how his wish to extend that debate, 'to locate translation at the heart of human communication . . . to explore . . . the philosophic enquiry into consciousness and the meaning of meaning' (Steiner 1998, ix–x), had been resisted. Steiner establishes his ground by translating/interpreting four texts in the first part of

Chapter One in the manner of close reading exercises. Though they are not literally foreign language texts, in Steiner's view they are because all are to a degree removed from current English usage – 'out of the past of one's own language' – and as such they are therefore subject to 'a manifold act of interpretation' (Ibid., 18).The passages come from Shakespeare's *Cymbeline*, Jane Austen's *Northanger Abbey*, there is a sonnet by D. G. Rossetti and an extract from Nöel Coward's *Private Lives*.The need for interpretation relates not only to a notion of historicism (where the past may be the very recent past), but also to sociocultural origins which predicate a process of interpretation/translation.

Steiner argues that interpretation is a concomitant of translation, regardless of whether the 'translation' be from another language:

> Any thorough reading of a text out of the past of one's own language and litera-ture is a manifold act of interpretation. In the great majority of cases, this act is hardly performed or even consciously recognised. At best, the common reader will rely on what instant crutches footnotes or a glossary provide.When reading any piece of English prose after about 1800 and most verse, the general reader assumes that the words on the page, with a few 'difficult' or whimsical exceptions, mean what they would mean in his own idiom. In the case of 'classics' such as Defoe and Swift that assumption may be extended back to the early eighteenth century. It almost reaches Dryden, but it is, of course, a fiction. Language is in perpetual change. (Ibid., 18)

No discussion of translation theory since the 1970s has been able to proceed without some degree of reference (approving or otherwise) to Steiner's work, and in recent years his presence seems to have grown all the more significant. In 1988 Susan Bassnett revisited Steiner's proposed division of the stages of development of translation theory into four overlapping periods.

Steiner proposed a first phase from Cicero and Horace through to Hölder-lin's discussion of his own attempts to translate Sophocles in 1804. A second phase is initiated by Schleiermacher's essay on translation of 1813, *Über die verschiedenen Methoden des Übersetzens*, and continues into the early twentieth century. Steiner's third phase begins with 'the introduction of structural linguis-tics and communication theory into the study of translation' (Bassnett 1988, 46), while the fourth phase is triggered in the 1960s by the work of Heidegger and Gadamer, and the belated impact of Benjamin's essay, *Die Aufgabe des Über-setzers* (1923). He depicts the third and fourth phases as existing alongside each other, the fourth phase being characterized by 'a reversion to hermeneutic, almost metaphysical inquiries into translation and interpretation' (Steiner 1998, 250). That particular turn, one that might be described as a throw-back to the theologically grounded hermeneutics of Schleiermacher which were to be subjected later to a more objective, 'scientifically' informed methodology, is an important one to appreciate. Steiner's work is built along the lines of a 'meta-physical inquiry', and the criticism his book has received owes a good deal to scholarly scepticism on that score.

Few have been more dismissive of Steiner and Benjamin than Douglas Robinson, who describes them ironically as heirs to a Romantic tradition of language theory whose creed preserves the belief that 'we were once gods . . . and we will become gods again, as soon as the romantic poet/translator/saviour has undone the verbal magic that traps us in impotence' (Robinson 1991, 89).

In her commentary on Steiner's suggested four periods, Bassnett argues that any periodization is inevitably arbitrary and ultimately unhelpful (Bassnett 1988, 46). She goes on to outline how T. R. Steiner, André Lefevere, F. O. Mattieson, and Timothy Webb, have all produced equally valuable but equally variable models for the way the theory and practice of translation has evolved. Lefevere, for example, in *Translating Literature: The German Tradition* (1977), emphasizes the importance of the tradition that starts with Luther and links Gottsched, Goethe, the Schlegels, Schleiermacher and ultimately Franz Rosenweig, a contemporary of Benjamin.

One facet of the phenomenon of translation is all too easily forgotten in the process of constructing models such as these. Antoine Berman wrote (in the context of reading Steiner), 'It is impossible to separate the history of translation from the history of languages, of cultures, of literatures – even of religions and nations' (Berman 1992, 2). I would wish to add to this that where there is a market for literature in translation (and we have already seen how this was so in eighteenth- and nineteenth-century Germany) entrepreneurial forces will take a hand. Commercial translation, as Hilary Brown has shown, became a major activity in Germany after 1770; the word for it was, aptly, 'Übersetzungsmanu-fakturen' (Brown 2005, 26). In these circumstances neither translators nor publishers may be expected to take time out to reflect on theoretical issues attached to the mode of translation adopted. Though this is not to suggest that translation becomes divorced from theory, it is certainly to introduce a materialist aspect into the theoretical debate in line with the approach of Bassnett, Lawrence Venuti, and María Calzada Pérez, as opposed to the spiritual and numinous nuances that are central to the work of Benjamin and Steiner. Equally important is an awareness of a context that recognizes the political situation of the time, be it the aftermath of the Napoleonic Wars and the current of German Nationalism that was a preoccupation of the Jacobsen chapters, the volatile years of the 1840s that significantly moulded the work of Ferdinand Freiligrath, or the somewhat different European instabilities that were surfacing towards the end of the century, when Marie Gothein produced her biography and anthology of William Wordsworth.

It is the complex, frequently contradictory relationship between nationalism encapsulated in language, and the translator's task, which lies at the heart of this study. A work of translation may either have the effect of challenging the solidity of those nationalist barriers, or emphasize the difference between peoples where that difference lies rooted in linguistic difference. Indeed, a translation may be understood to be capable of performing both tasks simultaneously; confirming the existence of distinct national identities to some of its readers, while also revealing what Benedict Anderson described in 1983 as 'imagined communities'. Theorists from Dryden to Tytler, Schleiermacher to Nietzsche, Arnold to Pound, Richards to Steiner, Rosenweig to Venuti, all work in response to pressures of this kind specific to the times in which they live. Translators are frequently thrust into an indeterminate no-man's land, a realm of endless, and at times contradictory, negotiation. Maria Tymoczko's response to this is to emphasize the impossibility of 'neutral' translation: 'the ideology of translation is indeed a result of the translator's position, but that position is not a space between' (Tymoczko 2003, 201).

The translator's problem in this respect is summed up by Berman:

The very aim of translation – to open up in writing a certain relation with the Other, to fertilise what is one's own through the mediation of what is foreign – is diametrically opposed to the ethnocentric structure of every culture, that species of narcissism by which every society wants to be a pure and unadulterated whole. (Berman 1992, 4)

It was presumably this brand of narcissism that prompted Goethe to claim that the German language would eventually be spoken by everyone because 'other nations . . . will realise that in this way they can . . . save themselves the apprenticeship of almost all other languages'. 'The force of a language,' he added, recalling St Jerome, 'is not to reject the foreign, but to devour it' (Ibid., 11–12). A. W. Schlegel was equally confident: 'It is . . . no mere sanguine optimism to suppose that the time is not far distant when the German language will become the speaking voice of the civilized world' (Robinson 1997i, 60). Concurring with his contemporaries (for once) that German retained far more of the purity of the early, great languages of civilization, Schopenhauer was inclined to be more specific: 'languages degenerate gradually from the noble Sanskrit down to the gibberish of English' (Robinson 1997ii, 246).

Contemporary translation studies of the kind which primarily engage critics like Tymoczko, Jerry Palmer and Roberto Valdéon (in Salama-Carr 2007), have arisen largely in response to the need to raise awareness of the pressures and dangers that translators, a frequently invisible and peculiarly vulnerable company, are facing in the context of twenty-first-century global conflict. Christopher J. Hall notes that because translation involves 'using one grammar and then recording the meanings they activate using the grammar of the second', it is reasonable to point out that 'languages rarely express exactly the *same* meanings in the same ways (if they do at all)' (Hall 2005, 232). The political implications of this are far reaching. Robert C. Young argues that 'The initial act in colonization was to translate significant indigenous written and oral texts into the colonizer's language. In this way, translation transformed oral cultures into the webs and snares of writing' (Young 2003, 140).

There is much this contemporary debate can offer, however, when studying the evolution of the practice of translation from the eighteenth into the nineteenth century. The symbiosis is particularly pertinent when acts of translation are linked to a study of the development of Nationalist ideologies, linked as such ideologies will inevitably be to the assumptions that surround notions of literary cultures peculiar to the nations that produce them. In the case of Germany, it is appropriate to look in more detail at Luther's approach to biblical translation, before considering the impact of seventeenth- and eighteenth-century British theorists on German translation practice.

Luther's German Bible was an act of defiance against the autonomy of the Roman Catholic Church. He sought to justify his actions through an essay on translation, the *Sendbrief vom Dolmetschen* of 1530. Here, Luther made the case for clarity in relation to the target reader; in the process he rejected a word-for-word discipline in favour of a vernacular rendering of the subject text in order to prioritize meaning. His intention was, to adopt a maxim used later (but not endorsed) by Schleiermacher, to bring the text to the reader. While St. Jerome in the fourth century had made a similar argument for translating the scriptures, Jeremy Munday points out that the difference for Luther lay in the political implications of his use of 'the language of ordinary people', and thus in the impact his translation would make on the sense of unity among those 'ordinary people' (Munday 2001, 23). Bassnett draws attention to the revealing fact that in the *Letter*, Luther 'uses the verbs *übersetzen* (to translate) and *verdeutschen* (to Germanize) almost indiscriminately'. His priority is summarized as the production of 'an accessible and aesthetically vernacular style', and beyond that, of course, a spiritually liberating experience (Bassnett 1988, 53–4). Bassnett concludes:

> The task of the translator went beyond the linguistic and became evangelistic in its own right, for the (often anonymous) translator of the Bible in the sixteenth century was a radical leader in the struggle to further man's spiritual progress. The collaborative aspect of Bible translation represented yet another significant aspect of that struggle. (Ibid., 55)

Despite the influence of Enlightenment thought and the quest for objectivity and scientific method evident in much post-Romantic theorizing, translation theory has remained a field in which a sense of the numinous has found a ready ingress. A belief that language is a site where we engage with a mystery that may justifiably be contemplated in theological terms is evident in the work of Benjamin, Steiner, and Paul Ricoeur. The lost innocence of Eden is epitomized in the Babel sounds of linguistic difference beyond which lies the tantalizing dream of a unity created by fusion into one common language; with that dream of restored linguistic unity comes the dream of a one world faith, and a one world nation. Luther's job, of course, was to create a unified scripture for his fellow Germans. Roger Paulin comments on how translation rendered this a two-way process in the evolution of a unified literary German language. 'It was Luther's aim', he writes of Luther's use of the vernacular, 'to reduce the strangeness of "the culture of salvation" by searching for German equivalents' (Paulin 2003, 110). At the same time, however, he endorses Goethe's view that Luther's translations resulted in a significant enrichment of the target language.

Paulin is here identifying a link between translation and what he refers to as 'cultural annexation' (ibid., 101), a phenomenon that the majority of contemporary translation theorists see as an inevitable consequence of translation. As Germany gradually broke free from the dominance of French literary influence through the eighteenth century, the English writers who gained prominence were frequently translators. Of these, John Dryden was particularly significant, and he produced a series of influential essays on translation in the form of prefaces to *Ovid's Epistles* (1680), *Sylvae* (1685), *The Satires of Juvenal and Persius* (1693), *Examen Poeticum* (1693), *Virgil's Aeneid* (1697), and *Fables Ancient and Modern* (1700). Among the issues discussed by Dryden are the level of expertise needed by a translator, and the extent to which the character of the subject text should be preserved. Should the translator judge and if need be amend the subject text? Should the subject text be modernized in the process of translation, and should the resulting target text be 'foreignized', or assimilated into the target culture so that it serves the needs of the target reader? On the issue of methodology, Dryden identified three main approaches to translation: 'metaphrase' (word for word), 'paraphrase' (translation with latitude), and 'imitation'; he became primarily concerned with establishing a set of guidelines for paraphrase, relaxing his initial concern for faithfulness to the subject text.

He was prepared to modernize, but he maintained that the translator must be fully competent in both languages, and should always seek to display the individuality of the translated author. In his essay on Virgil (1697) he recognizes the tensions that arise when the translator feels obliged to make his author appear 'as . . . if he had been born in *England*, and in this present age' (Hopkins 2005, 63). No clearer illustration may be found of the instinct for 'cultural annexation' accompanying literary translation than this. Having stressed the tensions that can exist between the translator and his target author in the context of Virgil, in the Dedication to *Fables* Dryden introduces a sense of the numinous when he discusses metempsychosis, the situation where the translator feels such intense sympathy for his author that it seems their souls have mingled, and they write with one voice. Dryden provided much of the theoretical framework that informed the eighteenth-century debate on translation in England and Germany, and at the heart of that was a sense of national identity, regardless of the respect that might have been felt for the subject author and text. Louis Kelly describes him as 'product-oriented'; his discussions on translation 'list criteria by which a translation may be made acceptable as a piece of English literature' (Kelly 2005, 67). Despite the vigorous debate that ensued through the eighteenth century on the precise nature of those criteria, Kelly summarizes the general view as one where 'the translator should exploit his own stylistic resources to acclimatize his author's strengths to his home culture' (Ibid., 68).

Dryden began to be known and read in Germany at the same time that Shakespeare was making his appearance; Paulin cites references to him by Daniel Georg Morhof in the early 1680s (Paulin 2001, 12–13). His views on translation became widely known through the eighteenth century, when he was recognized as a kindred spirit by Johann Gottsched, whose vision of establishing a single German language based on the Saxon tongue included the creation of a national poetry and drama rooted in the French model. The issue of national identity permeates the entire debate. Once the translator sets about his or her work, who owns the text, and for what purpose? Is an English Virgil being created to serve the ends of England? Dryden confessed that he had edited out what he felt was inappropriate material, while admitting that he had embellished and added to the original in other places, and then claimed that he had done all this in the spirit of the original; but did the 'original' really have anything to do with this? Was this not an act of cultural appropriation hedged around by a few lame gestures towards 'foreignizing' the target text? Much later in the eighteenth century, Wieland, Bürger and Goethe continue to debate the issue, this time in relation to 'a *German* Homer'. Bürger's use of blank verse to translate Book Six of the *Iliad* won the approval of Wieland and Goethe because, as Wieland put it, 'iambic verse is, in our opinion, the old, natural and heroic metre of our language'. Later in the same letter Wieland refers to what Bürger is doing as creating a 'German Homer' (Kristmannsson 2001, I, 253–5). In the same year that Schleiermacher published his essay on translation, 1813, Goethe – using Schleiermacher's terminology – summed up the plethora of theoretical issues as essentially a matter of two choices:

> . . . one requires that the author of a foreign nation be brought across to us in such a way that we can look on him as ours; the other requires that we should go across to what is foreign and adapt ourselves to its conditions, its use of language, its peculiarities . . . Our friend [Wieland], who looked for a middle way in this, too, tried to reconcile both, but as a man of feeling and taste he preferred the first maxim when in doubt. (Weissbort 2006, 200)

An enlightened view might be expected to recognize and indeed celebrate difference as an enriching experience, or at the very least seek out the middle way so that translation, while it dismantles a fundamental component of difference (language), nevertheless honours its origins. In the event, however, 'Our friend Wieland' does what in practice all men of 'feeling and taste' do according to Goethe: he brings it home! Those terms, 'feeling' and 'taste', relate to a sense for one's own culture, which is to say here specifically, one's native language. As we study examples of British poetry translated into German in the nineteenth century, we need to be constantly aware of the survival of an influential cosmopolitan ideal which exists in a state of tension with what might be termed the *realpolitik* of translation as colonization.

Two important translators who moved the debate forward towards the end of the eighteenth century, and were influential in Germany, were Sir William Jones (1746–94), and Alexander Fraser Tytler (1747–1813).

Jones's translations have on occasion been dismissed as little more than mock-oriental English poetry that owe very little to their supposed originals. He was in every respect a true son of the Enlightenment, cosmopolitan in outlook and intensely patriotic. Clive Holes is prepared to accept that he genuinely came to believe that his own language and culture stood in need of enrichment, and that this could be achieved by the translation of eastern poetry (Holes 2005, 443–55). Tejaswini Niranjana offers a far less sympathetic reading of Jones:

> The most significant nodes of Jones' work are: (a) the need for translation by the European, since the [Indian] natives are unreliable interpreters of their own laws and culture; (b) the desire to be a lawgiver, to give the Indians their 'own' laws; and (c) the desire to 'purify' Indian culture and speak on its behalf. (Robinson 1996, 134)

Regardless of how his attitude is interpreted, Jones's motive for translation remains essentially one of appropriation; he made it very clear that an inevitable consequence of the negotiations that took place between the subject text, the target text, and the reader, were bound to result in a significant distortion of the subject text. His practice was generally to provide both prose and verse translations in recognition of the multifaceted nature of translation and interpretation.

He is generally recognized as the first Briton to take a genuinely scholarly interest in the languages and cultures of India, though Chairs of Arabic had been established at Cambridge in 1632 and at Oxford in 1634. In due course he came to challenge the widely held view that Hellenistic civilization was superior to Persian. In 1760 he published, in French, a translation of Mahdi Khan's biography of the Persian ruler, Nadir Shah; it had been commissioned by Christian VII of Denmark. In 1772 he published *Poems Consisting Chiefly of Translations from the Asiatick Languages*. The contents were poems inspired by, rather than translated from, Jones's reading of the Arabic, Persian, and Turkish originals, and the collection played a significant role in establishing an exotic perception of 'the Orient' for generations to come. Jones himself was imagining his Orient at this point; it was not until ten years later, in 1782, that he went to India to take up the post of Judge at Bengal. To comply with Warren Hastings' decision that the Indians were to be ruled according to their own laws, he undertook to translate the Hindu legal code from Sanskrit into English. This alerted him to a strong affinity between Sanskrit and Greek and Latin. His theory that there had at one time existed a single language beyond these three from which may also have sprung Gothic, Celtic, and Persian was to have a lasting influence on nineteenth-century philology, nowhere more so than in Germany, where it was adopted by A. W. Schlegel and the Grimm brothers, among others. In the twentieth century, Jones's theory has been recognized as a key breakthrough in modern linguistics (Holes 2005, 451).

Jones's approach to translation may still appear cavalier, and the part he undoubtedly played in reinforcing a stereotype of the 'Orient' has understandably won him enemies. What makes his career of considerable importance here, however, is the way in which he showed himself keenly aware of the issues that attended translation. He was sensitive both to the cultural debate and to market forces. He translated the *Sacontalá* (a collection of Sanskrit fables) first into Latin, because he felt this enabled him to reproduce the original most faithfully, then into English, where his free treatment of the text pretends to do nothing more than adapt the original for the English target reader. This version owes far more to Shakespeare than it does to the author, Cálidás (Ibid., 451). We can therefore see how Jones came to develop the idea that 'translation' might be considered a form in itself, preparing the ground for the German theorists (his work began to be translated into German in the 1790s). Against the accusations of Said and others that he was instrumental in reinforcing a negative image of the Orient, is the fact that he portrayed the Orient as a place possessing a cultural and linguistic heritage of inestimable worth and beauty. As Clive Holes has pointed out, he expressed dislike for the term 'Oriental', preferring 'Asiatic'. 'Oriental', he wrote, 'is in truth a word merely relative, and, though commonly used in Europe, conveys no very distinct idea.' (Ibid., 454). On the one hand, as Holes concedes, Jones was engaged in interpreting his subject texts for a classically grounded readership (rather as William Hodges had painted Indian locations and Pacific islands with a distinctly Claudian touch in the eighteenth century); on the other, he is promoting a view that the 'Asiatic' is worthy of study for its own sake. Crucially he displayed the translator's craft as a complex, many faceted occupation that lies at the heart of cultural evolution, not at its periphery.

In his *Essay on the Principles of Translation* of 1797, Alexander Tytler acknowledged his debt to Dryden in his attempt to codify key principles for the practice of translation. His four main 'rules' (set out as chapter headings) may be read as a summary of the major issues which form the basis of the nineteenth-century debate. First he states: 'A Translation should give a complete transcript of the ideas of the original work'. Second, 'The style and manner of writing in a translation should be of the same character with that of the original.' Third, 'A translation should have all the ease of original composition'. Fourth, 'The genius of the Translator should be akin to that of the original author'. In a more general statement in his first chapter, he proposes that a good translation is:

> That, in which the merit of the original work is so completely transfused into another language, as to be distinctly apprehended, and as strongly felt, by a native of the country to which that language belongs, as it is by those who speak the language of the original work. (Tytler 1797, 14)

Where 'the ideas of the original' are concerned, he seems to be very clear; there is to be no censorship, and he requires the style to suggest the original. If some degree of 'cultural annexation' (Paulin's term) is inevitable, Tytler suggests that a translation should preserve a sense of the foreignness of the text. However, he also requires a translation to have the 'ease' of the original, which implies a degree of licence to deal with what might be the stylistic awkwardness of a too literal rendering. We should note also that (no doubt from his reading of Dryden) he subscribes to the idea of metempsychosis in so far as 'The genius of the Translator should be akin to that of the original author' (ibid., 375).

Tytler's goal is to create a unifying experience through translation, a moment in which the barriers between nations and between historical periods, manifest in linguistic difference, are bridged. This accords with what Mary Anne Perkins (2001) has referred to as a spirit of 'liberal Nationalism' that existed through the Romantic Period. One year after Tytler's *Essay* was published, George Campbell published his 'Preliminary Dissertations to a new Translation of the Gospel' and this, combined with Tytler's work, encapsulated the major issues attendant on translation as they appeared at the turn of the century. Particularly significant for the German reception of Tytler and Campbell (not least with respect to Schleiermacher), was their recognition of the need for an imaginative engagement of the translator with the 'genius' of the original text.

As an introduction to an assessment of the significance of Friedrich Schleiermacher in relation to the theory and practice of translation, it is helpful to note that Paul Ricoeur summarized the multiple problems created by translation as the 'faithfulness/betrayal dilemma', arguing that the dilemma was insoluble. He refers to Rosenweig in order to pin-point the primary issues: 'to translate', he says, 'is to serve two masters, the foreigner in his strangeness, the reader in his desire for appropriation'. This eternal paradox of translation, Ricoeur claims, had been encapsulated by Schleiermacher in his essay of 1813 when he described the choices faced by a translator: '"bringing the reader to the author", "bringing the author to the reader"' (Ricoeur 2006, 22–4).

Schleiermacher's essay on translation was predicated on his work on hermeneutics (prompted by his theological studies), and on his undertaking to write a study of Plato in conjunction with a translation of the complete works. He believed the translator's task was to bring the reader to the author. In other words, he acknowledged the text as foreign, and believed that the reader of the translation should experience it as such. It follows from this that the translator must seek to establish an 'alienating' style in translation, as opposed to a 'naturalizing' one. Two important consequences of this considered by Schleiermacher are, first, that different readers must be expected to interpret the text in different ways, according to 'the level of education and understanding' they possess (Munday 2001, 28); and second, Schleiermacher speculates that there may evolve a distinct language for translation as the task is pursued, a language that will be forged in the process of the translator's imaginative engagement with the subject text. The translator's job is to convey the subject text into a target text in terms of its spirit, and in doing so capture the essence of its otherness. This is Schleiermacher's way of attempting to resolve the paradox of difference described by Ricoeur and Rosenweig as the dilemma of 'faithfulness/betrayal', a problem noted also by Schleiermacher's contemporary, von Humboldt, in the following way:

> Any translator must inevitably encounter one of the following obstacles: he will cleave with too much accuracy either to the original, at the expense of his people's language and taste, or to the originality of his people, at the expense of the work to be translated. (Berman 1992, 1)

For Ricoeur, such difference is not to be regretted; he sees in it a positive force from which we may learn how to understand and cope with the inherent state of difference that is our destiny as human beings. We have already noted that Tymoczko argues persuasively against any unrealistic notion that there might be an in-between language or place that the translator might inhabit. Tourey, on the other hand, has argued that it is possible to conceive of neutral laws of translation (Munday 2001, 108). Hall's contribution to this debate is to draw attention to Larry Selinker's work on what he calls 'interlanguage' – systems used for basic communication with speakers of other languages which tend to be individualized rather than for group use (Hall 2005, 234–5). Venuti insists that, while a degree of neutrality may be attached to the technical work of the translator as he or she produces a series of translated texts, it is inevitable that what finally gets written on the page 'will also include a diverse range of domestic values, beliefs and social representations which carry ideological force in serving the interests of specific groups. And they are always housed in the social institutions where translations are produced and enlisted in cultural and political agendas' (Venuti 1998, 29).

Schleiermacher's belief that the reader should be taken to the text, along with the idea that the translator might create a specialized language for the translation in hand, suggests an idealistic model for translation that in reality (Venuti would argue) is an impossibility. But it is also true that Schleiermacher contemplates the implications of the way a translator is bound by his own language and national identity: 'just as a man must decide to belong to one country,' he writes, 'so [a translator] must adhere to one language' (Tymoczko 2003, 184). What Schleiermacher is most concerned to understand and resolve is how to translate/interpret for his target reader the difference between the original text and the text in translated form. Unless the reader experiences the otherness of the text and of the target author, the translation will not perform its proper function. It was this that pushed Schleiermacher into the conviction that translation had to be considered as more than an objectively mechanical process. As a theologian, this was not a particularly difficult step for him to take. Julia A. Lamm argues that at the root of Schleiermacher's theory of translation was the conviction that 'interpretation and explication are an art':

> Much more than learning a foreign language, therefore, the interpreter must have a 'living awareness of language, the sense of analogy and difference.' Hence the art of understanding Plato begins in scholarship – in particular, in philology – but such scholarship always requires art. It can be extended to non-specialists if the translator-interpreter is an artist. (Lamm 2005, 96–7)

For all Schleiermacher's sense of difference, however, and his belief that the reader should be taken to the text, the end product remains in essence a Germanizing one.

Roger Paulin argues a similar case in connection with Heinrich Voss's translations of Shakespeare. Voss produced a German Shakespeare using coinages ('a bracing cold shower of Germanisms') that made his German text as testing for his German readership as Shakespeare (with his 'difficult Latinisms') would have been for his English audiences. Compared to his rival, A. W. Schlegel, Voss was foreignizing his text, taking his reader (as Schleiermacher would have him do) to the text through his use of unfamiliar, frequently archaic German words to establish the otherness of Shakespeare. What we need to appreciate, however, is that the end result of this exercise is nevertheless perceived as ultimately a Germanizing process. Voss advocated that when a translator encountered difficulties in the subject text, they should be rendered in the target text through 'the choice if need be of locutions which Shakespeare "might have chosen were he German"'. The key phrase here is '. . . were he German'. The recognition and indeed celebration of difference, as opposed to appropriation, remains an affirmative act on behalf (in this instance) of German culture (Paulin 2003, 342).

The complexities surrounding the act of translation were being analysed in early nineteenth-century Germany in a way that was to provide the basis for all subsequent scholarship. An important driving force at the heart this new initiative was the development of the concept of modern, post-Enlightenment nationhood. Gauti Kristmannsson sees this illustrated in the shift in Germany from adherence to the models provided by seventeenth-century French classicism to English models. Referring specifically in this respect to Lessing, Herder, Goethe and Hegel, he claims that:

> They invented a new aesthetic through the interpretation of Shakespeare . . . or rather through the translational synthesis of the Greeks, Shakespeare and recent British aesthetics (Shaftesbury, Blackwell, Burke, Blair), as well as recent British philosophy and historical approaches (Hume, Roberston, Warburton, Lowth, Hurd, Percy). In the process they invented nothing less than a new German nation of the nineteenth century. What became the political Frankenstein of the twentieth century may, however, have begun more modestly as a ghost, ghost-written for the German spirit desiring a body it did not have. (Kristmannsson 2001, I, 248)

Despite confusing Frankenstein with his monster, Kristmannsson's point provides a context for the theory. Schleiermacher and his contemporaries were doing their thinking, and their translating, in a Germany whose quest for nationhood rivalled other, already long-established nations in its ambitions; and that quest was predicated above all else on language, as Mary Anne Perkins argues:

> Friedrich Schiller went so far as to claim that 'Our language will rule the world. Language is the mirror of a nation; when we look in this mirror we are faced with a great and noble reflection of ourselves'. He extolled 'the delicious treasures of the German language, which expresses everything, both the deepest and the most superficial, the spirit, the soul, and which is suffused with meaning'. (Perkins 2001, 194)

In like manner Fichte wrote: 'we have preserved our language and literature, and we will always remain a nation on this basis' (Seeba 2003, 4).

In one respect, the work of men like Humboldt, Goethe, Lessing, Hegel and Schleiermacher appears to represent the development of an increasingly sophisticated appreciation of the complexities of translation and interpretation, where Ricoeur's post-colonial sensitivity to a 'faithfulness/betrayal' dilemma becomes possible. Lawrence Venuti, however, argues for a less rose-tinted version of the ideology of translation. His argument, as relevant to the European situation as to Anglo-American practice, is summarized by Hatim and Mason:

> Distinguishing between 'domesticating' and 'foreignizing' translation, he [Venuti] shows how the predominant trend towards domestication in Anglo-American

translating over the last three centuries has had a normalizing and neutralizing effect, depriving source text producers of their voice and re-expressing foreign cultural values in terms of what is familiar (and therefore unchallenging) to the dominant culture. (Hatim 1997, 145)

Intentional or not, Venuti explains, the result is the same: 'to assimilate to a dominant – or even "hegemonic" – culture all that is foreign to it' (ibid., 145).

In his work on hermeneutics, Schleiermacher could argue (as we have seen Steiner doing) that everything the reader encounters is, in effect, 'foreign'; everything stands in need of interpretation/translation, and in this respect the notion of 'truth' or accuracy becomes almost irrelevant. Understanding is a matter of negotiation, and that process moves the work of the translator towards the realm of art and creativity, inspiration and imagination. Schleiermacher believed that interpretation must involve 'the empathetic attempt to "feel one's way" into the mind of an author' (Bowie 2005, 75). A. W. Schlegel wrote that to achieve the highest form of translation, one that reveals 'the pure and perfect character of the individual work of art', the translator 'must be an artist himself' (Robinson 1997ii, 213). Taking the idea a step further, and in the process reversing the points of reference, Novalis wrote, 'Am Ende ist all Poesie Übersetzen', 'all poetry is translation' (Bernofsky 2005, 43). Steiner, as we have seen, and also Benjamin, inherited this conviction, and thus challenged the reductionist tendencies of theorists like Venuti, Bassnett, and Hatim and Mason.

In an essay published in 2001, Mary Anne Perkins argues that an important legacy of the Romantic Period theorists of language and translation, notably in Germany and Britain, is the ideal of 'liberal nationalism' (Perkins 2001, 191). Schleiermacher, she suggests, was one of many 'who engages in the struggle to reconcile particular nationhood with a universal cosmopolitan ideal' (ibid., 197).

Xenophobic nationalism and the Romantic Period are, Perkins suggests, frequently linked, and nowhere more so than in relation to Germany in the nineteenth century. Remembering passages from Wordsworth's *Excursion* already considered in the previous chapter, this may seem an unfair emphasis, but of course this relates to what we have seen Kristmannsson refer to as the 'Frankenstein' of fascism. To look more closely at this, Perkins focuses on the issue of how translation is a key factor. She returns to Luther for an insight into the function of language more generally: 'Luther . . . linked nationhood to language and truth in a way which became irresistible to the Protestant nationalisms of the Romantic period' (ibid., 191); 'the divine word', associated by Luther with the purity of the German language, comes to be perceived as the sole arbiter of fundamental truths. 'In this way the origin and evolution of the language of a people, a *volk*, was imbued with a spiritual character; it became the medium and the manifestation – the incarnation – of national spirit' (ibid., 192). Language is perceived as a living, defining power. When we read Hamann, Böhme, Fichte, Schiller, Goethe and others developing a mystique of the German language into a conviction that their emerging Nation had a divine calling, it is all too easy, Perkins argues, to draw a line that neatly connects a German theory of language (and translation) to the rise of German fascism in the twentieth century. This model has undoubtedly influenced post-war scholarship in its assessment of nineteenth century German history and culture, and specifically in relation to its engagement with cultural exchanges during that period. Kristmannsson discusses the way this area is now being revisited, and how in consequence eighteenth-century nationalism in Germany is being reassessed, after the period had been 'de-nationalised after 1945 to rescue the greats of the Enlightenment from the shadow of national ideology' (Kristmannsson 2001, I, 15).

Perkins suggests that the compelling nature of the German example may lead us to underestimate the significance of the relationship between language and nationalism in other countries. The *Logos* in Coleridge's thought, she claims, 'becomes the very symbol of nationhood itself' (Perkins 2001, 193). Perkins, however, is concerned to note that Romantic nationalism also contains within it the ideal of 'distinction-in-unity'; she writes:

> . . . the insistence of the Romantics on the particularity and uniqueness of nation-
> hood can no longer automatically be associated with exclusivity and chauvinism.
> It must rather be seen as *one* aspect of a struggle to realize both nationhood and
> a cosmopolitan, humanitarian ideal. (Ibid., 195)

The paradox of sustaining a belief in nationhood alongside 'a cosmopolitan, humanitarian ideal' is precisely what we have already witnessed in Jacobsen's response to Wordsworth. Fichte, Novalis and Humboldt all insist that their ulti-mate goal is the greater good of universal humanity, while Schleiermacher wrote: 'I saw clearly that each man is meant to represent humanity in his own way, combining its elements uniquely, so that it may reveal itself in every mode, and all that can issue from its womb be made actual in the fullness of unending space and time'. Perkins adds, 'This model is extended to a paradigm of distinct, unique nations uniting in a universal human community' (ibid., 197).

The tensions and contradictions that accompany the evolution of theories of nationhood in nineteenth-century Europe are manifold, not least because the Napoleonic wars were to leave different nations in very different circumstances. The cultural unification of Germany was accompanied by a powerful convic-tion that its language was superior to all others, and that it was still evolving towards becoming a language that would eventually eliminate all others. We are confronted with what Perkins describes as an 'uncomfortable dichotomy', but she insists that 'these thinkers recognized the importance of the apparent dichotomy of nationhood and human community and the importance of the attempt to find a basis of reconciliation' (Perkins 2001, 199).

In the three examples of Wordsworth translated into German that follow, it will be possible to see how the translators reflect aspects of this uncomfortable dichotomy at different periods of the nineteenth century.

Jacobsen, Freiligrath, and Gothein: Translation in Practice

> *'A translator requires mindful awareness of potential conflicts and cultural difference, but
> beyond this there are no identifiable off the peg optimal solutions, and the individual has
> his/her way in tackling intercultural conflicts'.*
>
> Tang in Salama-Carr 2007, 135

I begin by returning to the final short passage which Jacobsen quotes towards the end of his account of *The Excursion* in the *Briefe an eine deutsche Edelfrau* (1820). His way of presenting a foreign text alerts us to a context for translation that none of the theorists so far mentioned consider. Jacobsen was far from being the only German writer and anthologist of English poetry to present the reader with the poem in its original language, and as such it could hardly have been more 'foreignizing':

> Earth is sick,
> And Heaven is weary of the hollow words
> Which States and Kingdoms utter when they speak
> Of Truth and Justice.
> (Jacobsen 1820, 151; Wordsworth 2007, 178)

The prose translation at the foot of the page, however, performs the function that all his translations in this book do; they render the 'alien' English into a very accurate, but wholly Germanized, account of the original. A German reading the following without knowing it was a translation would not be expected to realize that it was anything but German in origin:

> *Die Erde ist krank und der Himmel ist müde der hohlen Worte, welche Staaten und Königreiche von sich geben, wenn sie von Warhrheit und Gerechtigkeit sprechen.*

Where, then, does this place Jacobsen in the context of his translation agenda? He does indeed seem in accord with Perkins' notion of a Romantic period 'liberal nationalist'; he expresses a complex, contradictory ideology of nationalism and reconciliation, where the notion of 'World Literature' is a genuine ideal, but one ultimately defined by a notion of the uniqueness and destiny of German language and culture across the globe. Within that matrix, we have seen how Jacobsen clearly had a sense of a special relationship between Germany and Britain. We should also remember that he writes for a group of readers he knows to be proficient in English; this means that for his immediate target readership there would not be the same impact of Wordsworth's 'otherness' that otherwise would have been the case. He is an Anglophile preserving the 'Britishness' of British poetry in the main body of his text. At the foot of the page, he proceeds to render that difference as insignificant as possible for his German reader. Here we do have an act of appropriation: Jacobsen's British poets are being worked into his vision of an ever-expanding, powerful, civilizing German Nation. It is a Nation defined as much by its Protestant Christian tradition as by its language, hence the strength of his affinity with Wordsworth. Here there is no middle way for the translator. The poetry is either in English, or it is in German prose, at which point it is absorbed into the larger vision of a universal German Nation.

None of this should blind us, however, to the fact that Jacobsen's writing carries within it evidence of his strong attachment to the eighteenth-century tradition of cosmopolitanism. We would expect nothing less from an inhabitant of Altona, dominated by the Hanseatic ports. Jacobsen, in his way, will have been aware of the contradictions embedded within his work, but given the fact that he had successfully survived the deprivations of French occupation, he was content to live with them, savouring his freedom to read, write, and travel where he chose. What he was not prepared to undertake as a translator, was the attempt to translate form in poetry as well as content. He therefore set to one side an issue that continued to be a major concern for German theorists and practitioners of translation; it emerges as an important point for discussion when we consider our remaining German Wordsworthians up to the outbreak of the First World War.

Freiligrath published his *Gedichte aus dem Englischen* in 1846. It contains just two poems by Wordsworth, 'Yew Trees' and 'The Solitary Reaper'. In his translations, Freiligrath undertook to reproduce the form of the poem as well as its content. For a number of reasons, 'Yew Trees' seems at first an odd choice; it is a very English poem if only because in the course of the first five lines there are references to family and place names (Lorton Vale, Umfraville, Percy) that might be expected to puzzle a German reader, though the references that follow to 'Scotland's heaths', 'Azincourt', 'Crecy', and 'Poictiers' would be familiar enough.

The appeal of this poem for Freiligrath undoubtedly lies in the way Wordsworth links his patriotism to his love of nature. The opening lines draw attention to the role played by the trees in supplying the longbows that had been used with such devastating effect against Germany's traditional foe:

> There is a Yew-tree, pride of Lorton Vale,
> Which to this day stands single, in the midst
> Of its own darkness, as it stood of yore:
> Not loth to furnish weapons for the bands
> Of Umfraville or Percy when they marched
> To Scotland's Heaths: or those that crossed the sea
> And drew their sounding boughs at Azincourt,
> Perhaps at earlier Crecy, or Poictiers.
>
> (Selincourt 1969, 146–7)

I am tempted to think that a reading of these lines will have stirred a sufficiently powerful sense of metempsychosis in Freiligrath to spur him on. Forests had long been a powerful symbol of German national identity. Commenting on early nineteenth-century German literature and art, Simon Schama writes, 'Religion and patriotism, antiquity and the future – all came together in the Teutonic romance of the woods. Figures asleep for centuries might stir into life, not least Germania herself'. Elsewhere he points out that 'by the time the German forest was being identified as the authentically native German scenery, much of it was fast disappearing under the axe', a fact that intensified the process of recreating the German forest through the 'literary and visual imagination' (Schama 1996, 95, 107), The tree, a thing of beauty in its native landscape, here becomes also a source of weaponry when it is time to defend your country.

Having begun work on the poem, I imagine Freiligrath becoming increasingly exasperated with Wordsworth as he struggled to translate the rest of the piece, determined, as was his practice, to retain as much of the formal structures of rhythm and metre in the source text as possible, and in this instance preserve one of Wordsworth's most interminably convoluted sentences that runs from line 14 for the remaining 25 lines of the poem. The consequence of this engagement with the subject text results in what might be considered the emergence of a third, intermediary language of translation, the consequence of which is that the German reader is in receipt of four extra lines of poetry by the end of the piece!

To what extent is Freiligrath engaged in 'taking the reader to the text', or in 'taking the text to the reader'? The poem contains a patriotic message that Freiligrath judged appropriate for a German readership of the late 1840s. Given this, too much 'foreignizing' of his translation will diminish the poem's impact. Freiligrath's commitment to the integrity of the original lies primarily in his adoption of the original blank verse form. The content is linguistically Germanized as Freiligrath seeks to bring the text to his readers.

To assess this in more detail, we will look again at the first eight lines of 'Yew Trees', but this time in Freiligrath's translation, which extends to nine lines:

> *Ein Eibenbaum, der Stolz des Lortonthals –*
> *Bis diesen Tag steht einsam er, inmitten*
> *Des eignen Dunkels, wie er vormals stand,*
> *Als er den Scharen Umfraville's und Percy's,*
> *Eh' sie nach Schottlands Haiden gingen, willig*
> *Geschosse reichte; oder jenen, die*
> *Das Meer durchkreutzen, und bei Azincourt,*
> *Vielleicht auch früher noch, bei Poictiers*
> *Und Crecy, dumpf die Bogen tönen liessen.*

(Freiligrath 1846i, 303–4)

Freiligrath's German retains – as far as possible – the iambic pentameter discipline of the English blank verse line. Though not an unusual discipline in German verse, translating blank verse in the way Wordsworth tends to use it is another matter. Faced with the need to concede to a Germanizing word order, Freiligrath relocates family and place names. The extra line that turns Wordsworth's eight lines into Freiligrath's nine begins to grow from line 4. By lines 6 and 7 it has become inevitable, by which time it is also clear that the demands of grammatical construction are putting increasing strain on the relationship between the source and target texts. This becomes very evident at the end of the passage, when Wordsworth chooses to disrupt the iambic beat in line 8, a process initiated by his use of the word 'earlier' which problematizes the scansion of 'Crecy', and leaves 'or Poictiers' to be read as though they were the final words of a prose sentence. Dismantling the metre in this way was a device Wordsworth did occasionally employ; here it throws into dramatic relief the expansive, exclamatory lyric flow of the following two lines, where every syllable counts: 'Of vast circumference and gloom profound/This solitary tree!' Confronted with Wordsworth's metrical irregularities in line 8, Freiligrath works against his source text in a bid to retain a metrically orthodox line, moving 'Poictiers' up to the previous line, bringing the reference to 'Crecy' after it, and finishing his ninth line with one easily assimilated extra syllable in 'liessen'. Wordsworth's displaced 'drew their sounding bows' is relocated in a comfortable place for the target readership, almost preserving intact the metre that it was Wordsworth's deliberate intention to disrupt.

Freiligrath's German priorities as a translator were not always to be driven quite so firmly by his desire to instruct his readership. His translation of 'The Solitary Reaper' that appears with 'Yew Trees' arguably shows him more willing to take his reader to the text. In general, however, both Jacobsen and Freiligrath appear to cast doubt on the idea that translation is a broadening or liberalizing activity. Instead, we find ourselves witnessing a situation where the target language seeks to absorb and make its own as much of the subject text as possible.

If 'Yew Trees' remains one of Wordsworth's least known poems, then the fragment from *The Prelude* first published in 1809 under the title 'The French Revolution: As it appeared to enthusiasts at its commencement' must number among his most frequently anthologized pieces. It first appeared in print in Coleridge's Journal *The Friend* in 1809, and was subsequently included in the 1815 *Collected Poems* before appearing as a section of Book XI of the 1850 edition of *The Prelude*. Marie Gothein included it in her anthology of Wordsworth's poems (1893):

Oh! pleasant exercise of hope and joy!
For mighty were the auxiliars which then stood
Upon our side, we who were strong in love!
Bliss was it in that dawn to be alive,
But to be young was very heaven! – Oh! times,
In which the meagre, stale, forbidding ways
Of custom, law, and statute, took at once
The attraction of a country in romance!
When reason seemed the most to assert her rights,
When most intent on making of herself
A prime Enchantress – to assist the work
Which then was going forward in her name!
Not favoured spots alone, but the whole earth,
The beauty wore of promise, that which sets
(As at some moment might not be unfelt
Among the bowers of paradise itself)
The budding rose above the rose full blown.

(Wordsworth 1979, 397)

Gothein's translation is:

O froher Schwung der Hoffnung und der Freude!
Welch mächt'ge Hilfe war auf unsrer Seite,
Wir, die wir stark und fest in Liebe waren!
's war Freude nur den jungen Tag zu sehn,
Doch damals jung zu sein, war reiner Himmel!
O Welche Zeit, da all der trockne Zwang
Von Sitte, von Gesetz und von Statuten
Sich wandelte in ein romantisch Land,
Wo die Vernuft auf ihre Rechte pochend
Sich selbst als erste Zauberin berief,
Um eifrig so das stolze Werk zu fördern,
Das unter ihrem Namen sich entfaltet.
Nicht nur ein Ort, o nein, die ganze Erde
Sonnt' damals sich in hoffnungsvoller Schönheit,
In jener Hoffnung, wie im Paradiese
Sie wohl zu Zeiten noch gefühlt mag werden,
Wo man die Knospen über Blüten stellt.

(Gothein 1892, II, 151)

From the first three lines it is apparent that Gothein does not translate the sense of excitement and urgency which Wordsworth creates using the run-on from line 2 into 3: 'For mighty were the auxiliars which then stood/Upon our side . . .' Each line of her blank verse tends to function as a finished statement, or if not, pairs of lines will divide the sense of a statement equally between them. In line 13 we can see her working to preserve the formal presentation of the line against the precise sense of the original with her additional 'o nein': 'Nicht nur ein Ort, o nein, die ganze Erde/Sonn't damals sich in hoffnungs- voller Schönheit'; 'Not favoured spots alone, but the whole earth,/The beauty wore of promise . . .' Attention to accuracy of form, which will make the poetry appear the same to the eye on the German and English pages, works against Gothein bringing the German reader to the English text. The ecstasy implicit in the famous phrase, 'Bliss was it in that dawn to be alive' translates somewhat tamely, and the climax that follows is then (once more) hastened forward by Wordsworth into the next line, an effect lost in Gothein, who finishes line 5 with 'Heaven', whereas Wordsworth picks up the next wave of enthusiasm at the end of line 5 and runs it on into line 6: 'But to be young was very heaven! – Oh! times,/In which the meagre, stale, forbidding ways . . . ' Gothein's line 5 and 6 are: 'Doch damals jung zu sein, war reiner Himmel!/O welche Zeit, da all der trockne Zwang?/Von Sitte . . . ' The momentum is lost, and also a sense of the miracle that Wordsworth manages to suggest. In the original we read of a transformation of what is already there. The 'meagre, stale, forbidding ways/Of customs, law, and statute' are not replaced by, they are transformed into ('took at once/The attraction of') 'a country in romance'. Gothein's translation suggests that the old ways were moved out to be replaced by 'a romantic land'. The German lacks a sense of Wordsworth's magic:

> . . . *da all der trockne Zwang*
> *Von Sitte, von Gesetz und von Statuten*
> *Sich wandelte in ein romantisch Land* . . .

In line 9 Wordsworth touches on an issue that was of great importance to him in relation to his own initial enthusiasm for the French Revolution. Until the mid-1790s, he nurtured the Godwinian belief that the power of reason underpinned what was an inevitable march of progress, reform, and revolution. By the time he was writing these lines in 1804, he had abandoned rationality as his central creed. Consequently lines 9-12 sound a qualified note crucial to his meaning (my italics): 'When Reason *seemed* most to assert her rights'. Gothein has nothing for 'seemed', 'Wo die Vernuft auf ihre Rechte pochend . . . ', 'reason insisted on her rights'. For Gothein, Reason is the female magician who promotes the project or scheme 'Which flourishes in her name', 'Das unter ihren Namen sich entfaltet'. She adds the adjective 'proud' to 'project/scheme'. There is no suggestion of the Wordsworthian nuance encapsulated in his use of 'seemed' here. The more we look at Wordsworth's lines in this passage, the less we see of his poetic meaning in the German translation:

> When Reason seemed the most to assert her rights,
> When most intent on making of herself
> A prime Enchantress – to assist the work
> Which then was going forward in her name!

The implied mismatch of 'work/Which *then* was going forward *in her name!*' is not in Gothein. Wordsworth's Revolution has been hi-jacked by a spurious Enchantress called 'Reason'. It is 'going forward' in her name, and the neutral implications of that phrase 'going forward' become all the clearer when we look at how Gothein translates it, only to realize that she is interpreting/translating an enthusiasm that is subtly with-held in the original. 'Unfold/entfaltet', with the connotation of 'open out' or even 'blossom', is not the same as 'going forward'.

At this point we should recall Schleiermacher's perceptive observation that readers must be expected to interpret the text before them exercising a significant degree of independence from the author/translator, and according to 'the level of education and understanding' they possess (Munday 2001, 28).

A consideration of the way both Freiligrath and Gothein pursued their commitment to translate form as well as content makes clear how subtly, and to a degree idiosyncratically, Wordsworth manipulated his blank verse. It also shows how difficult blank verse used in this way is to translate into German. It could, arguably, only be done with a considerable degree of foreignization. Neither Freiligrath nor Gothein were prepared to make Wordsworth seem as difficult as that would require. These poems are to have a meaning for their target reader-ship that brings them and their author towards the German, and away from the English. The final five lines of *The Prelude* passage illustrate this well:

> Not favoured spots alone, but the whole earth
> The beauty wore of promise, that which sets
> (As at some moment might not be unfelt
> Among the bowers of paradise itself)
> The budding rose above the rose full blown.

The parenthesis points up a celebrated and characteristically telling Wordsworthian image for the French Revolution. The phrase which ends line 14, 'that which sets', is suspended by two lines in brackets referring to 'the bowers of paradise'. This gives the resolution of 'that which sets', 'The budding rose above the rose full blown', a complex meaning. Because the final sentence of the poem is interrupted by a reference to Paradise in its specific biblical con-text, we have both the promise of bliss contained in Nature, and therefore sanctified, and a sense of poignancy that, like Paradise, it is already lost. We should recall that the sub-title Wordsworth gave this extract prepares us for this moment. This is about the French Revolution 'as it appeared to enthusiasts at its commencement'. The implicit equivocation of 'appeared' plunges the Wordsworth scholar (in possession of the appropriate 'level of education and understanding') into the debate about Wordsworth's radicalism, the charge of apostasy, the significance for him of Godwin and the consequences of his disenchantment with rationalism.

What, however, does Gothein's German reader find here? The parenthesis is discarded, and no attempt is made to hold the sense in suspense:

> Not just the place, but the whole earth
> In these times basked in hopeful beauty,
> In the kind of hope which might have been felt
> During times long gone in paradise
> Where buds were considered more important than blossoms.

The universalism of 'the whole earth', '*die ganze Erde*', is retained. Gothein makes it explicit that paradise is in the past, 'times long gone', and (however it might be construed) her prosaic rendering of Wordsworth's poetic 'budding rose above the rose full blown' attaches the notion that the promise of beauty is of more worth than beauty itself to the past: to Paradise. It is also associated with what is now an historically distant moment of revolution back in 1789. In Wordsworth's poetry Paradise remains free from the past tense to which Gothein attaches it. Wordsworth's 'moment' in line 15 is suspended in the bracketed parenthesis, still potentially available, still in existence somewhere, if not here: 'As at some moment might not be unfelt'.

Having made these judgements, however, Marie Gothein, an experienced translator of English poetry, her mind saturated by poetry she clearly admired, was undoubtedly translating Wordsworth's lines into German with Wordsworth every bit as much as her potential German readers in the forefront of her mind. But again, we should remember that Wordsworth, though far from unknown in nineteenth-century Germany, was a minority interest and, as her biography makes clear, Gothein fervently wished to win him a wider German readership. One consequence of this is that her translations of Wordsworth are marked by an attempt to bring the text to the reader.

Taken together, these three examples of translation illustrate the wide-ranging significance of the evolution of Anglo-German translation theory for an appreciation of the important relationship between literature and nationalism in nineteenth-century Germany. At the same time we have been reminded of the constant need to take into account the divide that needs to be bridged between theory and practice. This latter concern has been made particularly clear from a reading of the debates taking place in contemporary translation studies, a rapidly expanding body of work that owes its origins not just to the consequences of the technologies of a global media network, but also to the contentious claims of those who inherited the traditions of the nineteenth century hermeneuticists, notably Benjamin and Steiner.

6 Wordsworth among the Romantic Poets in Mid-Nineteenth-Century Germany

Anthologists and Translators

> *The spiritual parentage between Britannia and Germania has very early awakened my sympathy for English poetry.*
>
> Ploennies 1843, xii

A German visitor to England in the 1850s, using G. Knight's English primer, would have been able to engage in literary small-talk with the following request: 'You will oblige me by purchasing for me "A Selection from the Poetry of John Dryden"', adding (with due solemnity), 'It is true, Dryden is dead in body long ago, but he will live as long as Pope and Milton and many others.' You are advised that you may then terminate the conversation with, 'Well, maybe he will, I don't care' (Knight 1854, 17–18). Knight's English primer for Germans living and working in London has relatively little by way of advice on cultural small-talk, but what it does have reminds us that the German appetite for English Literature reached back over many years, and that some ability to discourse on literary topics was thought desirable for every visitor, regardless of the reason for their stay. It also seems, however, that Knight is keen to help his student avoid getting into too much detail. The topic of conversation turns far more regularly to practical issues: mending gowns, hemming handkerchiefs, selecting the appropriate needle, buying groceries. There is also room for explaining why you are in London rather than Paris, 'The French are too conceited to be taught' (ibid., 57).

The healthy nineteenth-century market for English primers is also a reminder of how many Germans continued to live and work in England, travelling between the countries on a regular basis. This migratory population were moving the printed word back and forth across Europe. Franz Thimm, for example, worked first in Berlin for Asher & Co., booksellers and printers. In 1839, aged 19, he came to London and built up his own business primarily around the production of German Language primers. His *History of the Literature of Germany* was published in 1844 in London by another German, David Nutt, and in Berlin by Asher, whose modern and antiquarian bookselling business was based in London and Berlin. Thimm, who also produced a book on the Shakespearean literature of England, Germany, France and other European countries, became a naturalized British subject. It is not therefore surprising that the interest in English language poetry in Germany remained as strong as it had ever been in the eight-eenth century, and that it extended widely across the spectrum of 'Romantic' period writing in England and America.

High profile English literary figures visited Germany throughout the cen-tury, all of whom might be expected to have encouraged this appetite. George Eliot first travelled to Germany in 1854; she returned in 1867 while working on her blank verse drama, *The Spanish Gypsy*. Matthew Arnold grudgingly travelled to Germany in 1865 as an Assistant Commissioner to the Taunton Commission on Schools. Unlike Arnold, who wrote to William Slade of the 'hideousness and commonness' of the Germans, Julian Fane, who became an attaché in Berlin in 1844 (his father was British Minister to Prussia) and Robert Bulwer were enthusiasts for German culture (Arnold 1997, 457). Fane was par-ticularly interested in Heinrich Heine, suggesting in an article of 1855 that Heine's *Book of Songs* contained lyrics that combined simplicity and profundity in a way that was reminiscent of Wordsworth (Liptzin 1924, 44).

Arnold and Eliot were, like Fane, Wordsworthians. Eliot's *The Spanish Gypsy* is a blank verse drama that reflects in part her lasting debt to Wordsworth; *Silas Marner* (1861) was originally planned as a blank verse narrative poem in the manner of Wordsworth's *Michael* and the tales of rural life that provide the back-bone of *The Excursion*. Frederick Karl argues for the formative influence of Wordsworth on Eliot: '[He] would in time fill her mind and replace her formal religious spirit with his own brand of nature's spiritual qualities' (Karl 1995, 39). German hosts, happy to discuss their own great writers alongside the English Language poets they were reading, will certainly have had it confirmed that Wordsworth ranked among the major poets of his native country.

One of the earliest German translators of Wordsworth after Jacobsen was Ferdinand Freiligrath, an Anglophile who became a prolific translator of Eng-lish language poetry; his career will form the focus of the second part of this chapter. Freiligrath epitomizes the link that exists between the reception of English language poetry in Germany and the evolution of German National-ism. Few, if any, of the enthusiasts for British poetry considered in this chapter were as deeply embroiled in the politics of nationalism as Freiligrath during the early part of his career. While the political context by no means explains every-thing about this aspect of Anglo-German cultural exchange, an awareness of it is an important factor when seeking to understand both the abiding popularity of a wide range of British poets in Germany, and – as Susanne Schmid has illus-trated with particular reference to Shelley – frequently the way in which the poetry was translated (both literally and figuratively) into German (Schmid 1999).

The task has been made more difficult by a reading of European history since the Second World War that extrapolates the rise of German fascism and its con-sequences directly from the course taken by Germany's path to nationhood in the nineteenth century. After the Second World War there was a powerful ten-dency to write out as much Anglo-American involvement in German history and culture as possible. Wordsworth is just one of many British poets whose dis-appearance from the German literary landscape seems to be the consequence of the kind of revisionary literary history undertaken by René Wellek, who recog-nizes 'similarities and even deep affinities' existing between German and English Romanticism, but – with the exception of Coleridge and De Quincey – rejects all notion of what he terms 'historical contacts' during this period (Wellek 1965, 11). We cannot distance ourselves from Germany in this way; Jacobsen's eclectic enthusiasm in 1820 gives us a clear picture of 'historical contacts' in place well before his book was published, and this was perpetuated by translators and anthologists, by German visitors to England and English visitors to Germany, for the rest of the century.

Oskar Ludwig Bernhard Wolff, Freiligrath's senior by twenty-one years, was born in Altona in 1799. Jacobsen's work will have been well known to him. As well as pursuing an academic career, which was rewarded by a Professorship at Jena in 1838, Wolff wrote novels and poetry, and also offered evenings of extempore recitations. His books included a history of the novel, and a travel guide for the English tourist (written with H. Doering), where Hamburg is described:

> Commerce is, indeed, the main spring, which sets the whole machinery of active life in Hamburg, in motion; yet, the commercial spirit does not exclusively permeate, and the artist and man of learning, will find a residence in Hamburg extremely agreeable, if they do not raise their expectations too high. (Wolff 1837, 66)

Wolff's collected works, when they appeared in 1841–3, ran to 14 volumes. He became best known to the wider German reading public as the producer of a series of anthologies of verse. His enthusiasm for English Language poetry is evident in his collection of folk songs, published in 1835. Working with C. Schütz, he began a periodical anthology in 1836, *A Choice Selection of the Most Celebrated English Authors both Ancient and Modern.* All the poetry is in English, and Wolff's selection throughout the series is predictable. Scott, Burns, Moore, Hemans, Landon and Southey are all well represented, as is Byron, though he by no means outstrips the others. Wolff had, however, published a separate collection of Byron's poetry in 1830. Shelley makes an appearance in 1839. In 1837, No. 32 included Wordsworth's 'Simon Lee', and No. 30 for 1838 included 'We are Seven' and 'The Farmer of Tilsbury Vale'. No. 30 carried Wordsworth as its featured poet and, in keeping with the regular format, this entitled him to a biographical sketch which has every appearance of drawing on Jacobsen's biography very closely, including a reference to Bridgewater as the location of his Somerset home in 1798. We may safely assume that Wolff had the 1828 Galignani edition of Wordsworth to work from, but by this time copies of Wordsworth in his English published form were available.

The inclusion of 'Simon Lee', 'The Farmer of Tilsbury Vale', and 'We are Seven' suggests that Wolff is making his own selection while also including poems made familiar to him by Jacobsen. A further suggestion of Jacobsen's influence in the biographical note is his assertion of the importance of *The Excursion* and *The White Doe of Rylstone*. 'We are Seven', however, is not mentioned by Jacobsen, and Wolff may be credited with having 'discovered' it for later anthologists. It was a 'Lyrical Ballad' (along with 'Simon Lee') that earned Wordsworth much adverse criticism in England from readers annoyed by Wordsworthian 'simplicity'.

In its first manifestation in the *Lyrical Ballads* of 1798, 'We are Seven' begins with one of Wordsworth's most provocative lines. If the ballad in its sentimental eighteenth-century narrative form had become a comfort zone for the reader, Wordsworth's intention was to destabilize that reader, as here, for example, in 'Simon Lee':

What more I have to say is short,
I hope you'll kindly take it;
It is no tale; but should you think,
Perhaps a tale you'll make it.

(Wordsworth 1992, 67)

The opening stanza of 'We are Seven' reads:

A simple child, dear brother Jim,
That lightly draws its breath,
And feels its life in every limb,
What should it know of death?

(Ibid., 73–4)

Wordsworthians have long known that the reference to 'brother Jim' originates in a conversation between Wordsworth and Coleridge in which the latter coined the first line in order to present Wordsworth with the challenge of making the first verse of this poem from it – which he duly did. 'Jim' (or 'Jem') referred to a mutual friend, James Tobin (Fenwick 1993, 3–4). The reader of 1798 is dropped without warning into a conversation between the poet and 'brother Jim'. By the time Wordsworth was preparing the collected edition of 1815, however, he recognized that this was a perverse way to begin the poem. In a bold move (with, it might be argued, no less a degree of perversity) he removed 'dear brother Jim', moving 'a simple child' to the right hand margin, thereby creating a gap of four syllables in the first line which he filled only with dashes. With brother Jim present (though not mentioned again) the reader had been made to feel like an eavesdropper. Now he/she had to settle for a poem that appeared to start half way through the first line. Wordsworth not infrequently manages to locate his reader in an uncomfortably ambivalent role, suggesting that it is their job to fill in the blanks and complete the story. Wolff reproduced the 1815 version.

The content of the three poems chosen by Wolff might all be expected to appeal to his German readership on several counts. All are in ballad form, all have a rural theme running through them. They also possess qualities that a German reader would associate with his own native literary traditions; they are poems that puzzle and tease the reader's imagination with a form of riddling. In 'Simon Lee' the poet helps the old man with an act of manual labour that is beyond him; but the excess of Simon's gratitude creates an unexpected conclusion, compounded by the poet's final, paradoxical statement:

– I've heard of hearts unkind, kind deeds
With coldness still returning;
Alas! The gratitude of men
Hath oftener left me mourning.

(Ibid., 93–6)

In 'We are Seven' we have the mysterious insistence from the child that, though two of her six brothers and sisters are dead, seven of them remain.

'The Farmer of Tilsbury Vale' may seem to be different in kind from the other two poems; but towards the end we realize that – in a playful, contradictory, and riddling manner – Wordsworth challenges us with the claim that the old farmer, Adam, is still able to live in the country while being in the city. His abandonment of the country – the result of his lackadaisical management – is something we are expected to condemn: 'You lift up your eyes! – but I guess that you frame/A judgement too harsh of the sin and the shame' (ibid., 290). In the revised 1815 version of this poem (the one Wolff is reading), Adam's dishonesty towards his neighbours, who lend him money, is made to sound slightly less extreme (not to say controversial) than it was in the original version of 1800 where he is described as a 'merciless Jew' (ibid., 290). By cutting that reference, Wordsworth gives himself a marginally easier job when he sets out to rescue him from our rejection, on the grounds that 'his heart all the while is in Tilsbury Vale'. The poem ends with a blessing on him as he approaches death.

All these poems wind their riddling games around the theme of mortality: the farmer and Simon Lee are near the end of their lives, the child's brother and sister lie buried in the churchyard. This latter point makes Julian Young's comments on Schopenhauer's use of the riddle particularly apposite:

> In the first book of *The World as Will* . . . Schopenhauer says that the problem of philosophy is to say 'what' the world is. Sometimes he says that it is to solve the 'riddle' of what the world is. Given the rootedness of this word in German folk tales where solving a 'riddle' is often a matter of life and death, this suggests that an answer to the question, rather than merely satisfying the curiosity of armchair investigators, will have existential implications, will have an effect on our lives. (Young 2005, 17)

With men like Schütz and Johann Michael Doering, Wolff had become a prime mover in the English poetry industry in Germany. Inevitably he came to know Freiligrath, and in 1842 contributed an essay to Freiligrath's memorial publication on Karl Gustav Immermann (1796–1840), a hero of the Napoleonic wars. Immerman's most successful play, *Das Traverspiel in Tirol* (1828) was revised in 1834 and renamed *Andreas Hofer*, a name we have already seen as deeply evocative for nationalist writers. Wordsworth's sonnet to Hofer, 'Of mortal parents is the Hero born' occurs in a sequence that praises Hofer's resistance in the Tyrol; it was published in Coleridge's *The Friend* in 1809. Wolff's inclusion among the contributors to Freiligrath's tribute is indicative of his political sympathies. Immermann subsequently became best known for his satirical novel *Münchhausen* (1838–9).

In 1848, Wolff published *A Treasurehouse of English Poetry: from Chaucer to Bayly*, and the role-call of Romantic Period poets continues to look very similar to Jacobsen's selection. Wordsworth's introduction praises him for the depth of his religious feeling, and for perceiving profound truths in what might otherwise be thought trivial circumstances (poems like 'We are Seven' are clearly implied by this). He is represented by 14 poems, more than any of the others (there is no room for Coleridge at all). Wordsworth's poems are: 'Sonnet: Adieu, Rydalian laurels!', the *Ode: Intimations of Immortality*, 'Three years she grew', 'Scorn not the sonnet', 'It is a beauteous evening', 'The world is too much with us', 'London 1802', 'Composed upon Westminster Bridge', 'Great men have been among us', 'To a skylark', 'She dwelt among th'untrodden ways', 'We are Seven', 'The Seven Sisters', and 'Ruth'. Though sonnets predominate, the length of the *Immortality* Ode and the final three poems give Wordsworth a marked prominence alongside his contemporaries.

From this selection we can see that Jacobsen's Wordsworth remains centre stage in 1848, the year of revolutions. He is a patriot, expressing both his political commitment and an intensity of religious feeling primarily through his love of nature:

It is a beauteous Evening, calm and free;
The holy time is quiet as a Nun
Breathless with adoration . . .

(Wordsworth 1983, 150–1)

Suzanne Schmid's assessment of what appealed to German readers in their own authors is applicable to what they sought elsewhere, not least in Wordsworth:

In an age of urbanization and industrialization, technical and social change, descriptions of rural idylls satisfied a demand for a harmonious space, free from conflicts. English constructions of nature in that period were imbued with an ideology that regarded the rural countryside as a mythic source of national strength, supporting the building of the empire. (Schmid 1999, 346)

More controversially, perhaps, she goes on to claim (as Perkins does) that 'The German discourse of nature was not tied up with imperialism' (ibid., 346). This seems a too prescriptive judgement, particularly in the light of the way Jacobsen reflected on his vision of the future of Germania in the *Letters*. On the evidence of Wolff alone, Schmid is clearly mistaken to include Wordsworth among the poets who 'never achieved much fame in Germany' (ibid., 346).

Five years before Wolff's *Treasurehouse* was published, Luise von Ploennies (1803–72) published a parallel text selection of British poetry, *Britannia: A Selection of British Poems Ancient and Modern*. Ploennies' motivation is rooted in the conviction that Germany and England share a common political destiny. The book is dedicated to Queen Victoria, and in her Preface she explains why she has come to love English poetry:

. . . the mighty strains which owe their birth to the green and free shores of Albion have a sympathetic charm for me, because they are so like the deep and soul-cap-tivating lays of my own native land. They are both branches of the same tree, which on the green Isle, where thoughts and words are allowed to grow up in unbounded strength, have attained such simple and striking beauty. The spiritual parentage between Britain and Germania has very early awakened my sympathy for English poetry. (Ploennies 1843, xvi)

Felicia Hemans is singled out for particular praise, her 'deep and soul-breathing poetry is lit up by the ray of faith . . . Her strains have moved my heart with deepest feeling and sympathy' (ibid., xxiv).

Fifty-three poets are represented. The parallel text format implies a wish to maintain a balanced relationship with the target text. The translations Ploennies uses (many are her own, but she uses Freiligrath for Coleridge's *Ancient Mariner*) attempt to reproduce the formal qualities of the poetry in a way similar to that already seen in the cases of Freiligrath and Gothein. Ploennies describes Wordsworth as the 'contemplative "favourite of Nature", who holds with her a mysterious intercourse as did Numa with the nymph Egeria' (ibid., xxii). Against Moore's 24, Byron's 17, and Hemans' 13, Wordsworth has just five poems. They are 'Three years she grew', 'She was a phantom of delight', 'Song of the Wandering Jew', 'The Seven Sisters' and, yet again, 'We are Seven' (Ploennies uses the 1815 version of the first verse). By the middle of the century we can see a German Wordsworth canon emerging. Set against that, the odd one out in this selection is 'Song of the Wandering Jew', but we know that Freiligrath had translated it in the early 1830s.

Compared to Wolff, who in 1848 included some politically explicit sonnets in his selection, Ploennies anthologizes a Wordsworth who contemplates nature and domestic felicity. This is reinforced by her decision to create her own titles for the first two poems: 'Nature's favourite', and 'The Perfect Woman'. 'Song for the Wandering Jew' is not overtly a political poem, and though for Freiligrath it reflected his own experience of exile, at the time he translated it his melancholy was the result of domestic, not political, circumstances. The poem accords well with Ploennies' love of Wordsworth's evocation of nature:

> Though the torrents from their fountains
> Roar down many a craggy steep,
> Yet they find among the mountains
> Resting places calm and deep.
>
> (Selincourt 1969, 131)

The political theme of the volume as a whole, however, is confirmed with a poem of her own – dedicated to Hemans – with which she concludes the collection. It begins with a quotation from Georg Herweg, the radical German poet. In line 5 she alludes to Theodor Körner, the poet killed fighting against Napoleon in 1813 (there is a note drawing our attention to a poem she has written on Körner's death). It is called 'What is Poetry?/Was ist Poesie?':

> All, all that's high and worthy she claimeth as her own,
> She lends immortal glory to fame and greatness gone;
> The memory of heroes is honour'd by her lyre,
> And even from the ashes she wakes celestial fire.
> Where oaks are proudly shading the youthful minstrel's grave,
> He of the sword and lyre, the bravest of the brave,
> There does she oft at twilight entwine a glorious crown,
> On which, with dews of evening her tears are trickling down.
>
> (Ploennies 1843, 667)

Ploennies writes across the language divide; there is no central 'third text' here. The poet/translator may be envisaged as passing two texts through each other to her two sets of target readers.

In 1863 Ploennies published another collection of English poems, *Englische Lyriker des neunzehnten Yahrhunderts*. This time the poetry is all in German translation, and this time (as the title announces) they are all from the nineteenth century. Speculating on why the parallel format is dropped, it may be that by the 1860s her publishers were of the opinion that the market favoured a more unambiguously German publication. Thirty-six poets are represented, and the collection is divided into three main sections: 'Poems by Men', 'Poems by Women', and 'American Poetry'. The first section begins with the sub-heading, '*Dichter der Lake School*'. In the Contents pages, a short wavy line inserted between Charles Lamb and Walter Scott signifies the end of that section. There are no other sub-groupings, a fact that indicates Ploennies' sense of the unique place these poets had in the development of modern British poetry. The 'Lake Poets', in the order they appear, are Wordsworth (five poems), Edward Quillinan (Wordsworth's son-in-law; Ploennies includes a sonnet dedicated to Wordsworth and Dora, and three others), Coleridge (five poems), Southey (two poems), and Charles Lamb (one poem). Moving on then to Scott, 20 more poets are represented. These include predictable names, but also minor poets presumably picked up from English periodicals and other anthologies. Each poet has a brief introduction, and in most cases some biographical matter is included.

Wordsworth stands at the head of this collection as the chief poet of the Lake School. The most poems any of the other men get is seven, and that is Byron. Charles Wolfe, the Irish poet, gets six. Each section begins with a representative quote from the poet followed by an introduction. In Wordsworth's case Ploennies begins with her own translation of a passage from Book One of *The Excursion*. It was a poem she had clearly studied closely, and the first poetry by Wordsworth after the Introduction consists of 112 more lines from *The Excursion* Book One which she calls 'From the Deserted Hut'. This begins at line 81: 'Oh! many are the Poets that are sown/By nature . . .', and finishes at the point where the Wanderer is about to begin his narration in the shadow of the ruined cottage at line 465 (Wordsworth 2007, 50–61). Included here is the passage on the Wanderer already discussed in the context of Jacobsen's *Briefe*: 'O then what soul was his, when on the tops/Of the high mountains, he beheld the sun/Rise up . . .'. We have noted that Jacobsen picked this passage up from *Blackwood's*, and that it was later to be adopted in the pirated Galignani edition as quintessentially 'Wordsworthian'. Ploennies' lengthy edited extract describes the Wanderer's childhood and education, appropriating the poetry as a powerful statement in the tradition of the German *Bildungsroman*. Her biographical account of Wordsworth suggests her continued debt to Jacobsen; Wordsworth's 'poetic isolation' in the West Country is still situated near Bridgewater. Other than that he is a poet inspired by lakes and mountains. 'The common people with whom he interacted became dear to him, and his poetry thus brings together the sublimity of nature and the joys and griefs of common folk.' Wordsworth, she explains, is now remembered both for his philanthropy and his poetry (Ploennies 1863, 4). The other poems she includes by Wordsworth are 'To a Highland Girl', three verses from 'The Fountain', 'March Song', and 'Scorn not the Sonnet'.

The extract from 'The Fountain' appears to have been lifted directly from Jacobsen's *Briefe*, unless, like Jacobsen, she copied them directly from the *Blackwood's* essay of 1818 'on the Lake School of Poetry'. It is a German rendering of the same fabricated 12-line verse discussed in Chapter 4. Free as she tends to be with her translations, it is very clear that Ploennies has Jacobsen (or possibly *Blackwood's*) in front of her. Ploennies simply calls these lines 'Song', and translates so as to retain the rhyme and metre of the original. Where the content is concerned, however, she has no qualms about adapting the original to her own (and, we assume, her reader's) taste. The humble Blackbird is rejected. We begin with the Lark, that now 'rises to the sun', where Wordsworth had simply noted it 'upon the hill'. Ploennies opts for the more romantic Nightingale to replace the Blackbird:

> The blackbird in the summer tree,
> The lark upon the hill,
> Let loose their carols when they please,
> Are quiet when they will.

Thus becomes:

> Die Lerche, die zur Sonne steigt,
> Im Busch die Nachtigallen,
> Ein Jedes singt, ein Jedes schweigt,
> Nach seinem Wohlgefallen.

(Ibid., 13)

Ploennies' decision to include Edward Quillinan's sonnet 'Wordsworth's Home' is worth noting. Quillinan (1791–1851) married Wordsworth's daughter Dora in 1841. Dora died in 1847. In 1850, when Wordsworth died, Quillinan, still deeply mourning his wife's death, wrote a sequence of four sonnets in memory of Dora. In 'Suspiria: Wordsworth's Home', he elides Dora's death with that of Wordsworth and the consequent sadness that permeates the poet's house, Rydal Mount. It is a complex sonnet that reflects on the way that – for Quillinan – Wordsworth's legacy as a poet has been blighted by the untimely death of his favourite daughter. There is no mention of Dora's death in Ploennies' bio-graphical note, and it would appear that she read, and then attempted to translate this poem, as a tribute to Wordsworth alone. The German reader would cer-tainly have missed much of what Quillinan was attempting to achieve. What her inclusion of this poem also indicates is the accessibility of Quillinan's poetry in Germany.

In 1835 Johannes Scherr published the first edition of what became a popu-lar, monumental anthology, *Bildersaal der Weltliteratur*. True to its name, Scherr includes sections for 'Oriental', 'Greco-Roman', 'Troubador', 'Italian', 'Spanish', 'Portuguese', 'French', 'English', 'German', 'Dutch', 'Scandinavian', 'Bohemian' and 'Hungarian' poetry. All the poetry is in German translation. If we look at how Scherr's project had developed by 1855, when a new edition came out, we find that Germany, not surprisingly, has the lion's share (460 pages), followed by England (137 pages), a pattern that was evident from the start. Though well behind the leader, England occupies a comfortable second place. Amongst the English, Byron is awarded celebrity status among the modern poets. Burns is described as having introduced a new style to English writing. Wordsworth is the English poet who excels in nature description, and therefore Scherr's deci-sion to represent him through 'We are Seven' (his only contribution) might seem to us surprising. However, this helps suggest what the concept of 'nature poetry' meant to a German reader at this time. Scherr will have read a poem in which an innocent, 'natural' child living in the countryside, speaks a truth from her heart that links the world of nature (of life and death) to the world of the spirit.

The translation of 'We are Seven' was done by Karl Ludwig Kannegiesser, a distinguished translator of Shakespeare and Dante. He responded to the prob-lem of Wordsworth's eccentric revision of the first line by taking the text to his German readers in a translation that restores the regularity of metre and rhyme throughout. In English it reads:

> A simple song, a childrens' song
> Of life and of death!
> He who feels life in every limb,
> Does he feel death?

After what is therefore a significant rewriting of the first verse, which nevertheless accurately reflects the poem's preoccupations, the rest of the translation is a skilful rendering of Wordsworth in this whimsical mode. Scherr's project accords with the ideology of a Germanic-centred concept of 'World Literature'; from the weighting of his selection he seems to share Ploennies' view that England and Germany have most in common, and that the future – at least in so far as it involves cultural evolu-tion – lies in a negotiation between the Anglo-German peoples.

In 1851 Ludwig Herrig published an anthology of *Englische National-Literatur*, dividing the poetry into 'Chaucer to 1558', 'Elizabethan', 'The Age of Transition: Waller to Dryden', 'Queen Anne to 1780: Prior, Pope, Gay, Young', and 'Modern Literature from 1780'. The modern writers are divided between 20 English and 12 Scottish poets. All the material, including Herrig's Preface, is in English. His motivation is educational; this is a book for students, and it reflects a somewhat stereotypical image of the workings of the German scholarly mind:

> In order that the pupil may be enabled to garner up the knowledge thence derived, the selections for reading should be made with a constant view to unity of purpose and arranged according to their natural order. The various subjects thus grouped and classified should be studied by the pupil in such a manner as to render him sensible of their necessary connexion . . . to give him a faithful impression both of their relative value and of the whole, composing this great variety of individual parts. (Herrig 1851, vii)

Herrig believed that learning English should be a priority for all young Germans, and he assures us that he has made his choice of authors with far greater care for the good of his readers than is the case with the majority of Anthologies currently available in Germany. The reason for learning the English language is to learn how the English think. Given the lack of discerning anthologies, he insists, the student's 'knowledge of English life, customs, manners and feeling is needlessly stinted; nor is he so well able to appreciate and to enter into such elements of thought and action as may be termed peculiarly English' (ibid., viii).

Herrig argues that by learning a language we avoid all the problems inherent in a 'translated' text:

> . . . we must hear the orator deliver his harangue in the senate and on the platform, we must feel political parties grow hot in their controversy, we must watch the rural sport on the village green and listen to the country maiden's evening song; the rich and the poor, the powerful and the humble, the wise and good as well as the low and scurrilous must pass before our eyes, each arrayed in his own dress and speaking his own language. Then we shall not only have learnt words, rules of grammar and a literature, but we shall have comprehended the innermost being and spirit of a nation. (Ibid., viii–ix)

This is a necessary preparation, Herrig seems to suggest, for peace or war. It should come as no surprise either, having noted the reference to 'the country maiden's evening song' to learn that he included Wordsworth's 'The Solitary Reaper' in a collection of poems all of which, in his eyes, depicted the English national character in all its variety, its strengths, and its weaknesses.

Going on the numbers of poems alone, Herrig's strategically constructed pantheon is headed by Thomas Moore, who has 27 poems; he is followed, some way behind, by Hemans with nine. Byron and Kirke-White each have eight, and Wordsworth is next with seven poems. He begins with 'We are Seven', and given what has already been explained about Wordsworth's decision to redraft the first verse for his 1815 collection, Herrig's use of the original *Lyrical Ballads* verse with its introduction of 'brother Jim' is important. Firstly we must assume that Herrig had access to an original edition of the *Ballads*. Secondly we may be sure that the meticulous Herrig had compared the two versions, and opted for the one that fulfilled his avowed intentions for the anthology. The German reader is to be taken by an uncompromising editor to the author. Wordsworth is here seen 'arrayed in his own dress and speaking his own language'.

The remaining six poems are 'I heard a thousand blended notes', 'To a Skylark', 'The Solitary Reaper', 'Ruth', 'Lines written while sailing in a boat at evening', and the sonnet 'Where lies the land to which yon ship must go?'. Given what is clearly Herrig's determination to stand apart from the run-of-the-mill anthologizers, it is not surprising to find two notably 'non-canonical' poems at the end of his selection. This is also a reminder that English poetry was available in English editions in Germany.

The final volume to be considered in this brief review of anthologized English language poetry is Karl Elze's collection, *Englischer Liederschatz*, first published in 1853. In the spirit of Germany's sense of a shared heritage with England, Elze explained that he wanted to achieve 'a faithful expression of the Anglo-Saxon tribe's lyrical view of the world and of life in the first half of the nineteenth century' (Schmid 2004, 65). The poems are in English, and the anthology was sufficiently popular to run through several editions on into the 1860s. He groups the poetry in six sections, 'Homeland and the Home', 'The World and Nature', 'Life', 'Love', 'The Epic', and 'Miscellaneous'. Elze's favourite poet reminds us yet again of Jacobsen's account: it is Moore with 21 poems, followed by Hemans with 20. Byron is given the same number as Wordsworth, eight, which is five more than Coleridge. Wordsworth's sonnet 'Upon Westminster Bridge' is located in 'Homeland and the Home'; 'Lines Written in Early Spring', 'I wandered lonely as a cloud', and 'To the Cuckoo' are in 'The World of Nature'. 'We are Seven' (using Wolff's 1815 version) is in 'Life', while 'She was a phantom of delight', and 'She dwelt among th'untrodden ways' are in 'Love'.

Elze includes brief biographies of his poets. At 18 lines, Wordsworth is reasonably well served, though he by no means receives the most attention. Elze confirms the portrait that Jacobsen had first sketched in 1820; Wordsworth is a poet of nature, but also a poet who engages with the political world he inhabited. For all that, he is primarily a lover of the countryside, honoured by his Nation with the Laureateship, and commemorated in his own hand by the posthumous publication of his autobiography in verses, *The Prelude*.

Elze's use of the term 'Epic' to describe his penultimate section is somewhat misleading. In the first place, 'Epic' here does not refer to length. The section is divided into sub-sections, the first of which contains verse with a heroic subject matter; for example Macaulay's 'The Armada', Longfellow's 'The Warden of the Cinque Ports', and Scott's 'Young Lochinvar'. This section is followed by seven poems on religious themes including Byron's 'Jeptha's Daughter', and Hood's 'Mahmoud'. The next group are probably best described as soldier's tales; they include Macaulay's 'The Battle of Ivrey'. Finally there is a group of 22 poems which is primarily concerned with themes of liberty and labour. It is here, alongside Elizabeth Barrett Browning's 'The Cry of the Children', Thomas Hood's 'The Song of the Shirt', Ebenezer Elliott's 'Preston Mills', and Shelley's 'Liberty', that we find Wordsworth's 'The Solitary Reaper'. The poem has thus been politicized; the reaper is not a romantic highland girl devoid of a context apart from the scenery in which she stands, she is an isolated labourer whose language the poet cannot understand, and as such she reminds us of the hardships of rural labour. Tennyson's 'Mariana' may seem an even more unusual poem to place in this group, but when we see that Elze has put it with Wilson's 'The Widowed Mother', we appreciate that again he appears to be thinking about abandonment and betrayal in a social, as much as a sentimental, context. His method of grouping texts establishes an intriguing dynamic for the collection.

There can be no doubt that Wordsworth was among the English poets widely recognized in Germany as important literary figures, and that he was known in literary circles through the continued publication of his poetry, and not just by reputation. In his *Memoir* of Wordsworth published in 1851, Christopher Wordsworth comments on a flattering letter of 1840 that the poet received from Johann Lappenberg, 'the celebrated historian of Hamburg', assuring him of his intention of translating a selection of Wordsworth's poems, adding that both he and Ludwig Tieck regretted that not more of his work was available for German readers (Wordsworth 1851 II, 66).

The selection of British poets by German translators and editors discussed here was taking place in the context of a market inevitably influenced by increasingly turbulent political events. The poet and translator who brought the political life of the German nation most directly to bear on his choice of English language poetry for a German readership was Ferdinand Freiligrath. His influence can be traced across all the collections mentioned above, and through many more that cannot be dealt with here. It is to his contribution, and in particular to his response to Wordsworth, that we now turn.

Ferdinand Freiligrath

The feeling which impels a poet to devote his genius to forward what he believes a great political cause deserves honour: but it is doubtful whether any such cause has thus been greatly served.

McCarthy 1868, 204–5

Ferdinand Freiligrath (1810–76) was one of the most prolific German publicists for English language poetry in the middle period of the nineteenth century, and his career vividly illustrates the connections between 'translation' and nationalism. He was born in Detmold, Westphalia. As a child he became fascinated by the circus and the world of fantasy it conjured up; he read travel books avidly, and loved tales of the Orient (ibid., 176–9). Initially, however, it seemed that there would be little opportunity for him to indulge these passions because his father decided that he should train as an accountant. Like many Germans of his generation, he was keen to travel to Britain and had hopes of working for a wealthy uncle in Edinburgh; but his uncle died, and in 1832, at the age of 21, he was sent to Amsterdam to work as a book-keeper for a Dutch firm (Liddell 1949, x). This was his first experience of exile, and much of his writing reflected that mood.

Discovering his gift for languages encouraged his ambitions to translate English, French and Italian poetry into German. His choice of British Romantic Period poets clearly reflects Jacobsen's pantheon. After 1832, a preoccupation with loneliness and exile that the Amsterdam job occasioned also influenced his preferences. Like many of his compatriots, his enthusiasm for English language poetry was accompanied by a particular interest in Scotland, and the disappointment of not being able to travel to Scotland was rendered all the more intense by his early love of Scott and Burns. Writing to Schwab in 1835 he commented, 'I used to translate a lot of Burns – my favourite poet – but didn't have it printed because I thought somebody else must already have done that' (Spink 1932, 5). It was not long before he also began to read and translate Felicia Hemans. At this time he was also working on a translation of Shakespeare's *Venus and Adonis* (ibid., 5). He found an outlet for much of this work in Cotta's *Morgenblatt* (Ashton 1986, 79).

Besides Jacobsen, Freiligrath also had H. L. Broenner's *The British Poets of the Nineteenth Century* to draw on (1828). He continued his reading of travel books, becoming particularly interested in James Fenimore Cooper's stories of the American frontier, and William Robertson's *History of America* (1833). All this material answered to his personal sense of isolation, and with this in mind it is not surprising to find him translating Wordsworth's 'Song for the Wandering Jew' in 1830, along with Hemans' 'The Parting Ship', 'The Better Land', and 'Song of Emigration'. Probably his best known translation on this theme was Coleridge's *The Ancient Mariner* (1830). Even more ambitious, however, was his translation of Hemans' *The Forest Sanctuary*, a tale of religious persecution and exile, which he published in 1846.

Franz Thimm's estimation of him in his *Literature of Germany* brings much of this biographical material together:

> He has risen into repute by his ingenious and original, though fantastic, compositions, and especially by curious pictures of the manners and feelings of exotic nations and tribes, as well as by descriptions of the wild beauties of nature . . . (Thimm 1844, 257)

The success of his first book of poems in 1838 prompted him to attempt to make his living as a writer; he became editor of *Das Rheinische Jahrbuch für Kunst und Literatur.* By this time Wordsworth was among the poets he found most inspiring. Gerald W. Spink notes him writing enthusiastically to Heinrich Kunzel in 1838 about how deeply Wordsworth's nature poetry had influenced him. Wordsworth 'is wholly unsurpassable' ('ganz unübertrefflich') as a poet who knows and can express what a true feeling for nature ('Das Naturgefühl') entails:

> Das Naturgefühl, das namentlich in Wordsworths Dichtungen weht, ist ganz unübertrefflich, und ich denke noch immer mit stiller Freude an die Zeit zurück, wo ich ihn zuerst kennen lernte und mit ihm und Coleridge einsam Wald und Feld durchschweifte. (Spink 1925, 9)

Freiligrath continued to yearn for the opportunity to travel to Britain; in March 1838 he wrote to Schwab about his intention to visit London, in July he wrote to Immermann that he hoped to visit the Shetlands aboard a Dutch warship (Spink 1932, 5). Writing again to Kunzel (then living in London and planning to publish a journal called *Britannia*) he claims he would be prepared to do anything to be able to escape from 'the accursed merchant bribing society' of his homeland and move to London, even if it meant working in the docks. 'However,' he concludes, 'I would need half the day to walk, to stare into the fireplace and to write poetry' (Spink 1932, 6; Ashton 1986, 80).

The section of English poems included in his 1838 *Gedichte* comprises Coleridge's *Ancient Mariner*, 26 poems by Moore (by now well ahead of Burns), slightly fewer by Scott, and a few each by Southey, Campbell and Burns. Lamb, Keats and Hemans have one each. Although we have seen that he was reading and translating Wordsworth, he is not represented here. Worthy of note is the exclusion of Byron; like Jacobsen, Freiligrath found Byron's morals suspect, and his political cynicism disturbing.

In 1838 Freiligrath was by no means at his most politically engaged; he was, however, committed to German Nationalism, and believed that Friedrich Wilhelm IV would bring about the necessary reforms. Like Georg Herwegh (who chided Freiligrath in verse in the 1840s for being lukewarm in his commitment to reform) his growing political sympathies lay with the reforming, liberal middle classes, but within this group there were divided aims. Although there was general opposition to the powerful position of the landed class, regional and historical differences between the German states made any united front impossible, a situation readily exploited by those in power. The opposition was divided along lines that involved dislike of Austrian control, mistrust of Prussian ambition, rivalry between Lutheran states, the Catholic south and the Rhineland. Some liberals wanted a stronger federal state; others, like Freiligrath, were more radical in their ambitions, notably when it came to disposing of the monarchy. Against this we should set Franz Thimm's account of German politics and literature, observed from the vantage point of England in 1844:

> The state interests are sedulously kept from [Germans], as if indeed 'deutsche Biederkeit' were no longer trustworthy. The movements of their statesmen are matters of mystery . . . The public press is heavily fettered; and by this means, among others, they are prevented from talking over or inquiring into the condition of public affairs. The one thing wanting to circulate an unbroken rein of patriotism through the entire German community, to complete the prosperity of its literature, and render that prosperity permanent, is the deliverance of the press from the disabilities that have hitherto weighed upon it, and its exalture into a state of perfect and unconditional freedom. (Thimm 1844, 242)

Ten years before Thimm's lament, Heine remarked that 'if we wish to announce in the *Hamburger Correspondent* "My dear wife has given birth to a daughter, fair as freedom," Herr Doctor Hoffmann picks up his red pencil and strikes out the freedom'. His essay on 'The German Censors' consists of the opening phrase, 'The German censors of the press'; this is followed by multiple deletions, with only one word left uncensored in the middle of the page: 'blockheads' (Heine 1943, 119, 47). Freiligrath would have concurred with this diagnosis, and in due course attempted to bring about a cure.

In the years following the publication of the 1838 *Gedichte*, Freiligrath became increasingly radical in his political views. At the same time he became known as an upright family man of moral integrity. His admiration for Wordsworth is therefore easy to understand. Jacobsen had shown Wordsworth to be a great patriot and a stalwart defender of the Protestant faith, and his book illustrated how the poet's love of his homeland was expressed in poetry imbued with a sense of the spiritual power of Nature. Freiligrath married Ida Melos in 1841. Domestic life cooled his political ardour for a while, and the pension he received in 1842 further dulled what radical tendencies he might previously have had. It was not long, however, before Friedrich Wilhelm's reactionary policies drew him back into political life along with many of his contemporaries, and in 1844 he resigned his pension and published what became one of his best known collections of poetry, *Ein Glaubensbekenntnis*. Rosemary Ashton argues that, 'The volume was hardly objectionable; it included some vague nationalist rhetoric, much quoting from and reference to Schiller, and some adaptations from such British poems as Burns's 'Is there, for honest poverty', and Thomas Campbell's 'England to Germany' (Ashton 1986, 28). He moved to Brussels for six months, and from there to Switzerland where he published a collection of six political poems under the title of *Ça Ira*. From Switzerland he moved to London where he stayed for two years working in an Anglo-German bank. 'Poor Freiligrath has come to England in great poverty and in a very friendless state,' Varnhagen von Ensè wrote to Monckton Milnes in 1846. He was not long making contacts with the literati, however, and in 1847 von Ensè was able to report, 'Freiligrath pleases much those that see him, but that is few, for he is kept hard at work at his counting-house all the week', an ironic situation for the young poet who wished to be free of 'the accursed merchant bribing society' (Spink 1932, 26–7).

An important and enduring friendship sprang up between the Freiligraths and the Quaker writers and publicists William and Mary Howitt. William Howitt described him as a poet 'whose imagination enclosed the world in its grasp'. The Howitts first met him in Germany when they were travelling there from 1840 to 1843, and it seemed to them then that 'England or America were the only countries in which he could live with safety ... There scarcely ever was any man who came to this country, who lived so long in it, and who returned hence in a manner so erect, so manly, so honourable, and so independent, as Ferdinand Freiligrath!' (Spink 1932, 28–30). The Howitts' reading of Wordsworth mirrored the view of him to be found in both Jacobsen's and Freiligrath's comments. In *Homes and Haunts of the most Eminent British Poets* (1847), William Howitt declared that Wordsworth 'followed the stream of life as it led him down the retired vale of poetic meditation', he expressed 'a poetic Quakerism' which 'believes the Divine Spirit which fills the universe, to have so moulded all the forms of visible nature, as to make them to us perpetual monitors and instructors' (Howitt 1847ii, 273). It is unlikely that Wordsworth was particularly gratified to find himself enrolled as an honorary Quaker by the Howitts, but in many respects their broadly humanitarian politics were appreciated by him, as they were by Charles Dickens who invited them to contribute to *Household Words*.

As Paul Giles has suggested, in the period that links Romanticism to Modernism – from Byron to James Joyce – 'exile' has been associated with 'a form of intellectual empowerment' (Giles 2004, 31). Exile certainly continued to inform Freiligrath's judgement in relation to his choice of poems for translation into German. His *Gedichte aus dem Englischen* of 1846 was compiled in exile (though published in Germany). It marks the completion of his translation of Felicia Hemans' *The Forest Sanctuary*, a poem of 169 stanzas, and it appears with 36 shorter pieces by Hemans. Hemans had a keen interest in European poetry, drama, and prose, which she read as reflecting the great political changes that were taking place. Among other poems with German themes, she wrote two tributes to Theodor Körner, the young poet killed fighting the French in 1813:

> A song for the death-day of the brave –
>   A song of pride!
> The youth went down to a hero's grave,
>   With the sword, his bride.

He went, with his noble heart unworn,
          And pure, and high;
An eagle stooping from clouds of morn,
          Only to die.

(Hemans 1914, 454)

In later years she moved from her initial enthusiasm for Staël, Shelley and Byron, to become an admirer of the by then far more respectable and morally sound Wordsworth (Hemans 2002, 61).

The Forest Sanctuary is headed with a quotation from Schiller's *Die Jungfrau von Orleans* and Coleridge's *Remorse*; Hemans describes it as a poem charting 'the mental conflict, as well as the outward sufferings' of a Spaniard in exile in North America with his child (Hemans 2002, 228). He is the victim of religious persecution in the sixteenth century. In many ways Hemans' poetry—idealistic, nostalgic, patriotic and frequently naïve in tone – had much in common with Freiligrath's work, though the latter produced poetry with a far more direct and angry political content in the 1840s and early 1850s.

In addition to the poetry by Hemans (by now a widely translated poet in Germany), Freiligrath's 1846 *Gedichte* contains six poems by Elizabeth Landon, three by Mary Howitt, one by William Cowper, eight extracts from Southey's *Thalaba* with three other poems, and one each from John Wilson, Barry Cornwall, Robert Monckton Milnes, Ebenezer Elliott, and Tom Moore. Tennyson has 15 poems, Longfellow four, and there are two by Wordsworth. This list reflects the people Freiligrath was meeting in London. On receiving an autographed copy of the 1846 collection, Tennyson wrote to Freiligrath, 'I knew that you were a celebrated German poet and lover of liberty: therefore was my satisfaction great to receive . . . a copy of your works with your own friendly autograph', and he went on to praise Freiligrath's work as 'full of living warmth, in fact a Poet's translation of poetry' (Spink 1932, 28). It should be added that some of the translations (as Freiligrath points out in the Introduction) were by his wife.

Freiligrath's reputation as a prolific poet and translator thrived on the basis of his appeal to a liberal, progressive readership. His choice of English poems for translation ensured that his target German readership would frequently be reminded of his own politically embattled situation. Whether in England or Germany, he donned the mantle of Wordsworth's alienated wandering Jew, and of Heman's exiled Spaniard of *The Forest Sanctuary*. German readers of Freiligrath's English poems invariably discovered a more reflective and contemplative poet than the one likely to assail them when he wrote in his native language.

From the variety of poets that he chose to translate, it is clear that Freiligrath would certainly have wished to challenge René Wellek's assertion (made some 120 years later) that apart from Byron, no English poet 'has the sense of . . . life as a Nothingness, of the artist as an outsider'; Freiligrath did not need to resort to Byron for a soul-mate in this respect; Hemans, Coleridge, and Wordsworth were worthy alternatives (Wellek 1965, 22). Wordsworth brought to Freiligrath's pantheon a profound sense of patriotism that linked love of country organically to nature itself. He also articulated an energetic opposition to the activities of autocratic foreign invaders. The two poems included in the 1846 *Gedichte* by no means reflect the extent of his work on Wordsworth. As he explains in the Introduction to the volume, his translations were subject to long periods of revision, only eventually published when he was sure of their quality. Everything, he writes, must be 'put in order . . . and passed through a sieve' (Freiligrath

1846i, v). We know, for example, that he was translating the *Evening Voluntaries* of 1835, and sonnets from the *River Duddon* series through the 1840s; 'The Danish Boy', 'Written in March' and 'The Tables Turned' were also among the poems on his work-bench around this time (Spink 1925, 25, 30).

It is not unreasonable to assume that Freiligrath's decision to include 'The Solitary Reaper' and 'Yew Trees' in the 1846 volume was intended to display Wordsworth's range as both lyric poet, and a more stern patriotic poet. 'The Solitary Reaper' is probably best known by Anglo-American critics as a poem that expresses Wordsworth's sensitivity towards the relationship between word, sound, and meaning. Having described the beauty of the reaper's song, in the third verse Wordsworth makes it apparent that she sings in Gaelic, and therefore he cannot understand the song. It might be about 'old, unhappy, far-off things,/ And battles long ago', it might be far less elevated subject matter, 'some more humble lay', or it might be about 'Some natural sorrow, loss, or pain,/That has been, and may be again!' (Wordsworth 1983, 185). The final verse of the poem, however, suggests that there is a deeper, more profound meaning conveyed in the sound of the voice that by-passes the need to understand the language. 'Resolution and Independence' explores the same theme, as does the poem Freiligrath was also working on around this time, 'The Danish Boy':

> A harp is from his shoulder slung;
> He rests the harp upon his knee,
> And there in a forgotten tongue
> He warbles melody.
>
> (Wordsworth 192, 240)

As we have already seen, in his anthology of 1853, Karl Elze groups 'The Solitary Reaper' with poems of labour, including Elliott's 'Preston Mills', Hood's 'Song of the Shirt', and Elizabeth Browning's 'The Cry of the Children'. The beautiful setting and the ravishing music are combined with a politicized image of the girl as a solitary worker, a point of greater significance for Freiligrath than for most, if not all, later critics. This may well be why it was this poem rather than 'The Danish Boy' that he chose to publish in 1846. 'The Danish Boy' is very similar indeed to 'The Solitary Reaper', differing only in the fact that that the boy is a ghostly presence, his sole function is to sing. The solitary reaper is undoubtedly a flesh-and-blood working girl. Both poems, of course, convey a powerful sense of exile.

Two years after the 1846 *Gedichte* was published, Freiligrath returned to Germany. Here he co-edited the Marxist *Neue Rheinische Zeitung*, establishing a close friendship with Marx, and he continued to write overtly political poetry in the wake of the revolutionary upheavals (Ashton 1986, 30). In 'Hamlet' (translated in the 1869 *Poems from the German by Ferdinand Freiligrath* by William Howitt) he wrote:

> Deutschland is Hamlet! Solemn, slow,
> Within its gates walk every night,
> Pale, buried Freedom to and fro,
> And fills the watchers with affright.
>
> (Freiligrath 1869, 201–4)

I suggest this is a darker rendering of Ludolf Weinbarg's description of Goethe's *Faust* in his *Ästhetische Feldzüge* of 1834: 'Faust is Germany struggling to be liberated, indeed he is the liberated Germany as it anticipates the victory of its freedom' (Seeba 2003, 187).

We know that around this time Freiligrath's reading of English political poetry started to include the Chartist poet Ernest Jones. In 1848 his own defiant poem memorializing the victims of the fighting in Berlin, '*Die Toten an die Lebenden*' triggered his arrest for sedition. He was tried and acquitted, but soon after emigrated to England where he found work in a Swiss Bank. He wrote on German literature, contributing frequently to *The Athenaeum*. With the collapse of the Revolution, Freiligrath's political fervour had been severely tested, as it was for many around him, and indeed as it had been for many of Wordsworth's generation in the wake of the French 'Terror' of 1792. Where Wordsworth was concerned the case has already been made (specifically in relation to *The Excursion*) that his conservative turn is by no means a straightforward matter, and that he retained a fundamental belief in liberty over a long period of personal political adjustment in rapidly changing times. Hence the lines that caught Jacobsen's eye:

> Earth is sick,
> And Heaven is weary of the hollow words
> Which States and Kingdoms utter when they talk
> Of truth and justice.
>
> (Wordsworth 2007, 178)

We may set Freiligrath's decision to come back to England in the light of the lines which follow the quotation above. There seemed to be little left for the poet of *Die Toten an die Lebenden* in his native land when he looked around him for signs of hope in the future:

> Turn to private life
> And social neighbourhood; look we to ourselves;
> A light of duty shines on every day
> For all; and yet how few are warmed or cheered!
> How few who mingle with their fellow men . . .
>
> (Ibid., 178)

Writing of Freiligrath and his fellow exiles, Kinkel, Tausenau and Struve, Ashton suggests that 'They came to England with a mental picture formed by reading Shakespeare, Byron, Shelley and Dickens, as well as the numerous travel books about England by previous German visitors like Prince Pückler-Muskau, who published his English travel diary in 1831 and was immortalized as "Count Smorltork" by Dickens in *Pickwick Papers*' (Ashton 1986, 35). In Freiligrath's case, anxiety for his own safety, regardless of what he might now write or indeed say, was compounded by his sense of responsibility to his wife and daughter. The family arrived in London in 1851, and stayed for 16 years, during which time he finally managed to meet Wordsworth (Bömig 1906, 79). An early twentieth-century biographer and editor of Freiligrath, M. F. Liddell, was of the opinion that 'the financial struggles and troubles of these later years virtually killed the poet in him' (Liddell 1949, xv). It might be added that it also threatened to kill his political radicalism, and despite his continued friendship with Marx, Freiligrath declined to join the Communist International in 1864. His literary labours were now primarily concerned with editing marketable anthologies of poetry of his own, and contributing items to anthologies edited by others specifically aimed at a burgeoning middle class readership in Britain, Germany, and America. Though Freiligrath's appetite for political conflict had undoubtedly been blunted, the extent to which he had abandoned his political ideals remains a moot point. George Eliot, despite her reformist sympathies, viewed his work with suspicion when Andrew Johnson suggested the possibility of translating some of Freiligrath's poems into English at this time (Karl 1995, 133–4).

Whatever his political views were, there was never any diminution in his commitment to the belief that translation was to be understood and respected as a branch of literature in its own right. Liddell noted that in the *Collected Works*, for every three German poems, Freiligrath has four translations, adding that the proportion would have been even more in favour of translation, had he not been so scrupulous about achieving the standard he set himself (Liddell 1949, xliv).

Two years after his arrival in England, Freiligrath produced a weighty anthology of English language poetry. *The Rose, Thistle and Shamrock* was an anthology of English, Scottish, and Irish poetry, first published in Stuttgart in 1853. All the poetry is in English. There were at least five editions of this version, with Freiligrath's wife and daughter involved in editing. Some idea of the extent to which Freiligrath became a respected figure in both countries may be had from Charles Timothy Brooks' decision to include a translation of Freiligrath's 'The Lion's Pride' in *The Dial* of 1842, attempting (as a tribute to Freiligrath's skill in translation) to replicate the formal qualities of the original. When he undertook to back-translate Freiligrath's German rendering of Burns' 'Farewell to his Native Land', he claimed that it was only the Scots dialect that had prevented Freiligrath achieving a perfect match between the English and German languages (Boggs 2006, 28). A volume of Freiligrath's poems published in England in 1870, however, met with little success. The *Athenaeum* pronounced him a second-rate poet, given to vague and cliché-ridden rhetoric and excessive indulgence in rhyme (Ashton 1986, 91).

The Preface to the revised 1874 edition of *The Rose, Thistle and Shamrock* notes that after more than 20 years in print, the anthology was still popular. The collection provides us with a reliable indication of which poems by Wordsworth had become familiar to an English reading German public in the 1860s and 1870s. In section 1, 'Poesy and the Poets', there are eight poems by Wordsworth from a total of 52. These are 'Though the bold wings of poesie', 'If thou indeed derive thy light from heaven', 'Resolution and Independence', 'A Poet's Epitaph', 'Scorn not the sonnet', 'Remembrance of Collins', 'At the Grave of Burns', and 'To the Sons of Burns'. In section 2, 'Home and Country', he includes the sonnet 'Composed upon Westminster Bridge'. Wordsworth is here anthologized as a poet who writes lyrically about poetry and nature. However, in Section 4, 'Society, Work and Progress', there are three extracts from *The Excursion*, and it is here that, once again, political issues are given prominence. Freiligrath turned to Book VIII, 'The Parsonage' for his passages, beginning at line 87 where the poet reflects on the consequences for the countryside of industrial change:

> An inventive age
> Has wrought, if not with speed of magic, yet
> To most strange issues. I have lived to mark
> A new and unforseen creation rise

> From out the labours of a peaceful Land
> Wielding her potent enginery to frame
> And to produce, with appetite as keen
> As that of war, which rests not night or day,
> Industrious to destroy
>
> (Wordsworth 2007, 261)

Freiligrath called this extract 'The Manufacturing Spirit'. The second passage is headed 'The Factory at Night', and begins at line 170:

> . . . at the appointed hour a bell is heard
> Of harsher import than the curfew-knoll
> That spake the Norman Conqueror's stern behest –
> A local summons to unceasing toil!
>
> (Ibid., 263)

Finally, in 'The Working Classes', beginning at line 262, we read of the destruction of the rural family by industrialization:

> Domestic bliss
> (Or call it comfort by a humbler name,)
> How art thou blighted for the poor man's heart!
>
> (Ibid., 265–6)

Here we have evidence of the persistence of Freiligrath's political convictions, and his belief that Wordsworth's voice should be included here, as well as among the nature poets. The rest of Wordsworth's poetry in the anthology does, however, confirm him as primarily a nature poet. It also affirms his persistent presence in the German pantheon. The section called 'Changes of Life' includes 'My heart leaps up' ('The Rainbow'); 'Love and the Affections' has Wordsworth's version of Chaucer's 'The Cuckoo and the Nightingale', 'She was a phantom of delight', and (inevitably) 'We are Seven'; 'Nature and the Seasons' has 'A Night Piece', 'I wandered lonely as a cloud', 'To the Cuckoo', and 'The Solitary Reaper'; and in 'The Sea and the Sailor' Freiligrath included 'The Sailor's Mother'. Later revisions saw just two Wordsworth poems dropped, but the passages from *The Excursion* remained.

Freiligrath's declared intention (stated in the Introduction to the 1853 edition of the Anthology) was that this collection of poetry should be 'a welcome present to every lover of English poetry' in Germany, England, and America. Genteel and politically neutral as this may sound, his choice of *Excursion* extracts alone indicate that political motivation born of the conflicts that marked the evolution of nineteenth-century German Nationalism were never far from the surface of Freiligrath's mind, despite the fact that by this time Marx had written him off as the 'mercantile poet' (Ashton 1986, 90). Throughout his second, long period of exile, Freiligrath gained respect and affection in England and America, and never lost a devoted following in Germany. It was through the financial support of friends and admirers that he was eventually able to return to Germany in 1867, when he settled in Cannstadt, near Stuttgart. Some intriguing parallels between his career and that of Wordsworth present themselves. Both poets experienced the bitterness of exile, and although Wordsworth's case was far less extreme than that of Freiligrath, his brief period spent huddled miserably over the stove in freezing Goslar arguably contributed to inspiring some of his greatest work, not least *The Prelude*. Both poets struggled with nagging financial worries, both poets had devoted women in attendance to ease their way, and not least, both poets committed themselves to radical political programmes, only to see the promise of a new dawn fade in the light of changing circumstances. Both poets were therefore liable to the charge of apostasy, and both poets undoubtedly did change their opinions in relation to their earlier convictions. Against the unremittingly gloomy and reactionary prognostications of Wordsworth's 'The Warning', however (published in 1835 in the wake of the Reform Act of 1832), Isabella Fenwick noted down a comment from Wordsworth in 1843 that seems at the very least to absolve the Chartists from their radical 'ardor and perseverance', given the absence of 'wiser and more brotherly dealings' from 'the wealthy few' (Fenwick 1993, 90). M. F. Liddell, commenting on Freiligrath's late poetry, is in no doubt that he was 'an unrepentant democrat to the last' (Liddell 1949, xv).

7 Cultural and Political Disruption: Wordsworth's Voice in Late Nineteenth-Century Germany

Introduction

The German looks upon his nation not only as a people, but as a race, almost as a formal religion . . . In order to build up his patriotism the German has been taught systematically to dislike first the Austrians, then the French, now the English: and let not the American suppose that he likes him any better . . .

Collier 1914, 539

By the late nineteenth century the circumstances in which the British Romantic poets were read in Germany were profoundly different from those enjoyed by Friedrich Jacobsen, celebrating a Europe newly liberated from the threat of French imperialism. Following the creation of the North German Confederation in April 1871, the way in which German Nationalism exerted an influence on political and cultural life underwent significant changes. By the 1870s the readership for English language poetry was beginning to include an increasingly specialized academic, scholarly sector, while anthologies catering for the general reader were being supplemented by collections for specifically educational purposes within schools. In addition, the shifting pattern of relationships between an increasingly influential German State and her neighbours was reflected in its reading, and translating, of foreign language texts.

In 1871 the constitution of the North German Confederation became the constitution of a united Imperial Germany under Wilhelm I. In 1888, after the brief reign of Frederick III, Wilhelm II became Emperor, and with the departure of the Chancellor, Bismarck, the instability of this 'diverse young nation with intense growing pains' was compounded, as Steven Ozment explains, by 'the growth of both the military budget and the liberal voter turnout' coupled with a dramatic rise in population (60% from 1871 to 1914) (Ozment 2005, 228). German government was bedevilled by contradictory forces, summarized by Stephen. J. Lee:

> The autocratic traditions of the Prussian-based monarchy and ruling élite appeared incompatible with the more recent concession of Parliamentary democracy. The ruling class lived in fear of revolution from below . . . The working class, which had been considerably enlarged by Germany's massive industrial growth, resented the almost feudal class structure . . . The middle class shared the régime's fears of socialism, but were fully committed to upholding Parliamentary democracy. (Lee 1982, 141–2)

Mary Fulbrook suggests the cultural implications of this:

> Not only imaginative writers, but also social thinkers, explored the implications for personality and family life ... in the shift from what was seen as an 'organic', traditional 'community' to a more alienating, individualistic 'society' (the distinction between *Gemeinschaft* and *Gesellschaft*). (Fulbrook 2004, 145)

Germany found itself torn between two contradictory models of statehood and politicians and intellectuals, like Eberhard Gothein (1853–1923), attempted to work for social reform on behalf of the working class without disturbing the Prussian commitment to capitalism and state order. The belief that this was possible became the manifesto of the so-called *Kathedersozialismus* movement (Maurer 2006, 1).

Gothein was one among many who feared that factional pressure threatened to fragment the state:

> Inward-looking professional associations and leagues multiplied in trade and industry, agriculture and farming, the civil service and the military. Political parties developed hard core constituencies among such groups, which in turn created their own government lobbies. Among socially rising groups, the industrial proletariat found a home in Marxist Social Democracy, which, after 1890, became the largest German political party, taking a third of the vote in 1912. (Ozment 2005, 230)

There remained, however, a powerful ambition for national unity capable of inspiring belief in the destiny of Germany. This was a cultural phenomenon that could defy the many ideological and political fault lines of post-unification Germany. From 1890, *Deutschland über Alles* was being sung in schools across Germany, and was an obligatory adjunct to all national holidays. In his Taylorian Lecture of 1892 at Oxford, T. W. Rolleston stated that 'the idea of Fatherland must be the soul of every achievement in culture, and hence also the fundamental motive of culture'. He added, however, that Germany had become unhealthily obsessed with this idea in the absence of any literary figures of true greatness since Lessing and Goethe (Rolleston 1892, 97).

Writers were therefore working in a volatile context where influential voices such as Schopenhauer and Nietzsche were equally scornful of both the old and the new Germany. Novelists such as Theodor Storm (1817–88), Conrad Meyer (1825–98), and Wilhelm Raabe (1831–1910), were employing techniques and devices that emphasized the illusory nature of an objective, unifying perception of the human condition. Ozment describes a situation where 'young Germans wandered from soapbox to soapbox, on which influential demagogues, militarists, nihilists, and racists increasingly climbed' (Ozment 2005, 231). Against this, historians like Alfred Stern were using their research into English history to create a perception of revolutionary and turbulent periods of history as ultimately affirming continuity and order. Stern's detailed history of the English Civil War, *Geschichte der Revolution in England* (1881), combines cultural, political, and social history to present a sense of hope for future stability coming out of disruption and uncertainty. Stern's work belongs in the tradition of Germanic historical and philological scholarship that includes the work of Lappenberg, who, besides his historical work on England produced a massive study of the *Poetry of England* in 1834 which took all its 413 pages to arrive at the Norman period. In 1886 Jakob Schipper published a study of English and

German Philology, following it in 1908 with a volume on English culture and literature; his *History of English Versification* was translated into English in 1910. Hermann Paul's *Compendium of Germanic Language* was published between 1901 and 1909; equally monumental was Alexander Baumgartner's *Geschichte der Weltliteratur* of 1897. This was created by a team of writers, including the Coleridge enthusiast, Alois Brandl, and Moritz Brosch.

Enthusiasm for English culture and specifically literature persisted among the Germans, and enthusiasts for Wordsworth continued to make a case for him. In the 1880s Michael Bernays (1834–97) attempted (without success) to convince Paul Heyse of Wordsworth's greatness: 'der überragen Gröse William Wordsworth's zu überzeugen' (Prawer 1960, 11). Elsewhere Bernays claimed that 'he [Wordsworth] deals with more of life than Burns, Keats, Heine' (Bernays 1907, 177). The stumbling block for Heyse appears to have been Wordsworth's intrinsic Englishness. After 1888 it is clear that to be enthusiastic about English literature was controversial given Germany's changing European political policy. This is not without its relevance to the manner in which Wordsworth in particular was perceived in the decades that immediately preceded the outbreak of war in 1914. German readers of Wordsworth in this period, finding in *The Excursion*, *The Prelude*, and the lyric poetry, a powerful expression of nationalist fervour coupled with deep distrust of modernity set against a traditional agrarian society imbued with Christian values, would note the contrast between that and their contemporary world. Germany, in common with other European countries, was experiencing a widespread turning from belief in the religious sources of ideas of order and identity. The moral of 'We are Seven' had never seemed so timely when the consequent search for alternatives – spiritualism, hedonism, myth, and legend – seemed only to lead into a culturally fragmented wasteland. This is the Germany experienced by Adrian Leverkühn, the central character of Thomas Mann's *Dr. Faustus* (1947): 'Why does almost everything seem to me like its own parody? Why must I think that almost all, no, all the methods and conventions of art today *are good for parody only*?' (Mann 1999i, 134). If Leverkühn's thinking resembles that of anyone, it is Nietzsche's, as Georg Lukács has suggested, pointing out that 'the work of art itself is called into question' (Lukács 1964, 67); he goes on to argue that Leverkühn's music (as described in the novel) represents 'the concentrated expression of intellectual and moral decadence' (Lukács 1964, 67–8). In this particular instance Mann's doomed composer might well have been partly inspired by Richard Strauss. Strauss's opera *Ariadne auf Naxos* of 1912 (with a libretto by Hofmannsthal), was originally conceived of as an opera within a play, a parodic comment (using Molière's *Le Bourgeois Gentilhomme*) on the dichotomy of Reason and Imagination. Ernst Otto Nodnagel described Strauss's music as symptomatic of a 'new aesthetic orientation' which 'represented a terrible danger, the greatest living talent had turned his back on spirituality and now sought to bring about the "dissolution" (*Auflosüng*) of the art' (Youmans 2005, 4–5). This is a situation where, as Lukács suggests, 'The democracy which was won by revolution turns into a caricature of itself . . . Its outward forms, its ideologies of "freedom", become more hypocritical, contrasting ever more sharply with social reality . . .' (Lukács 1964, 63).

No German Wordsworthian considered in this chapter will have been reading the English language Romantic poets without a sense of where their voices belonged in this context. For those who felt themselves to be in any sense outsiders in relation to current political and cultural trends, the adoption of Wordsworth in particular had an appropriate resonance. Despite the fact that his place in the German pantheon of English poets appears never to have been under threat, writer after writer was wont to stress Wordsworth's lack of popularity in Germany. He had become a representative of the outsider; an endemically 'English' poet at a time when Germany's network of political alliances was becoming increasingly fragile, not least with regard to Britain, and when German national integrity and security was deemed more vulnerable than ever after the advent of Wilhelm II and the departure of Bismarck.

The comparison with Byron remained a touchstone, and the extent to which the admirable qualities of Wordsworth might be deemed to challenge those of Byron, was included in most of these late nineteenth-century German accounts, the first of which to be considered here was by an Englishman.

Henry Bernard Cotterill

> *Wordsworth stands amid a group of English poets who are not only epoch-making ('epochemachend') but who in a particular way (concerning our attitude toward nature) are the most important of all English poets, including Shakespeare.*
>
> Cotterill, 1883, 1

H. B. Cotterill was born in 1846. He was a prolific writer of textbooks, an essayist, editor, and a linguist. As a Cambridge Extension Lecturer he would have been expected to turn his hand to most things, and his translations include works by Virgil, Dante, and Goethe. He developed something of a reputation as a flamboyant speaker. His final work was an ambitious two volume *History of Art* published in 1922. Wordsworth was an abiding interest with him, and some measure of the respect in which his scholarship and translation skills were held is that his essay on Wordsworth was published in Dresden with T. W. Rolleston's essay on Walt Whitman as *Ueber Wordsworth und Walt Whitman*. Cotterill's target readership, however, is primarily non-specialist, the type he was most used to lecturing to.

He begins by asserting that Wordsworth is one of the most important English poets, to be ranked with Shakespeare. He is recognized by his compatriots as a great philosopher poet of nature, whose work reveals the restorative qualities of landscape. To illustrate this Cotterill translates lines 23–50 of 'Tintern Abbey' (apologizing for the inadequacy of his German version which reproduces the formal arrangement of the subject text). His intention is to establish a bond between the English poet and his German readership using an extract that combines a love of nature with philosophical reflection imbued by religious piety. The passage concludes with the evocation of:

> ... that serene and blessed mood
> In which the affections gently lead us on,
> Until, the breath of this corporeal frame,
> And even the motion of our human blood
> Almost suspended, we are laid asleep
> In body, and become a living soul:
> While with an eye made quiet by the power
> Of harmony, and the deep power of joy,
> We see into the life of things.
>
> (Wordsworth 1992, 117)

In drawing attention to the power and subtlety of Wordsworth's nature description, Cotterill compares him with Dante, knowing full well how respected the Italian poet was in Germany. It is above all the power of the simplicity of Wordsworth's poetry that Cotterill celebrates. He quotes from 'Yarrow Visited' and 'She dwelt among th'untrodden ways' to illustrate how his profundity is born of simplicity (Cotterill 1883, 21–2).

He then uses a passage from Book XI of *The Prelude* to encapsulate the outcome of the poet's experiences of the French Revolution; Cotterill's Wordsworth is in no sense a political animal. In Book XI, ll.297–305, Wordsworth appears to be abandoning his faith in being able to find a political solution to the evils of society:

> now believing,
> Now disbelieving; endlessly perplexed
> With impulse, motive, right and wrong, the ground
> Of obligation, what the rule and whence
> The sanction; till, demanding formal *proof*,
> And seeking it in everything, I lost
> All feeling of conviction, and, in fine,
> Sick, wearied out with contraries,
> Yielded up moral questions in despair.
>
> (Wordsworth 1979, 407)

Cotterill's translation of line 305 where Wordsworth states that 'moral questions' are being abandoned 'in despair' is not clear; the implication for a German reader is that the poet is putting his entire political engagement behind him. The final two lines of Cotterill's version read:

> *Ermattett, müde ewigen Widerspruchs,*
> *Verzweifelnd gab ich solche Fragen auf.*
>
> Weakened, tired of constant antagonism,
> Desperate I gave up such questions.
>
> (Cotterill 1883, 27)

The essay concludes with the 'Sonnet Composed Upon Westminster Bridge', quoted in parallel text, and with the poem Cotterill believes to be Wordsworth's finest, the *Ode: Intimations of Immortality*. He decides here to take the meaning of Wordsworth's poetry to as many of his German readers as possible, and therefore opts for prose translation.

Setting the political Wordsworth firmly to one side, the Wordsworth Cotterill offers as a far more serious and substantial poet than Byron, is a Wordsworth who stands alongside the greatest European poets in his firmness of religious conviction, and in the way he conveys his profound relationship with the natural world. In this the poet offers his readers a visionary sense of permanence and continuity; he also presents them with reasons to be wary of the disruptive spirit of modernity and change. The 1880s was indeed a time when nostalgia, and a sense of irreparable loss, might understandably exercise a particularly strong appeal. Using prose, Cotterill was able to reconstruct the Wordsworthian pain of loss very effectively:

> There was a time when meadow, grove, and stream,
> The earth, and every common sight,
>   To me did seem
> Apparell'd in celestial light,

> The glory and the freshness of a dream.
> It is not now as it has been of yore;
> > Turn wheresoe'er I may,
> > > By night or day,
> The things which I have seen I now can see no more.
>
> (Wordsworth 1982, 271)

> *Es gab einst eine Zeit, da Wiese, Wald und Strom, die ganze Erde und alles, was man sieht, mit himmlischem Lichte, mit hehrer träumerischer Schönheit für mich bekleidet war. Jezt ist's nicht mehr, wie sonst es war. Wohin ich mich auch wende, bei Tag und Nacht, was ich schaute, kann ich nicht mehr schauen.* (Cotterill 1883, 31)

Where translation includes the attempt to reproduce Wordsworth's original poetic form, the German reader has to negotiate a far more stilted expression of the meaning. This is evident when Cotterill's prose is compared to the first five lines of Marie Gothein's translation of the same poem:

> Einst war die Zeit, da schien mir Strom und Baum,
> Die Erde, jedes grüne Feld,
> > Der Weltraum
> > Von Himmelschlicht erhellt,
> In Glanz und Frische wie ein Traum.
>
> (Gothein 1893 II, 70)

Marie Gothein

> *The following is an attempt . . . to arouse some interest in a German readership for Wordsworth's life and poetical work.*
>
> Gothein 1893 I, 6

The most substantial study of Wordsworth to be published in nineteenth-century Germany was by Marie Gothein, the wife of the historian and sociologist Eberhard Gothein already alluded to. Gothein's two-volume *William Wordsworth, Sein Leben. Seine Werke, Seine Zeitgenossen* (1893) consists of a biography (374 pages) and an anthology (178 pages). The poems are in translation and all reproduce the formal arrangement of the originals. She insists that Wordsworth's reputation in Germany is wholly inadequate; and portrays him as a type of the perpetual outsider. The public is for the most part ignorant of Wordsworth, do not understand his work, and do not appreciate the translations of his poetry (ibid., v). She blames Byron as the originator of a prejudice against a poet who, as Ranke described him, was 'durch und durch englisch', 'English through and through', and thus very difficult to translate (ibid., iii). Here she makes it clear that the word 'translate' means both the literal act of moving from language to language, and the problem of translating from culture to culture. Behind this lies the bold step of an implicit criticism of Goethe; in this respect, Gothein herself assumes the role of an outsider. L. A. Willoughby summarized the situation:

> Goethe's attitude to his English contemporaries had been prejudiced by the hostility of [Byron's] *English Bards and Scotch Reviewers*, and Byron's letter from Ravenna . . . confirmed Goethe in his opinions: 'You do not know, perhaps,' Byron mocked, 'that this gentleman [Wordsworth] is the greatest of all poets past, present, and to come . . . his principal publication is entitled *Peter Bell* which he had withheld from the public for one and twenty years – to the irreparable loss

of all those who died in the interim – and will have no opportunity of reading it before the resurrection.' And not all the efforts of Freiligrath to popularise Wordsworth in Germany . . . have been able to eradicate the animosity of this judgement. (Willoughby 1938, 434–5)

Gothein undoubtedly overstates her case in relation to the sparseness of Wordsworth's reception in Germany. If we turn for a moment to Alois Brandl's *Samuel Taylor Coleridge und die englische romantik* (1886), we can appreciate that Wordsworth was certainly by no means marginalized in his German reception as Gothein appeared to need him to be. Brandl, who went on to discuss the relative merits of Wordsworth and Byron in an essay of 1896, describes Wordsworth as 'The great bard' who played a major role in founding English Romanticism. He was an enemy of the inequalities perpetuated by 'fashionable society':

> He had, moreover, what Southey had not, that which Coleridge especially required from the influence of a friend – firmness of character . . . Wordsworth had grown up among mountains and lakes, and had directly imbibed their quiet grandeur. Coleridge was the ivy which at last found the oak. (Brandl 1887, 164)

Wordsworth's poetry, he states, impressed Coleridge 'by the absence of all forced diction and imagery', in comparison with which, Coleridge's transcendentalism was more ambitious, but less healthy. No German reader would be left in any doubt of Wordsworth's merits. It should also be noted that he is aware of Cotterill's work, referencing the latter's interpretation of *The Ancient Mariner*, and no doubt also absorbing something of Cotterill's passion for Wordsworth.

Richard Wülker's *Gedichte der Englischen Literatur* of 1896 was equally unambiguous on Wordsworth's status. In the first reference to him he is linked to Byron as a major poet of nature in English, and this is confirmed in the section devoted to a review of his life and work. Wordsworth is then subsequently referred to frequently as England's 'first poet' of nature, a deeply philosophical and religiously devout writer 'of the highest rank': 'William Wordsworth steht als philosophischer Naturdichter an erster Stelle in der englischen Literatur' (Wülker 1896, 469). It is true that once Wülker moves on to the second generation of Romantic poets, he spends more time on Byron and Shelley than all the others put together, but this is not done at the expense of Wordsworth's reputation. Published shortly after Gothein's book, Wülker's *Gedichte* is a clear indicator of the status of Wordsworth in Germany during the time that Gothein was researching and writing her biography of this 'neglected' poet.

A brief consideration of Gothein's life will show that the marginalized Wordsworth she chooses to describe may in part be explained by the fact that she, like the politically radicalized and exiled poet Freiligrath, is only too happy to identify with a writer who can be perceived as a kindred spirit (Gothein 1893 I, iv).

Marie Gothein was born Marie Luise Schröter in 1863. She first met Eberhard Gothein, ten years her senior, while she was at private school in Breslau where he was teaching. They married in 1885. Unable to participate in formal education she took full advantage of her husband's willingness to tutor her. If there had been a brief period in late eighteenth-century Germany when some women had been able to challenge their traditional role in society, the influence of the Romantics (most notably Schiller, Fichte and Humboldt), ensured that this was destined not to last very long into the nineteenth century, when the 'docility' of women was confirmed to be a major social virtue (Brown 2005, 11). Gothein was highly gifted, and possessed an impressive aptitude for languages. As we have seen, Eberhard Gothein was particularly exercised by the fear that German society was in imminent danger of fragmenting along class lines; his response was to attempt to bring together representatives of the old leadership and bourgeoisie with the evolving world of an industrial society and capitalist economy. The fact that he encouraged his wife's academic ambitions, however, did not result in Marie accepting his belief in the need for compromise in the face of modernity. In her History of Gardening (1914), *Geschichte der Gartenkunst*, she comments that the publication of Jacob von Falk's *The Garden: Its Art and History* in 1884 'coincided with a phase of empty and meaningless art' (Gothein 1928, ix). She was referring here to the *Biedermeier* complacency she saw attacked by writers like Gottfried Keller (1819–90), then by Fontane and Storm, and by Marie von Ebner-Eschenbach (1830–1916), whose *Das Gemeindekind* (1887) includes a feminist theme woven into a story that depicts a paternalist society dominated by materialism and class prejudice (Finney 2000, 319).

As an outsider in the exclusively male dominated world of formal education, it was inevitable that a woman of Gothein's abilities should find the intellectual environment of her husband claustrophobic. She was attracted to the cynicism reflected in the writings of Nietzsche and Schopenhauer; she wrote on religion and poetry, enthusiastically researching and translating the English Romantics, in particular Wordsworth, but also Keats, Shelley, Burns and Elizabeth Browning. She learnt Sanskrit and translated Rabindranath Tagore. In Wordsworth's letters to Sir George Beaumont, Gothein understood at once Wordsworth's notion of garden design as a form of poetry. Wordsworth, she writes, requires that this kind of poet 'should weave into one sympathetic whole the joy of every living being, of men and children, birds and beasts, hills, rivers, trees, and flowers . . . Nature must take entire charge, so that everything we do is suited to her beauty' (Gothein 1914 II, 407).

Gothein combined an encyclopaedic programme of reading with an impressionistic approach to her work that stands in striking contrast to her husband's economically grounded scholarship. Eberhard's move to Heidelberg in 1904 gave Gothein the opportunity to absorb a cosmopolitan cultural atmosphere dominated by Max and Marianne Weber, Ernst Troeltsch, George and Camilla Jellinek, Georg Lukács, Karl Mannheim, Emil Lederer and Eugen Leviné. She travelled widely across Europe, and made frequent use of the British Museum on her visits to England. Among the academics she met was William Knight, who had founded the Wordsworth Society in 1880. He helped her gain access to manuscript material for her biography of the poet. In the *Geschichte der Gartenkunst* she notes with approval the decision of 'Swanley Agricultural College' in Kent (properly 'Horticultural' College) to admit women students in 1891; the college was the first of its kind anywhere to do so (Morrow 1969). She herself, however, saw female emancipation in a more abstract light, and not as a direct challenge to the traditional role of men in society. She had always been an outsider. Quite apart from her career as a writer, she was (with Eberhard) a member of the *Wander-Vögel* generation of hikers, and a sportswoman (she was among the first to take up skiing). Her biography of Wordsworth includes a lyrical account of walking and climbing in the Lake District, describing the views from Scafell and Helvellyn (Gothein 1893 I, 3). Wordsworth, the poet of nature, the youthful political renegade, ridiculed by reviewers and other poets, who had to wait until middle age before his genius was properly recognized by his compatriots, was a poet with whom Gothein found it very easy to identify.

The ten chapters of Gothein's biography of Wordsworth divide the poet's life into the period of childhood, student years and the French Revolution, Racedown and Alfoxden, the *Lyrical Ballads* and Germany, Dove Cottage, marriage and the political poetry of the war period, Wordsworth's travels, Wordsworth at the height of his creative powers, religion and politics in old age, tours on the continent and in Ireland, and the final years. Like all the German Wordsworthians she is fascinated by the political strand in his life, relating it to the way German society and culture have evolved. Equally she is fascinated by the poet-philosopher of nature, who appears to rise above matters of immediate political expediency. Just as Jacobsen's generation had been powerfully influenced by the English Reviews on the subject of the 'new English poetry', so this later generation of German writers were influenced by the Victorian Wordsworth described by William Knight, Matthew Arnold, and others. Arnold's seminal anthology of 1879 set *The Excursion* firmly to one side in keeping with his insistence that the didactic, political Wordsworth was inferior to the lyrical poet of nature. Knight's three-volume *Life* of 1889 praises *The Excursion* primarily for the way it offers solace through nature for a politically disillusioned generation.

Gothein begins her biography by insisting that even though Wordsworth came to be known early on as part of a group of poets, the 'Lake School' ('Seeschule'), he is best understood as a poet who stands alone, for whom no 'label' is appropriate. His philosophy, she later explains, 'is mirrored in his perception of nature' ('ist in seiner Naturauffassung enthalten'), and thus constantly shifts between different perceptions of God (Gothein 1893 I, 219). In *The Excursion* he will reflect monotheism, dualism or pantheism, depending on where he is led by his consuming sense of 'the rich life of nature' ('dem reichen Leben der Natur'). On several occasions she notes that there are striking similarities in this respect between Goethe and Wordsworth, regretting the fact that Goethe seemed to set his face against appreciating what Wordsworth was doing (ibid., 219–20). Wordsworth the outsider was not a systematic philosopher, his commitment to nature made that inevitable, but if he had a 'philosophy', it was built around ancient Greek wisdom: 'His ideal is the stoic wise man who, raised above all external coincidences, keeps his mind free of the stormy waves of passion and joy in proud independence' (ibid., 221). This leads her to identify Wordsworth's invocation to 'wise passiveness' (in 'Expostulation and Reply') as a key facet of his belief system.

Gothein's selection of extracts from *The Prelude* and *The Excursion* for her Anthology illustrate the influence on her of Knight and Arnold. She quotes five extracts from *The Prelude*, beginning with Book VIII, lines 468–75, a celebration of home-land, '*Ihr Heimatfluren! . . .*':

> Dear native Region, whereso'er shall close
> My mortal course, there will I think on you;
> Dying, will cast on you a backward look:
> Even as this setting sun (albeit the Vale
> Is no where touched by one memorial gleam)
> Doth with the fond remains of his last power
> Still linger, and a farewell lustre sheds
> On the dear mountain-tops where first he rose.
>
> (Wordsworth 1979, 299)

This is followed by the passage from Book I describing how the seemingly simple act of stealing a boat as a child to row out on to the lake at night turns into a profound experience of the mysterious presence of nature. Her third extract is from Book V, the child of Winander, a passage that tells of an intense communion with nature:

> . . . a gentle shock of mild surprise
> Has carried far into his heart the voice
> Of mountain torrents; or the visible scene
> Would enter unawares into his mind,
> With all its solemn imagery . . .

(Ibid., 173)

The fourth extract is a long passage from Book XIV, Wordsworth's dedication of thanks to his sister Dorothy, to his wife Mary, and to Coleridge, beginning at line 232.

> Child of my parents! Sister of my soul!
> Thanks in sincerest verse have been elsewhere
> Poured out for all the early tenderness
> Which I from thee imbibed . . .

(Ibid., 471)

Sixty-nine lines are revised into 56 of German verse celebrating (with that passing reference to 'Tintern Abbey') Dorothy, Coleridge, and Mary, the 'inmate' of his heart (l.269), describing how each helped to reveal to him the power and beauty of nature. As the line count indicates, Gothein is prepared to edit and adapt in her attempt to present a Wordsworth who is both manifestly an English poet, but an English poet for whom her German readers may feel a sense of recognition as he writes about love of homeland, and how immersing himself in the natural world has been a source of wisdom for him. The final extract, lines 105 to 121 from Book XI (wrongly attributed in Gothein to Book IX), has already been discussed at the end of Chapter 5.

Her choice of passages from *The Excursion* is concerned primarily with philosophical reflection and reveal little of the poem's engagement with political issues. The exception to this is the first of the four passages she selects (Book IX ll.293–309), where Wordsworth longs for a time when universal education will foster national unity. The State, 'prizing knowledge as her noblest wealth', should ensure that all children be taught 'The rudiments of letters':

> . . . and inform
> The mind with moral and religious truth,
> Both understood and practised, – so that none,
> However destitute, be left to droop
> By timely culture unsustained; or run
> Into a wild disorder; or be forced
> To drudge through a weary life without the help
> Of intellectual implements and tools;
> A savage horde among the civilised,
> A servile band among the lordly free!

(Wordsworth 2007, 283)

> *Gleich wilden Horden unter Bürgern lebend,*
> *Gleich einer Sklavenbande unter Freien!*

(ll.308–9)

Her second choice comes from Book IV (ll.1056–75), describing how the human soul possesses the ability to rescue the mind from the most extreme 'oppressions of despair'. The centre piece is a description of the transforming effect of moonlight on the landscape:

> As the ample moon,
> In the deep stillness of a summer even
> Rising behind a thick and lofty grove,
> Burns, like an unconsuming fire of light,
> In the green trees; and, kindling on all sides
> Their leafy umbrage, turns the dusky veil
> Into a substance glorious as her own . . .
>
> (Ibid., 159)

The opening lines of Book IX in which the Wanderer assigns 'An *active* Principle' to all things, 'Whate'er exists hath properties that spread/Beyond itself, communicating good,/A simple blessing . . .' (689 ll.10–12) follow this (she adapts the passage for her readers by omitting the second line: 'Thus calmly spake the venerable sage'). Her fourth passage is the description of sunset by the lake from Book IX (ll.590–608). This illustrates the importance of poetry understood as an inclusive form of expression:

> Already had the sun,
> Sinking with less than ordinary state,
> Attained his western bound; but rays of light –
> Now suddenly diverging from the orb
> Retired behind the mountain-tops or veiled
> By the dense air – shot upwards to the crown
> Of the blue firmament . . .
>
> (Ibid., 292)

This might be described as a Caspar David Friedrich moment, concluding with a statement that in nature (the sunset being reflected in the lake) we may perceive the unity of all things, '. . . was am Himmel sich entfaltet, spiegelt/Die feuchte Tiefe in erhabner Einheit', 'That which the heavens displayed, the liquid deep/Repeated; but with unity sublime!' (ll.607–8). Arguably Gothein does not make fully clear the significance of Wordsworth's reference to the lake as the 'liquid deep'. She also passes over Wordsworth's device of having the sun set 'with less than ordinary state' in line 591, in order to make the burst of light which comes from behind the mountain with renewed energy all the more dramatic. For 'less' in line 591, we have 'mehr' (more'):

> *Schon hat die Sonne*
> *Mit mehr als der gewohnten Pracht im Sinken*
> *Des Westens Saum berührt . . .*

Gothein includes 108 items in her anthology, in which most of Wordsworth's range is represented. She groups sonnets of different kinds (to Liberty, and Miscellaneous), she has a separate section for 'Lucy-Lieder', for poems dedicated to specific people, and, as we have seen, towards the end offers extracts from *The Prelude* and *The Excursion*. The way in which she translates 'Tintern Abbey' is characteristic of her intentions. While Wordsworth clearly remains of value to her as a peculiarly English poet, in her act of translation she does seek to Germanize him to the point where her readership may be drawn to meet him. Gothein's version of 'Tintern Abbey' ends with a question mark:

> *Wirst du nicht vergessen,*
> *Wie nach viel Wanderungen, vielen Jahren,*
> *Die fern ich war, mir diese steilen Klippen,*
> *Die grüne Landschaft rings noch teurer waren*
> *Um ihrer selbst, meher noch um deinetwillen?*

(Gothein 1893 II, 20)

Wordsworth's final lines in this poem are affirmative. The fact that Dorothy is with him in this landscape endorses their relationship. When she comes to remember the experience in the future, perhaps in times of difficulty, 'If solitude, or fear, or pain, or grief,/Should be thy portion . . .' (ll.144–5), she will experience a degree of healing through the remembrance of the landscape and her brother; and he concludes in the lines translated by Gothein above:

> Nor wilt thou then forget,
> That after many wanderings, many years
> Of absence, these steep woods and lofty cliffs,
> And this green pastoral landscape, were to me
> More dear, both for themselves, and for thy sake.

(Wordsworth 1992, 120)

Gothein introduces a wistful note of doubt into these lines. The suggestion is not that Dorothy will remember with joy the 'pastoral landscape', but that there is a possibility she might forget. Wordsworth's 'Nor wilt thou then forget' has been translated as 'Won't you forget . . .?' from which grows the terminating question mark. This has the effect of changing Wordsworth's poem into something more akin to a melancholy statement of a kind only too familiar in the German Romantic tradition:

> *Ich bin bei dir, du seist auch noch so ferne,*
> *Du bist mir nah!*
> *Die Sonne sinkt, bald leuchten mir die Sterne.*
> *O wärst du da!*

I am with you; however far away you may be, you are near me. The sun is setting, soon the stars will be shining down on me. If only you were here!

(Goethe, *Nähe des Geliebten*, in Forster 1957, 223)

Gothein does have a political agenda, and it becomes clear in her Introduction to volume one. Against the background of the volatile European political situation in the 1890s, she considers reasons for a renewed interest in England. You might do worse, she suggests, than study one of the greatest patriotic nature poets that England has produced, one whom Lappenberg, a historian of the English, admired, and whom Ranke is not ashamed to mention (Gothein 1893 I, iv). Equally, however, she shares her country's anxiety about the future of Germany as it finds itself surrounded by increasingly hostile nations. Her response to this threat (of which England is a part) is characteristically expressed through a reference to language as the bedrock of national identity. Translation, in this context, as Robert C. Young has argued, is the first step towards the subjugation of national identity: 'The close links between colonization and translation begin not with acts of exchange, but with violence and appropriation, of "deterritorialization"' (Young 2003, 140–1). Gothein alludes to a prophesy by De Quincey that the English language would colonize the world in the next 150 years, with the result that everyone would be reading *The*

Excursion with the ease and regularity that they now read Shakespeare (Gothein 1893 I, iv–v). Gothein is referring to a passage from De Quincey's essay on Wordsworth first published in *Tait's* Magazine in 1839, and subsequently in his *Reminiscences of the English Lake Poets*, where he claims that the English language is conquering the world: 'Even the German and the Spanish will inevitably sink before it; perhaps within 100 or 150 years' (De Quincey 1961, 111). Learning more about the English and their language is therefore important, and Gothein explains that she describes not only Wordsworth in her book, but also 'the cultural history of the English people. (Gothein 1893 I, vi). In this context we should remember that in the late 1890s at Freiberg, Eberhard Gothein's predecessor, Max Weber, was arguing that Germany should do all that was required of it to become a powerful nation state. Fulbrook comments that at this time 'Imperialism became a cultural given' (Fulbrook 2004, 149).

Bearing this political context in mind, we can now consider further the Wordsworthian persona that emerges from Gothein's Biography and Anthology. She mentions George Eliot as an inspirational source for her study of Wordsworth and English culture, but by far her most important contact was William Knight, founder of the Wordsworth Society in 1880. Knight belonged to a substantial British critical coterie of whom the most influential members were Leslie Stephen and Edward Caird. Others involved were Stopford A. Brooke, John Campbell Shairp, and Aubrey De Vere. It was this group that Matthew Arnold had particularly in mind when he launched his attack on 'Wordsworthians' in his 'Wordsworth' essay of 1888 (Arnold 1970, 366–85). Arnold caricatured the Wordsworthians as pious bores, people who did as Ruskin claimed he had done, 'use[d] Wordsworth as a daily text-book from youth to age, and lived, moreover, in all essential points according to the tenor of his teaching' (Gill 1998, 216). 'Wordsworth's poetry', Arnold countered, 'is great because of the extraordinary power with which Wordsworth feels the joy offered to us in nature …' For Arnold, any notion of an ethical system based on Wordsworth's poetry, described by Stephen as 'a scientific system of thought' by which we might live, was anathema (Arnold 1970, 381, 378). Ruskin, notwithstanding his personal admiration for the poet's teaching, was similarly scornful of the devotional excesses of the 'Wordsworthians', and for this reason welcomed Arnold's choice of poems in the 1879 Anthology.

Gothein casts Wordsworth in the role of sage and seer, a patriotic poet dedicated to the beauties of nature and the innocence of childhood. Her reading of Knight's edition of the poems and his biography (1888–9) will have confirmed the belief held by Knight and nineteenth-century English Wordsworthians that the poetry did indeed constitute a series of teachings by which one could live.

In her Introduction, Gothein emphasizes that a major problem in establishing the importance of Wordsworth for a German readership is the one of translating him. As a linguist she perceived a fundamental disjunction between the 'short and striking' effect of an English monosyllabic line, and the sound of 'German compounds'. The problem is made worse in Wordsworth by his 'strange mixture of intended simplicity and abstract philosophy'. His work possesses a 'poetic beauty and power of original expression' that is endemic to the language in which he writes (Gothein 1893 I, vi–vii). Gothein could offer her readers an English Wordsworth in the Biography, but when it came to the Anthology, she faced the same problems as all of her predecessors. Her personal agenda, as an isolated female scholar working in the unpredictable cultural and political atmosphere of late nineteenth-century Germany, coupled with her decision to translate the subject text's formal arrangement as well as its sentiment, resulted in a now familiar process of compromise. She appropriates and manipulates her source text, while still offering it as an alien presence that challenges the cultural orthodoxies of the society in which her target readership lives.

She concludes the biography with a free translation of the final 15 lines of Arnold's 'Memorial Verses' to Wordsworth (1850). Two important characteristics are evident from the first four lines. First, Gothein affirms Arnold's claim that Wordsworth is unique, and thus superior to both Goethe and Byron. Second, by removing Arnold's reference to Europe and in consequence to a sense of specific political issues by which poetic worth might be judged, she claims an a-political status for the poet. Arnold writes:

> Time may restore us in his course
> Goethe's sage mind and Byron's force;
> But where will Europe's latter hour
> Again find Wordsworth's healing power?
> Others will teach us how to dare,
> And against fear our breast to steel;
> Others will strengthen us to bear —
> But who, ah! Who, will make us feel?
> The cloud of mortal destiny,
> Others will front it fearlessly —
> But who, like him, will put it by?
>
> Keep fresh the grass upon his grave
> O Rotha, with thy living wave!
> Sing him thy best! For few or none
> Hears thy voice right, now he is gone.

(Arnold 1986, 139)

Gothein's translation (rendered line for line into English) reads:

> Time creates in its course
> Anew Goethe's wisdom, Bryon's strength,
> But when will afresh in late hours,
> Soothingly, Wordsworth's power be felt?
> Because others show us how to dare,
> To defend ourselves against weak fear,
> And others strengthen us while bearing;
> But who is going to teach us to feel?
> The cloud that is our mortality,
> Others brave it combatively,
> But who has liberated us from it?
>
> Let Rotha, your damp waves
> Swell the grass on his grave.
> Sing him your best, because like him
> No one will hear your voice any more.

(Gothein 1893 I, 368)

Andreas Baumgartner

Everybody was in good spirits now ... For the next hour was likely to be a jolly one. Not a soul felt any qualms before it, and it even promised occasion for entertainment and mischief. This was English, with Candidate Modersohn, a young philologian who had been on trial for a few weeks . . . There was little prospect, however, of his being re-engaged. His classes were much too entertaining.

Mann 1999ii, 586–7

Four years after Gothein's *Life and Work* of Wordsworth was published, Andreas Baumgartner produced a very much shorter book. We have seen how the translation of foreign literature was being driven to a significant degree by the expanding market for educational books. Baumgartner was a teacher and publisher of educational literature, and his Preface makes it clear that our 'better appreciation' of Wordsworth is on the one hand aided by the anthology being in parallel text format, presenting the poetry in German in the traditional way with attention to formal equivalence. As a linguist, however, he explains that the translations can do no more than convey an impression of the content of the poems; they will not be able to reproduce their beauty. The translation of a lyrical piece should adopt a lyrical mode, but this will have a 'beauty and music' of its own, rather than of the original. From the third and final paragraph of this brief Preface it becomes clear that he hopes his parallel text will encourage his readers to learn English.

The 12 poems chosen are 'We are Seven', 'Anecdote for Fathers', 'The Childless Father', 'There was a boy', 'I wandered lonely as a cloud', 'The Solitary Reaper', 'The Highland Girl', 'The Reverie of Poor Susan', 'She dwelt among th'untrodden ways', 'I travell'd among unknown men', 'The Tables Turned', and 'The Idiot Boy'. For the ubiquitous 'We are Seven', he uses Gothein's translation alongside Wordsworth's 1815 version of the poem. He is therefore not concerned to produce a precise rendering of the original, rather a German version which 'corrects' the metre of verse one.

The notes to Baumgartner's short biography of Wordsworth which accompanies the poetry bear witness to his extensive reading of British poets along with his reading of secondary material. The list includes Eduard Engel's *History of English Literature* (1882), F. W. H. Myers's *Wordsworth* (1881), and T. H. Ward's *English Poets* (1880) which had a General Introduction by Matthew Arnold and included material by Dean Church; he refers to Grosart's *Prose Works of William Wordsworth* (1876), and makes frequent use of George Brimley's *Essays* (first published in 1858, then in 1860 and 1882). Henry James Nicoll's *Landmarks of English Literature* (1883) is referenced on several occasions, as is James Logie Robertson's *A History of English Literature for Secondary Schools* (1894), Swinburne's *The Nineteenth Century* (1884), and three collections of essays by Aubrey de Vere published in the late 1880s. He also used Christopher Wordsworth's two-volume *Memoir* of 1851, while Arnold's Anthology of 1872 was a major source for the poems; he quotes from the Preface several times. He also expresses his debt to Gothein. One notable absentee from Baumgartner is William Knight; Arnold was clearly preferred. Of all the sources Baumgartner refers to, he appears particularly interested in the essays of Aubrey De Vere (1814–1902). He footnotes the *Recollections*, published the same year that his own book appeared, 1897. It is also possible to detect his use of two earlier publications, the two-volume *Essays, Chiefly on Poetry* (1887), and *Essays, Chiefly Literary and Ethical* (1889).

Baumgartner's book also provides evidence that there continued to be a market specifically for Wordsworth outside the educational sphere at this time in Germany. As well as the 'school' edition, Baumgartner's publishers decided that it was worth bringing out a version that consisted solely of the poetry, excluding the accompanying Preface and biography. Both versions were published in the same year.

Baumgartner's Wordsworth, although clearly shaped by Arnold's Preface to the 1872 *Poems*, is also De Vere's Wordsworth. De Vere's accounts of his meetings with Wordsworth in later life, and his correspondence with Sarah Coleridge on the virtues of the poet's late work clearly fascinated Baumgartner. He was reading of a Wordsworth who experienced a duality of 'mind' and 'heart': '. . . in Wordsworth's poetry it is impossible to say whether the mind or the heart is the predominant power' (De Vere 1889, 325). 'The wisdom and Truth of Wordsworth's poetry,' De Vere wrote, resides in his ability to combine 'Nature' with 'high philosophic thought and high moral principal' (De Vere 1887 I, 175). The tension between reason and imagination had continued to have a profound influence on cultural and political life in Germany throughout the nineteenth century; publicizing Wordsworth's response to this issue seemed increasingly worth the time and effort involved in research, 'translation', and publication. The Wordsworth Baumgartner is seeking to pass on to German teenagers in the 1890s is a poet given to meditation and submission to the rhythms of nature, one who also reflects a tension between the ideal of art, and its manifestation in a world of material realities. As De Vere put it, 'The woodland reed-pipe, besides those notes which charmed the shepherds and the nymphs, had its mystic strain . . . ' (De Vere 1887, 177). More than this, Wordsworth embodied the definition of a poet he gave to Lady Beaumont in a letter of 1807, quoted by Baumgartner in the book (and no doubt repeated frequently to his students): 'Every great poet is a teacher' (Baumgartner 1897, 31). Arnold's credentials as an educationalist will have been well known to him, and at the end of the book he translates into German Arnold's affirmation from the Preface to his Anthology that '[Wordsworth] is one of the very chief glories of English poetry; and by nothing is England so glorious as by her poetry' (ibid., 58).

Baumgartner attempts to deal with the problem of Goethe's dislike of Wordsworth by referring his students to Professor J. R. Seeley's work on Goethe (1894), noting his ability to find common ground in the genius of Shakespeare, Goethe, and Wordsworth (ibid., 58). In the early years of the twentieth century, however, the vexed issue of Wordsworth's relationship to Byron in the German canon continues to command attention.

Francis H. Pughe

'Wordsworth as an artist is perhaps the least understood of our great poets.'
Landor in Pughe 1902, 41

Henry Cotterill was by no means the only Englishman publishing material on Wordsworth in Germany at this time. Francis H. Pughe produced a 167-page monograph, *Byron und Wordsworth*, in 1902. Pughe's sources replicate those of Gothein and Baumgartner. His intention is to establish Wordsworth as – at the very least – a poet of equal weight to Byron, and also to suggest that his relative overshadowing is unjustified. He sets both poets in the context of English Romanticism, emphasizing the profound variety of work within what is anything but a unified aesthetic. Wordsworth is shown to have an immense range of poetic expression compared to Byron; German readers should realize that Wordsworth's preoccupations – nature, humanity, religion, and love of country – have far more to offer than Byron's cynicism, albeit he too can write movingly of nature.

Pughe divides his monograph into seven chapters: Wordsworth's influence on Byron; the degrees of cosmopolitanism and nationalism to be found in both poets; Byron, Wordsworth, and antiquity; Byron, Wordsworth, and Romanticism; Nature in Byron and Wordsworth; style and technique in Byron and Wordsworth; and Byron and Wordsworth as poets and thinkers.

Compared to any of the work so far considered, Pughe's is the first to present its material, and discuss its evidence, in a way that is recognizably 'academic' in the later, twentieth-century sense. Gothein's biography is referenced as an important source early on, but Pughe is working in a critical terrain that makes Gothein read like a *belle lettrist*. Attention to the 'life' alongside the 'work' is markedly absent; the context here is provided by a deconstructed literary historical idea of English Romanticism. Academically analytic as this is, it is clear that a perceived crisis in German cultural and political affairs is being addressed in the course of the identification of Wordsworth's superiority to Byron.

In the first chapter Pughe develops a broadly based discussion of the differences between the poets, making the point that Wordsworth was far more revolutionary and innovative in his approach to poetry. This is evident from *Lyrical Ballads*, both in the poetry and the Preface. Byron, by comparison, was essentially a neo-classicist, viewing innovation with suspicion and scorn. Wordsworth's poetry is rooted in his relationship to the natural world, producing work that Byron could not begin to rival. Wordsworth's persona is 'plain, patriarchal', he is known for his 'orderly moral conduct' which engenders a 'wise passiveness . . . in marked contrast to the unsettled spirit which pervades Byron's life as well as his poetry' (ibid., 6–7).

The contradictions in Byron make him interesting, but using Nichol's assessment of him in *English Men of Letters* (1888), Pughe makes it clear why Byron's poetry is flawed:

> It was thus natural for him to pose as the spokesman . . . of two orders of society – as a peer, and as a poet in revolt. Sincere in both, he could never forget the one character in the other . . . Byron's heroes all rebel against the associative tendency of the nineteenth century; they are self-worshippers at war with society; but most of them come to bad ends. (Ibid., 4)

Against this he sets the serenity of the philosopher poet, quoting the reference to 'wise passiveness' from 'Expostulation and Reply' that Gothein had emphasized:

> The eye it cannot chuse but see,
> We cannot bid the ear be still;
> Our bodies feel, where'er they be,
> Against, or with our will.

> Nor less I deem that there are powers,
> Which of themselves our minds impress,
> That we can feed this mind of ours,
> In a wise passiveness.

> (Wordsworth 1992, 108)

Pughe is very aware of the fact that the relationship between active engagement in day-to-day life and politics, and life in art, was a debate which had a particular resonance in Germany. Wordsworth is shown to possess what for many was a highly valued Germanic frame of mind, an 'affinity to introspective thinking' ('beschaulichen Nachdenkens') (Pughe 1902, 6).

The issues that lie beyond Pughe's immediate scholarly context are even more apparent when he goes on to emphasize the way Wordsworth's love of nature enables him to see a harmonious order beneath the troubled surface of everyday life. Wordsworth's poetry has a mission to heal and to console; he is stable where Byron is volatile, vain, and out of step with his time. He was everything Wordsworth was not, and, using Nichol as an authority once again, we are left in no doubt that what Wordsworth lacked compared to Byron made him the better poet:

> [Byron's] vanity and pride were perpetually struggling for the mastery, and though he thirsted for popularity, he was bent on compelling it; so he warred with the literary impulse of which he was the child. (Ibid., 9)

The hallmark of Romanticism as a movement was its variety; it was this that Byron could not recognize or accept. The differences between Coleridge, Campbell, Southey, Crabbe and Keats are explored over several pages, Pughe suggesting that Wordsworth, for all his 'wise passiveness', was not afraid to moralize; he is thus in accord with Matthew Arnold's dictum that poetry should be 'a criticism of life . . . a decorative expression in rhythmical language of abstract truth about life' (ibid., 13). He later includes Wordsworth's comment to Lady Beaumont that Baumgartner had welcomed, adding a further sentence: 'Every great poet is a teacher. I wish to be considered as a teacher, or nothing' (ibid., 15). This is what lies at the heart of Pughe's case for the greatness of Wordsworth, though he allows it can be difficult when, as a consequence, the poet seems to become overly engaged with his own personality. He refers to Church's comment that Wordsworth 'made himself avowedly the subject of his own thinking' (ibid., 18), but Pughe attempts to allay this criticism by first unleashing a brief barrage of quotations from the poet, each of which emphasizes the benign consequences of his tendency to introspection along with confirming the appropriateness of his philosophy for the present day: 'The child is father of the man, The light that never was on sea or land, the harvest of a quiet eye, Thoughts that do often lie too deep for tears, We murder to dissect, The weary weight of this unintelligible world (sic)' (ibid., 16) He then quotes from the 'Ode to Duty' to show that Wordsworth himself is not unaware of the problem:

> I, loving freedom and untried,
> No sport of every random gust,
> Yet being to myself a guide,
> Too blindly have reposed my trust . . .
>
> (Ibid., 19)

In chapter three Pughe presents his reader with a very different Wordsworth from either the nature lover or the patriot philosopher. Appealing to the German reader versed in Goethe's understanding of the way Germany's cultural heritage had evolved, Wordsworth is revealed as a poet who owes much to the classical tradition. In this respect, he is developing the thesis that Gothein proposed with respect to Wordsworth's indebtedness to Greek philosophy, particularly the Stoics. His classicism underpins the qualities he should be most valued for. Quoting Myers, Pughe affirms that Wordsworth once more proves to be a poet of far greater substance than the contradictory Byron: 'Wordsworth, whenever he is great as an artist, has the self control, the clear outline and the sane simplicity of classic art' (ibid., 41).

This leads Pughe to discuss poems not normally included in the established nineteenth-century German Wordsworth canon, most particularly, *Laodamia*:

> And thus it was that the study of Vergil, and especially of Vergil's solemn picture of the Underworld prompted in Wordsworth's mind the most majestic of his poems (*Laodamia*), his one great utterance on heroic love. (Ibid., 41)

Laodamia offers an object lesson in moral firmness and self-control against which Byron looks shorn of purpose. Pughe compares *Laodamia*, *The Excursion*, *The Happy Warrior*, and the *Ode to Duty* with the moral laxity of Byron's *Childe Harold*, *The Giaour*, *Marino Faliero*, *Sardanapalus* and *Don Juan* (ibid., 41).

There is no mistaking Pughe's anxiety about the times in which he lives; and in his concluding remarks he prescribes the study of Wordsworth as a guide to a better future. It is with Nations, he argues, as it is with individuals: we must 'turn away from Byron's negations and scepticism in order to find spiritual enlightenment and moral strength in the religious poets and thinkers' (ibid., 166). It is small wonder, he reminds us, that Mill found in Wordsworth's nature poetry restorative qualities 'that gradually revealed new untarnished sources of joy there for all to share, which revived the tired mind' (ibid., 166–7). If Pughe appears uneasy about the course that events in Europe seem to be taking, the remaining German Wordsworthians to be discussed were in little doubt that war between England and Germany had become inevitable.

8 War Clouds: Wordsworth in Germany 1906–1914

To those who have known Germany, and the manner in which the spirit of the nation has expressed itself in literature for many years back, the events of the War have brought a shock of astonishment and disgust . . .

Fernau 1916, 10–11

In the final years before the outbreak of the First World War, German interest in Wordsworth's life and poetry remained undiminished. The publication in 1906 of Karl Bömig's dissertation, *William Wordsworth im Urteile seiner Zeit*, is further evidence of a well-established academic interest in the poet. Bömig's bibliography reaffirms the extensive availability of English sources, at the centre of which remain Arnold and Knight. Additional material includes Saintsbury's *History of Nineteenth Century Literature* (1896), Morley's *Complete Works of William Wordsworth* (1888), Adams's *The Poet's Praise* (1894), William Wale's Dictionary of Quotations, *What Great Men have said of Great Men* (1902), and Ellis Yarnall's *Wordsworth and the Coleridges* (1899). There are also enough German sources to suggest that interest in Wordsworth in Germany was, if anything, increasing, notably Wülker's *Geschichte der englischen Literatur* (1896), Fels's *The Life and Poems of William Wordsworth* (1875), Matthes's *Naturbeschreibung bei Wordsworth* (1901), and Brunswick's *Wordsworth's Theorie der poetkunst* (1884). Although not included in the bibliography, Bömig references Jacobsen (Bömig 1906, 76). Bömig also used Emil Legouis' book on *The Prelude*, a seminal work on the relationship between Wordsworth's poetry and politics through to 1798, *La Jeunesse de W. Wordsworth* (1896). He also made use of Taine's *Histoire de la Littérature Anglais* (1897). Other German sources include Brandes, Baumgartner, Brandl, Gothein, and Pughe.

Bömig's thesis is a familiar one. Wordsworth is a poet of nature and religion; and as such he has an important role to play for contemporary German readers. Wale's *What Great Men Have Said of Great Men* includes the following entry on Wordsworth from Lytton's 'Intellectual Spirit of the Time':

> Wordsworth is the apostle, the spiritualiser of those who cling to the most idealized part of things that are – Religion and her houses, Loyalty and her monuments – the tokens of the Sanctity which overshadows the past: these are of him, and he of them. (Wale 1902, 476)

Bömig continues to insist that Wordsworth is little-known in Germany, although his subsequent account of his reception tends to contradict his case. He argues that the poet has been ignored because he does not offer poetry that can be easily understood: 'Wordsworth's beauty lies hidden, requires deep thought to be understood, and also lacks excitement and interest', 'Dennoch zeigen einige Werke aus neurer Zeit, wie die von Baumgartner und besonders von Gothein, dass Wordsworth auch einem deutschen Gemüte zugänglich gemacht werden kaun' (Bömig 1906, 83). Baumgartner, and particularly Gothein, have nevertheless shown that Wordsworth's deeply spiritual meanings can be made accessible to the German mind.

Picking up Gothein's reference to Lappenberg's enthusiasm for Wordsworth, he refers to his first meeting with the poet in 1814, and again in 1834 (ibid., 76). He has a good deal to say about Jacobsen's *Briefe*, praising the author's selection of poetry, but criticizing him both for his lack of critical discussion, and his decision to translate into prose (ibid., 77). Bömig takes the tale of 'Herr Kemperhausen's' visit at face value. Among the other German Wordsworthians he mentions are Knebel, who praised *The White Doe of Rylstone*, and Tieck, whom he quotes as saying 'Das ist ein englischer Goethe' (ibid., 78). He also refers to Freiligrath's enthusiasm for Wordsworth, before moving on to discuss his reception in France.

Paying tribute to the few Englishmen who were initially prepared to champion Wordsworth, Crabb Robinson, Coleridge, Southey and Scott, Bömig then relates how his standing gradually increased, as first *Blackwood's Magazine* praised him, then Macaulay, Mill, Bulwer and others began to support him; even Byron, he notes, 'the former derider, came under his influence' (ibid., 86–7). At the end of his account, Bömig's assessment of Wordsworth is very similar to that of Pughe: Wordsworth's poetry possesses a power of healing that is not just exerted on other literature, but on the spirit of the times:

> *Das aber war Wordsworths grösster und sicherster Erfolg, dass seine Dichtungen ihren Zweck erfüllt hatten, dass sie nicht nur auf die Literatur, sondern auf den Geist der Zeit überhaupt einen heilsamen Einfluss ausgeübt hatten; dadurch ist seine Stellung für alle Zeiten in der englischen Literatur gesichert. (Ibid., 88)*

Pughe and Bömig represent a significant advance on earlier nineteenth-century discussions of Wordsworth and the English Romantics in Germany with respect to their analytical engagement with the poetry. This is also the case with Dr Kurt Lienemann's substantial study of 1908, *Die Belesenheit von William Wordsworth*. Lienemann is heavily indebted to Knight, and in addition to Knight's many publications on Wordsworth, he has access to the transactions of the Wordsworth Society. The German reader is presented with what is in effect a 259-page catalogue detailing the range of Wordsworth's reading. The aim of the enterprise is to affirm that Wordsworth was much more than an unassuming, simple nature poet. Drawing heavily on Christopher Wordsworth's *Memoir* of 1851, Crabb Robinson's writings, and on Grosart's edition of the prose, Wordsworth is revealed as widely read in all the English literature that continued to be of such interest to German readers throughout the century. Lappenberg, Henry Paul (*Grundriss der Germanischen Philologie* 1901–9), Jakob Schipper (whose work on German and English philology in the 1880s and early 1900s was translated into English in 1910 as *A History of English Versification*), Moritz Brosch, Alexander Baumgartner and Helene Richter (*Geschichter der Weltlitaratur* 1897), all contributed to Lienemann's project.

Helene Richter's *Geschichte der Englischen Romantik* (1911), is a reminder that Wordsworth could indeed be considered of relatively little importance among what continued to be seen as the major writers of the English Romantic Movement. However, Richter does not adversely criticize Wordsworth; with Coleridge and Keats, he is simply mentioned in passing. Her roll-call of those she considers foremost in this group, however, would no doubt have puzzled an early twentieth-century reader (English and German) let alone a twenty-first-century reader. Her list includes Leigh Hunt, Lamb, Hazlitt, Christopher North (John Wilson), James and Horace Smith, Peacock, Hood, Praed, Crabbe, Cowper, Bowles, Rogers, Campbell and Procter (Richter 1911, 708).

The final example of German writing on Wordsworth to be considered here, is by Felix Güttler. Europe had convinced itself that war was inevitable for several years before its outbreak. Just what that war would entail, of course, was undreamed of, but for many the prospect nevertheless presaged a catastrophe recalling Heine's chilling words written in the period before the outbreak of the 1848 Revolutions: 'A play will be performed in Germany that will make the French Revolution seem like a harmless idyll in comparison' (Heine 1943, 53). Güttler's book of 1914, *Wordsworth's Politische Entwicklung*, was written under the cloud of impending conflict with England. It is divided into six chapters: Wordsworth and the French Revolution; Wordsworth the Republican; Wordsworth the poet of freedom; Wordsworth the High Church Tory; An overview of the condition of English society in the first half of the nineteenth century; and finally, Wordsworth's political socialism.

The contrast between this book and Gothein's *Life and Work* is a profound one. Güttler displays a scholarly rigour that contrasts with Gothein's impressionistic approach to analysis, while the circumstances in which it was written clearly help to establish a very specific agenda. Güttler's story is one that describes the growth of Wordsworth's political maturity; we are led through his youthful enthusiasm for political radicalism, witnessing how the poetry reveals a man who comes to blend his liberal convictions with Christian principals and a love of nature in the course of turbulent times. The end product is a poet whose mature work implicitly puts to shame the war mongering that drives European powers in the early twentieth century.

Güttler's bibliography is substantial compared with any of the previously discussed essays and books with the exception of Lienemann. It adds new names to those already considered doing work on Wordsworth in Germany, including Paul Sanftleben's dissertation on Wordsworth's *The Borderers* (1907), and Thomas Zeiger's essay on Wordsworth's reputation in German Literature (1901). More general literary histories that contextualize Wordsworth include Moritz Brosch's *History of England*, and Alfred Stern's *History of Europe* (1894–1911), already noted but appearing here for the first time in a bibliography. Güttler makes considerable use of Lienemann's work on Wordsworth's reading. He draws also on French texts including Charles Cestre's essay on the French Revolution and English poets (1906), Emile Legouis on *The Prelude*, and Raymond Gourg's book on William Godwin (1908). The source for both poetry and biography is dominated by William Knight, and after that, prominent members of the Wordsworth Society circle: Edward Dowden, H. Herford, Leslie Stephen, W. H. White, and Alexander Grosart. It is indicative of the readership Güttler is targeting that he quotes throughout in English. This is not an exercise in appropriating Wordsworth for a German readership; his intention is rather to put space between himself and this objective. This is what defines the politics of the book.

Wordsworth's 'Political Development' is couched in opposition to the political tradition that in many ways might be thought of as encapsulated by the process of translating and anthologizing foreign language texts in Germany throughout the nineteenth century.

Güttler uses Wordsworth's experience of the French Revolution as a timely reminder that though the seeds of revolt may be sown in the national mind as a result of justifiable resistance to oppression, thereafter that nation may be tempted to cultivate world-conquering ambitions that are fated to end in disaster. In the first chapter, he therefore uses *The Excursion* to set the Solitary's embittered experience of his misplaced faith in the Revolution against Wordsworth's youthful enthusiasm for the spirit of reform, emphasizing his point by quoting from the Ode of 1816, 'Who rises on the banks of Seine' (Güttler 1914, 16). We have moved well away from the familiar track beaten by the anthologies. The Ode is an expression of fear on Wordsworth's part that France's new and reassuring posture after the war masks the unreformed nature of a nation that in reality is still a threat:

> Her love ye hailed – her wrath have felt!
> But she through many a change of form hath gone,
> And stands amidst you now an armèd creature,
> Whose panoply is not a thing put on,
> But the live scales of a portentous nature;
> That, having forced its way from birth to birth,
> Stalk round – abhorred by Heaven, a terror to the Earth!
> (Selincourt 1969, 247)

It is not surprising to find Güttler eager to inform his German readership of Wordsworth's view that France can never be trusted, but he implies a broadening of the moral by then going on to quote from Wordsworth's poem of 1830, 'Presentiments', in which the poet reflects on the possible outcome of impending franchise reform:

> When some great change gives boundless scope
> To an exulting Nation's hope
>   Oft, startled and made wise
> By your low-breathed interpretings,
> The simply-meek foretaste the springs
>   Of bitter contraries.
> (Güttler 1914, 19)

Through Wordsworth's broad reference to 'an exulting Nation's hope', Güttler switches attention from the specificity of Revolutionary France to what may include the imperial ambitions of Germany. The 'Presentiment' becomes that of impending war in the twentieth century.

In chapter two he explores the radicalism expressed in Wordsworth's letters to William Mathews (1791–6), to the Bishop of Llandaff (1793), *Descriptive Sketches* (1793), and the influence on Wordsworth of the rationalist political philosophy of Godwin. From Knight he takes the view that the young poet was never wholeheartedly a radical. Knight claims to be able to find evidence in Wordsworth's writings to confirm that even when his commitment to Revolution was at its most extreme, he had 'a dim perception that there might be another side to it, and that there was something hollow in its aims' (Knight 1889 I, 62).

Chapter three moves Wordsworth forward into the period when England is threatened by invasion and the voice of the radical is fused with that of the patriot. Again, the influence of Knight's biography is evident. Wordsworth retained throughout his belief in the underlying principals of 'liberty, equality, and fraternity', principals 'to which he clung to the last, even when borne back on the full tide of a healthy conservative reaction' (ibid., 70–1). Alongside the war-time sonnets, Güttler turns to Wordsworth's pamphlet of 1809 *The Convention of Cintra*. This is a crucial document in the charting of Wordsworth's political journey; Wordsworth's anger is not occasioned by the fact that his own country had stifled the French Revolution and repressed reform at home, he was angry because England had failed in its duty to wage a war against France dictated by a recognition of the moral imperatives of the situation. Although in *The Excursion* Wordsworth does indeed rehearse once more the conviction that going to war with France in 1793 was wrong, in *The Convention of Cintra* his complaint is that the conduct of the war is being controlled by narrow materialistic ambitions, and also being used as a means for individuals to seek personal aggrandisement. In the political sonnets of these years we may see, with the invocation of the English heroes of the Civil War, Milton, Harrington and Sidney, Wordsworth relocating his radicalism from eighteenth-century France to a seventeenth-century English 'Commonwealthman' tradition. In this he knew he was still at odds with the establishment, as 'Character of the Happy Warrior' (1807) clearly illustrates (Williams 2005, 181–98).

Güttler's reading of this material, textual and biographical, is summed up in the sonnet of 1810, 'O'erweening Statesmen'. It might well be dedicated to the leaders of Germany in the years leading up to 1914:

> O'erweening Statesmen have full long relied
> On fleets and armies, and external wealth:
> But from *within* proceeds a Nation's health;
> Which shall not fail, though poor men cleave with pride
> To the paternal floor; or turn aside,
> In the thronged city, from the walks of gain,
> As being all unworthy to detain
> A Soul by contemplation sanctified.
> There are who cannot languish in this strife,
> Spaniards of every rank, by whom the good
> Of such high course was felt and understood;
> Who to their Country's cause have bound a life
> Erewhile, by solemn consecration, given
> To labour, and to prayer, to nature, and to heaven.
>
> (Güttler 1914, 46)

In a similar vein is 'Emperors and Kings' of 1816:

> Emperors and Kings, how oft have temples rung
> With impious thanksgiving, the Almighty's scorn!
> How oft above their altars have been hung
> Trophies that led the good and wise to mourn
> Triumphant wrong, battle of battle born,
> And sorrow that to fruitless sorrow clung!
>
> (Ibid., 53)

The war mongering of 'O'erweening statesmen', and the 'impious thanksgiving' of 'Emperors and Kings' has replaced the fruits of those who turn 'To labour, and to prayer, to nature, and to heaven' as their guide to understanding what constitutes 'a Nation's health'.

In chapter four, 'Wordsworth the High Church Tory', the poet comes of age. Güttler begins by quoting the poet's celebration of Church and State which opens Book VI of *The Excursion*:

> Hail to the Crown by Freedom shaped – to gird
> An English Sovereign's brow! And to the Throne
> Whereon he sits! Whose deep foundations lie
> In veneration and the People's love,
> Whose steps are equity, whose seat is law.
> – Hail to the State of England! And conjoin
> With this a salutation as devout,
> Made to the Spiritual fabric of her Church;
> Founded in truth; by blood of Martyrdom
> Cemented; by the hands of Wisdom reared
> In beauty of Holiness, with order'd pomp,
> Decent and unreproved. The voice, that greets
> The majesty of both, shall pray for both;
> That, mutually protected and sustained,
> They may endure as long as sea surrounds
> This favoured Land, or sunshine warms her soil.
>
> (Ibid., 60)

'In this enthusiastic hymn to the English State and Church', Güttler writes, 'Wordsworth already appears as a royalist subject and a fervent admirer of his fatherland and its institutions' (ibid., 60). He notes how, as Wordsworth had grown older, his circumstances had improved. He was no longer impoverished, and the patronage of Sir George Beaumont had given him the opportunity 'to appreciate the value of an old-established noble lineage'; he was bound in due course (in *The Excursion*) to lament the passing of 'old merit and honourable things' in the modern world (Güttler 1914, 61; Wordsworth 2007, 256).

Wordsworth is portrayed as a patriot no longer committed to an alien French creed of liberty, equality and fraternity, but to the preservation of the traditions of liberty and the Protestant Christian tradition embedded in England, specifically the tradition of free speech which relies on the freedom of the press. The leaders of the people must earn respect, and Güttler quotes here from Wordsworth's letter to Lord Lonsdale of December 1821:

> A free discussion of public measures through the press I deem the only safeguard of liberty; without it I have neither confidence in kings, parliaments, judges or divines . . . (Güttler 1914, 71)

These sentiments, however, do not predicate a Wordsworth prepared to countenance radical reform, as the lines already quoted from 'Presentiments' have indicated. Güttler stresses how nervous the prospect of Franchise reform made Wordsworth, and the extent to which he argued for the status quo. Quoting once more from Wordsworth's correspondence with Lonsdale in 1821, he explains the poet's argument against Catholic emancipation: it will encourage all the other dissenting groups, creating a situation that will harm, not help the spirit of toleration. The current Protestant religious Establishment of England, Wordsworth insists, is central to the 'propagation of civilisation in our own country' (ibid., 85).

Wordsworth's politics have become essentially a politics of moderation, suspicious of the ambitions of powerful, unchecked statesmen, and deeply anxious about an alienated working class, who, if denied any of the benefits of modern society, could be expected to seek the fall of the State. Güttler no doubt saw parallels here with the ideals of the *Kathedersozialismus* movement to which Eberhard Gothein belonged. Wordsworth's aversion to the human consequences of industrialization, and his commitment to the moral benefits of a rural economy are made clear in chapter five where Güttler quotes from Book IX of *The Excursion*:

> Our Life is turned
> Out of her course, wherever Man is made
> An offering, or a sacrifice, a tool
> Or implement, a passive Thing employed
> As a brute mean, without acknowledgment
> Of common right or interest in the end;
> Used or abused, as selfishness may prompt.
> Say, what can follow for a rational Soul
> Perverted thus, but weakness in all good,
> And strength in evil?
>
>   (Wordsworth 2007, 278)

He quotes at length from Wordsworth's letter of January 1801 to Charles James Fox, in which he lists the measures that are alienating the 'lower orders of society', in particular the 'small independent proprietors of land' otherwise known as 'statesmen'. Ironically, it is the grand 'Statesmen' of the land who through industrialization, tax on postage, work houses, 'houses of industry', soup shops, and a general rise in prices are instigating 'a rapid decay of the domestic affections among the lower orders of society' (Güttler 1914, 106–8). Güttler here incorporates part of the passage from Book VIII of *The Excursion* that Freiligrath had used in *The Rose, Thistle and Shamrock* to show how the core of the social order, family life, was being destroyed by industrialization:

> Lo! In such neighbourhood, from morn to eve,
> The Habitations empty! Or perchance
> The Mother left alone, – no helping hand
> To rock the cradle of her peevish babe;
> No daughters round her, busy at the wheel,
> Or in dispatch of each day's little growth
> Of household occupation; no nice arts
> Of needle-work; no bustle at the fire,
> Where once the dinner was prepared with pride;
> Nothing to speed the day, or cheer the mind;
> Nothing to praise, to teach, or to command!
>
>   (Ibid., 107)

Above all, Wordsworth is portrayed as a passionate opponent of the aggressive nationalism we have in fact seen does surface at times in *The Excursion*. Equally he is credited (more justifiably) with delivering a warning that the leaders of Nations should not allow themselves to be tempted to follow short term gain at the expense of forgetting, or sacrificing, the past and its traditions.

The subtext of Güttler's book is therefore very well served by his choice of Wordsworth's 'The Warning' (1833) as a poem that encapsulates the poet's mature political thinking. 'The Warning' offers a gloomy prognosis following the passing of the Reform Bill in 1832. It might be expected to touch a nerve for German students of cultural history who understood that the destinies of Germany and England were as closely entwined as were their racial roots. The patriotic Briton is one who reveres the historic traditions of his race:

> Whose infant soul was tutored to confide
> In the cleansed faith for which her martyrs died;
> Whose boyish ear the voice of her renown
> With rapture thrilled; whose Youth revered the crown
> Of Saxon liberty that Alfred wore,
> Alfred, dear babe, thy great progenitor.
>
> (Selincourt 1969, 395)

In the passage Güttler quotes, Wordsworth describes what happens if the leaders of a country submit to the pressures of the present without due recourse to the lessons of the past. If responsible leadership is overwhelmed by pressure to make concessions that undermine the traditions of the State, disaster will follow:

> Who shall preserve or prop the tottering Realm?
> What hand suffice to govern the statehelm?
> If in the aims of men the surest test
> Of good or bad (whate'er be sought for or profest)
> Lie in the means required, or ways ordained,
> For compassing the end, else never gained;
> Yet governors and governed both are blind
> To this plain truth, or fling it to the wind;
> If to expedience principle must bow;
> Past, future, shrinking up beneath the incumbent Now;
> If cowardly concession still must feed
> The thirst for power in men who ne'er concede;
> Nor turn aside, unless to shape a way
> For domination at some riper day;
> If generous Loyalty must stand in awe
> Of subtle Treason, in his mask of law,
> Or with bravado insolent and hard,
> Provoking punishment, to win reward;
> If office help the factious to conspire,
> And they who *should* extinguish, fan the fire –
> Then, will the sceptre be a straw, the crown
> Sit loosely, like the thistle's crest of down;
> To be blown off at will, by Power that spares it
> In cunning patience, from the head that wears it.
>
> (Güttler 1914, 79)

Telling as the whole passage is when set in an early twentieth-century context, the crucial lines come towards the end: 'If office help the factious to conspire/And they who *should* extinguish, fan the fire . . .' This is not a situation, in other words, where 'playing politics' is an appropriate response. As always, Wordsworth urges the political Establishment ('office') to proceed in accordance with disinterested moral principles. If not, Government will exacerbate, not resolve, the situation, and the working class, deprived of all hope and aware of the duplicity of their masters, will eventually seize a power it does not know how to use. Wordsworth lays the blame for the impending disaster squarely on the shoulders of those who are in power; a few lines further on he exclaims, 'O for a bridle bitted with remorse/To stop your Leaders in their headstrong course!' (Selincourt 1969, 396). We should be reminded here of the profession of sympathy Wordsworth made for the Chartists to Isabella Fenwick in 1843 (Fenwick 1993, 90).

The general tenor of Wordsworth's anxiety may also instructively apply to the twentieth-century reader. The beginning of the twentieth century has seen an irresponsible, weak leadership drawn into confrontational, opportunistic politics, the result of which will be a war between peoples that history and tradition teaches share a common, Saxon heritage. The sentiment here is a key note for Güttler's thesis on Wordsworth, the one-time revolutionary whose mature politics produce a poetry that teaches the wisdom of freedom attained through respect for the traditional values of Church and State, and temporal authority imbued with Christian virtue. In a section entitled 'Retrospect' which is set at the end of chapter four, 'Wordsworth, the High Church Tory', the situation is summarized thus:

> So then Wordsworth, the former revolutionary, has changed in every aspect; a republican and cosmopolitan has turned into a royalist subject and a shining defender of his fatherland who never tired of loudly proclaiming England's greatness and the excellence of her institutions. Nevertheless, he does not betray his previous ideals and he never wrote against his better insight. ('. . . und er hat nie gegen seine bessere Einsicht geschrieben.') (Güttler 1914, 96)

Five things in particular, Güttler claims, explain what had happened: Wordsworth had matured with age, he had got to know the aristocracy properly, he had learnt from the catastrophe of the French Revolution, he had learnt from the truly patriotic Englishmen around him, and he had learnt to identify with the rural population of his homeland (ibid., 96–7). Though he may have appeared to become reactionary in his old age, on 'the great questions of freedom and tyranny . . . he kept his old enthusiasm until death' (ibid., 97). Above all, Wordsworth had come to recognize the wisdom of having a firm rule of law; a people must be educated towards freedom before it can rule itself: 'Freiheit und Zügellosigkeit sind nicht dasselbe', 'Freedom and self-indulgence are not the same' (ibid., 98).

Güttler begins and ends the book with an appeal to the ideal of peaceful social evolution. Having rehearsed the cautionary tale of the Solitary's engagement with the French Revolution from *The Excursion* in chapter one, he goes on to quote from Book IV where the Wanderer reflects on the advantages enjoyed by modern man, and the way he seems intent on squandering the gifts of enlightenment. The Wanderer assumes the admonishing voice of nature itself in this extract, once more expressing a warning that could apply directly to the war-fixated leaders of European Nations, 'Ye aspire/Rashly, to fall once more':

> Vain-glorious Generation! What new powers
> On you have been conferred? What gifts withheld
> From your Progenitors, have Ye received,
> Fit recompense of new desert? What claim
> Are ye prepared to urge, that my decrees
> For you should undergo a sudden change;
> And the weak functions of one busy day,
> Reclaiming and extirpating, perform
> What all the slowly-moving Years of Time,
> With their untied force, have left undone?

By Nature's gradual processes be taught,
By Story be confounded.Ye aspire
Rashly, to fall once more . . .

(Ibid., 14)

In the final chapter of the book, Güttler quotes a long extract (33 lines) from 'Musings Near Aquapadente' (1837) which complements the sentiment of his material in chapter one, specifically developing the idea that this should be an enlightened age based on humane, Christian values, while in reality it seems to be anything but that. He introduces it by explaining that once Wordsworth had set his early enthusiasm for Godwinian rationalism to one side, he remained consistently opposed to utilitarianism, specifically as it related to education. A generation steeped in material interests and blind to the 'noble emotions of the soul' were in danger of making the same mistake as the beleaguered Solitary (ibid., 128–9). The extract begins:

> . . . yet we, who now
> Walk in the light of day, pertain full surely
> To a chilled age, most pitiably shut out
> From that which *is* and actuates, by forms,
> Abstractions, and by lifeless fact to fact
> Minutely linked with diligence uninspired,
> Unrectified, unguided, unsustained,
> By godlike insight. To this fate is doomed
> Science, wide-spread and spreading still as be
> Her conquests, in the world of sense made known.
> So with the internal mind it fares; and so
> With morals, trusting, in contempt or fear
> Of vital principle's controlling law,
> To her purblind guide Expediency; and so
> Suffers religious faith.

(Ibid., 129–30)

The poet of Aquapadente, who, in the opening lines of the poem gazes across the fertile landscape of Italy, the 'Bright sunbeams – the fresh verdure of this lawn/Strewn with grey rocks . . .' (Selincourt 1969, 278), is a moderate, reflective, political conservative of the late 1830s, but a poet also capable of delivering a telling comment on the eve of war in 1914, when the readers of this poem are once more faced with the imminent loss of the 'light of day'. It is a 'chilled age' of science 'most pitiably shut out/From that which *is* and actuates', fed only by 'Abstractions, and by lifeless fact to fact/Minutely linked with diligence uninspired'. It is a technological age devoid of religious vision.

> There lives
> No faculty within us which the Soul
> Can spare, and humblest earthly Weal demands,
> For dignity not placed beyond her reach,
> Zealous co-operation of all means
> Given or acquired, to raise us from the mire,
> And liberate our hearts from low pursuits.
> By gross utilities enslaved we need
> More of ennobling impulse from the past,
> If to the future aught of good must come
> Sounder and therefore holier than the ends

Which, in the giddiness of self-applause,
We covet as supreme. O grant the crown
That Wisdom wears, or take his treacherous staff
From knowledge.

(Ibid., 282)

For the 'Soul' to thrive we must engage all our 'faculties'. Unless we do this we remain in the 'mire', and our hearts will be shackled to 'low pursuits', enslaved by 'gross Utilities'. We need 'More of ennobling impulse from the past/If to the future aught of good must come'. As it is, 'the ends/Which, in the giddiness of self-applause/We covet as supreme' are godless, returning to the opening lines of the extract, they 'pertain full surely/To a chilled age . . . Unrectified, unguided, unsustained,/By godlike insight.' Against this, in the final lines of the poem, Wordsworth sets his poetry, 'the muse, whom I have served' (l.355). In sharp contrast to the aggressive, shallow beliefs of the present and its industrial landscape, the poet composes his lines 'under these chestnut boughs/Reclined . . .' (ll.358–9). This virtue of repose coupled to his love of beauty has enabled him to 'enshrine in verse/Accordant meditations' (ll.363–4) which will, he hopes, bring 'soberness of mind and peace of heart' to his readers 'in times/Vexed and disordered, as our own . . .' (ll.364-6). Against the prospect of war that faces his readers in 1914, times that are equally 'Vexed and disordered', Felix Güttler sets Wordsworth's poetry.

★

Wordsworth's poetry was far from being neglected in Germany in the way many writers, German, English, and American, would have us believe. The problem begins with Goethe's decision to deny Wordsworth 'Weltliteratur' status; Goethe was undoubtedly responsible for a cultural ambience in Germany that influenced the way in which Wordsworth tended to be translated and read. In the course of the nineteenth century, he increasingly came to be 'translated' as an English poet available to Germans who felt themselves marginalized, he was a poet among poets and intellectuals who, as Ezra Pound wrote of Hugh Selwyn Mauberley in 1920, was

> . . . out of key with his time,
> He strove to resuscitate the dead art
> Of poetry; to maintain 'the sublime'
> In the old sense . . .

(Pound 1959, 173)

Wordsworth had been established as a fixture in the German post-Napoleonic pantheon of British Romantic poets by Friedrich Jacobsen; besides enthusing over a philosophical nature poet whose Protestant religious pietism he found deeply attractive, Jacobsen was drawn to a poet whose British Nationalism he could admire without feeling threatened. Ferdinand Freiligrath recognized a kindred spirit in a philosophical poet who loved the natural world of his homeland, and opposed oppression. He understood that Wordsworth had suffered critical exile until relatively late in life. Marie Gothein's biography, indebted to Freiligrath's response, nevertheless steers Wordsworth into a changed Germany, one that is being forced to adapt to the loss of the guiding hand of Bismarck, and the increasing unpredictability of the future. By the end of the century Wordsworth could be co-opted by Germans as a poet at odds with social, political, and cultural modernity in all its dehumanizing and secularizing manifestations. He was a matured revolutionary, sadder and wiser than the young idealist who had been dazzled by French promises of liberty, equality and fraternity. This assured him a German presence until 1914, and he continued to be written about in Germany after the war.

Wordsworth's subsequent disappearance from German cultural histories that cover the nineteenth century to the present day is an omission that demands recognition and reassessment. Part of the explanation lies with an Anglo-American tendency to rewrite the nature of German participation in the cultural history of post-Second World War Anglo-American cultural exchange with Europe. This has been alluded to on several occasions in this book, specifically in relation to René Wellek's work. In Beat Wyss's essay on Caspar David Friedrich's painting, *Monk by the Sea* (c.1809), he draws attention first to Friedrich's unpopularity in Biedermeier Germany, then to his rediscovery for racially motivated reasons by the Nazis: 'Friedrich's blond *Monk by the Sea* became an Aryan soldier ... aware that he was a member of a "nation without space".' This once again rendered him unacceptable until the art establishment in the United States set about reconstructing German Romanticism in the 1970s as a cynical device that could be used (among other things) 'by American artists and critics' to diminish the influence of 'the École de Paris as the leading arts centre' (Wyss 2008, 54–5). Geoffrey Hartman explores this issue in more general terms in relation to post-war German history and culture in *The Fateful Question of Culture*, the published version of his Wellek Library Lectures of 1992. In 'Language and Culture After the Holocaust' he reflects on how 'revolutions, wars, disasters' may profoundly influence 'terms of discourse or sensibility':

> In matters of historical change we often give priority to a reference point drawn from revolutions, wars, disasters: from that kind of eventful history. In rare cases, such as Freud or German culture's infatuation with classical Greece (what E. M. Butler called 'the tyranny of Greece over Germany'), we include a crucial system of thought that has widely influenced terms of discourse or sensibility. When we periodize by concentrating on a catastrophic or epochal event, are we simply dramatizing historical change, enlarging it as it were, or are we actually seeking to explain that change? (Hartman 1992, 99)

Where the temptation has been, therefore, to think of Wordsworth as 'ours', as a Romantic Period poet whose English persona does not readily 'translate' into an alien culture, or across a period of 'historical change', we should be encouraged to think again. We should think again about the ubiquity of translation (starting ideally with the Bible in Europe, but at the very least with John Dryden and Alexander Pope), and look in considerably more detail than is often the case at how that relates to the history of reception, cultural exchange and literary critical activity in general, revisiting the past with an eye to our increasingly uncertain future.

Bibliography

Abrams, M. H. (1971), *Natural Supernaturalism: Tradition and Revolution in Romantic Literature*. New York and London: W. W. Norton.

Anderson, Benedict (1983/1991), *Imagined Communities*. London and New York: Verso.

Arnold, Matthew (1874), *Higher Schools and Universities in Germany*. London: Macmillan.

—(1879), *Poems of Wordsworth*. London: Macmillan.

—(1970), *Selected Prose*. Harmondsworth: Penguin Books.

—(1997), *Letters*, 2 vols. Cecil Y. Lang (ed.). Charlottesville and London: University Press of Virginia.

—(1986), *Matthew Arnold*, Miriam Allott and Robert. H. Super (eds). Oxford: Oxford University Press.

Ashton, Rosemary (1986), *Little Germany*. Oxford: Oxford University Press.

Barker, Juliet (2001), *Wordsworth: A Life*. Harmondsworth: Penguin Books.

Bassnett, Susan (1988), *Translation Studies*. London: Routledge.

Bassnett, Susan and Bush, Peter (eds) (2006), *The Translator as Writer*. London: Continuum.

Baumgartner, Alexander (1884), *Reisebilder aus Schottland*. Freiburg.

—(1897), *Geschichte der Weltliteratur*. 6 vols. Freiburg.

Baumgartner, Andreas (1897), *William Wordsworth Nach seiner gemeinverständlichen Seite dargestellt*. Zurich.

Beatty, Frederika (1939), *William Wordsworth of Rydal Mount*. London: Dent.

Behler, Ernst (1993), *German Romantic Literary Theory*. Cambridge: Cambridge University Press.

Beiser, Frederick C. (2003), *The Romantic Imperative: The Concept of Early German Romanticism*. Cambridge, Mass. and London: Harvard University Press.

—(2005), *Schiller as Philosopher: A Re-Examination*. Oxford: Oxford University Press.

Benjamin, Walter (1992), *Illuminations*, trans. Harry Zohn. London: Fontana

Berlin, Isaiah (1956), *The Age of Enlightenment*. London: Houghton Mifflin Press.

Berman, Antoine (1992), *The Experience of the Foreign: Culture and Translation in Romantic Germany*, trans. S. Heyvaert. New York: State University of New York Press.

Bernays, Michael (1907), *Briefe von und an Michael Bernays*. Berlin: B. Behr.

Bernofsky, Susan (2005), *Foreign Words: Translators-Authors in the Age of Goethe*. Detroit: Wayne State University Press.

Bewell, Allan (1989), *Wordsworth and the Enlightenment*. New Haven and London: Yale University Press.

Bishop, Paul and Stephenson, R. H. (2005), *Friedrich Nietzsche and Weimar Classicism*. New York: Camden House.

Bithell, Jethro (1959), *Modern German Literature*. London: Methuen.

Blackham, H. J. (1994), *Six Existentialist Thinkers*. London: Routledge.

Bloom, Harold (1970), *Romanticism and Consciousness: Essays in Criticism*. New York: W. W. Norton.

—(1997), *The Anxiety of Influence*. Oxford: Oxford University Press.

Boggs, Colleen (2006), 'Translation in the United States', in Peter France and Kenneth Haynes (eds), *The Oxford History of Literary Translation: Volume 4 1790–1900*. Oxford: Oxford University Press, 20–33.

Bömig, Carl A. (1906), *William Wordsworth im Urteile seiner Zeit*. Leipzig.

Bowie, Andrew (2003), *Introduction to German Philosophy*. Cambridge: Polity Press.

—(2005), 'The Philosophical Significance of Schleiermacher's Hermeneutics', in Jacqueline Mariña (ed.), *The Cambridge Companion to Friedrich Schleiermacher*. Cambridge: Cambridge University Press, 73–90.

Boyle, Nicholas (1991/2000), *Goethe, The Poet of the Age*. Oxford: Oxford University Press.

Bradley, A. C. (1909), *English Poetry and German Philosophy in the Age of Wordsworth*. Manchester: Manchester University Press.

Bramstead, Ernst K. (1964), *Aristocracy and the Middle Class in Germany*. Chicago: University of Chicago Press.

Brandl, Alois (1886), *Samuel Taylor Coleridge und die englische Romantik*. Berlin.

—(1887), *Samuel Taylor Coleridge and the English Romantic School*. London: Murray.

Brimley, George (1858), *Essays*. London: Macmillan.

Brink, Bernhard (1883–1896), *Geschichte der englischen Literatur, Early English Literature*, 3 vols. Vol. 1 translated from the German by Horace M. Kennedy, translation revised by the author. Vol. 2 translated by William Clarke Robinson. Vol. 3 edited by Alois Brandl, trans. L. Dora Schmitz. Strassburg: Trübner; London: Bell and Sons.

Brown, Hilary (2005), *Benedikte Naubert 1756–1819 and Her Relations to English Culture*. London: Maney Publishing.

Brown, Marshall (1979), *The Shape of German Romanticism*. New York: Cornell University Press.

Burleigh, Michael (2005), *Earthly Powers: Religion and Politics in Europe from the French Revolution to the Great War*. London: HarperCollins.

Burwick, Frederick, and Klien, Jürgen (eds) (1996), *The Romantic Imagination: Literature and Art in England and Germany*. Amsterdam: Rodopi.

Burwick, Frederick (1998), 'Romantic Madness: Hölderlin, Nerval, Clare', in Gregory Maertz (ed.), *Cultural Interactions in the Romantic Age*. New York: State University of New York Press, 106–127.

—(2007), 'The Reception of Coleridge in Germany to World War II', in Elinor Shaffer and Edoardo Zuccato (eds), *The Reception of S. T. Coleridge in Europe*. London: Continuum, 88–112.

Bushell, Sally (2002), *Re-Reading The Excursion: Narrative, Response and the Wordsworthian Dramatic Voice*. Aldershot: Ashgate.

Byron (1970), *Byron: Poetical Works*. Oxford: Oxford University Press.

Cardwell, Richard (ed.) (2004), *The Reception of Byron in Europe*, 2 vols. London: Continuum.

Carr, E. H. (1933/1998), *The Romantic Exiles*. London: Serif.

—(1964), *What is History?* Harmondsworth: Penguin Books.

Chase, Cynthia (ed.) (1993), *Romanticism*. London and New York: Longman.

Clarke, Robert T. jnr (1955), *Herder: His Life and Thought*. Berkeley and Los Angeles: University of California Press.

Clayden P. W. (1889), *Rogers and his Contemporaries*. London: Smith & Elder.

Coleridge, S. T. (1956), *Collected Letters*, 2 vols. Oxford: Clarendon Press.

—(1997), *Biographia Literaria*. London: Dent.

Collier, Price (1914), *Germany and the Germans from an American Point of View*. New York: Charles Scribner's Sons.

Cotterill, H. B. (1883), *Ueber Wordsworth und Walt Whitman*. Dresden.

—(1922–3), *A History of Art*, 2 vols. London: Harrap.

Curtis, Jared (ed.) (1993), *The Fenwick Notes of William Wordsworth*. Bristol: Bristol Classical Press.

Darnton, Robert, Fabian, Bernhard, Korshin, Paul J., and Wiles, Roy McKeen (1976), *The Widening Circle: Essays on the Circulation of Literature in Eighteenth Century Europe*, Paul J. Korshin (ed.). Pennsylvania: University of Pennsylvania Press.

Davis, John R. (1997), *Britain and the German Zollverein 1848–1866*. London: Macmillan.

De Quincey, Thomas (1961), *Reminiscences of the English Lake Poets*. London: Dent.

De Vere, Aubrey (1887), *Essays, Chiefly on Poetry*, 2 vols. London: Macmillan.

—(1889), *Essays, Chiefly Literary and Ethical*. London: Macmillan.

—(1897), *Recollections*. London: Edward Arnold.

Doering, Heinrich (1854), *Brittische Anthologie in metrischer Uebersetzung altenglischer Balladen*. Zerbst.

Donahue, Neil (ed.) (2005), *A Companion to the Literature of German Expressionism*. New York: Camden House.

Eichendorf, Joseph von (2002), *Life of a Good-for-nothing*, trans. J. G. Nichols. London: Hesperus Press.

Elze, Karl (1853), *Englischer Liederschatz aus englischen und amerikanischen. Dichtern vorzugsweise des XIX. Jahrhunderts mit Nachrichten über die Verfasser*. Dessau: Katz.

Engel, Eduard (1883), *Geschichte der englischen Literatur*. Leipzig.

Engell, James (1998), 'Romantische Poesie: Richard Hurd und F. Schlegel', in Gregory Maertz (ed.), *Cultural Interactions in the Romantic Age*. New York: State University of New York Press.

Esterhammer, Angela (2000), *The Romantic Performative: Language and Action in British and German Romanticism*. Stanford: Stanford University Press.

Evans, John (1807), *The Parnassian Garland, or Beauties of Modern Poetry*. London: Albion Press.

Evans, Richard J. (1987), *Death in Hamburg: Society and Politics in the Cholera Years 1830–1910*. Oxford: Clarendon Press.

Eyssenhardt, Franz (1886), *Barthold Georg Niebuhr*. Gotha: F. A. Perthes.

Fabian, Bernhard (1992), *The English Book in Eighteenth Century Germany: The Panizzi Lectures 1991*. London: The British Library.

Fabian, Robert (1976), 'English Books and Their Eighteenth Century German Readers', in Darnton (1976).

Fairley, Barker (1934), *Goethe and Wordsworth: A Point of Contrast*. Cambridge: Cambridge University Press.

Fairweather, Maria (2005), *Madame de Staël*. London: Robinson.

Fernau, Hermann (1916), *Because I am a German*, T. W. Rolleston (ed.). London: Constable.

Finney, Gail (2000), 'Revolution, Resignation, Realism (1830–1890)', in Helen Watanabe-O'Kelly (ed.), *The Cambridge History of German Literature*. Cambridge: Cambridge University Press, 272–326.

Fioretos, Aris (1999), *The Solid Letter: Readings of Friedrich Hölderlin*. Stanford: Stanford University Press.

Fischer, Christian August (1819), *Reise Livorno nach London im Sommer und Herbste*. Leipzig.

Forster, Leonard (ed.) (1957), *The Penguin Book of German Verse*. Harmondsworth: Penguin Books.

Franklin, Michael J. (1995), *Sir William Jones*. Cardiff: University of Wales Press.

Freiligrath, Ferdinand (1842), *Karl Immerman*. Stuttgart.

—(1844), *Ein Glaubensbekenntnis*. Mainz.

—(1846i), *Gedichte aus dem Englischen*. Stuttgart und Tübingen.

—(1846ii), *Ça Ira*. Herisau.

—(1853), *The Rose, Thistle and Shamrock, a Book of English Poetry, Chiefly Modern*. Stuttgart (revised fifth edn. 1874).

—(1869), *Poems from the German*, edited by his daughter. Leipzig: Bernhard Tauchnitz.

Fulbrook, Mary (2004), *A Concise History of Germany*. Cambridge: Cambridge University Press.

Furst, Lilian R. (1969), *Romanticism in Perspective*. London: Macmillan.

Galignani (1828), *The Poetical Works of William Wordsworth*. Paris: A & W Galignani.

Gaskill, Howard (1984), *Hölderlin's Hyperion*. Durham: Durham University Press.

Giles, Paul (2004), 'American Literature in English Translation: Denise Leverton and Others', *PMLA*, 119, (2), 31–41.

Gill, Stephen (1989), *William Wordsworth: A Life*. Oxford: Clarendon Press.

—(1998), *Wordsworth and the Victorians*. Oxford: The Clarendon Press.

Gillespie, Stuart and Hopkins, David (2005), *The Oxford History of Literary Translation in English Volume 3 1660–1790*. Oxford: Oxford University Press.

Gillies, R. P. (1826), *German Stories*, 3 vols. London: Blackwood.

—(1851), *Memoirs of a Literary Veteran*. London.

Girardin, Paul (1914), *R. P. Gillies and the Propagation of German Literature in England at the End of the Eighteenth Century and the Beginning of the Nineteenth Century*. Bern.

Goethe, J. W. (1981), *Selected Verse*. D. L. Luke (ed.). Harmondsworth: Penguin Books.

—(1998), *Faust: Part One*, trans. David Luke. Oxford: Oxford University Press.

—(2006), *The Sorrows of Young Werther*, trans. Michael Hulse. Harmondsworth: Penguin Books.

Goodman, Katherine R. (1999), *Amazons and Apprentices: Women and the German Parnassus in the Early Enlightenment*. Columbia: Camden House.

Goodwin, Albert (1979), *The Friends of Liberty*. London: Hutchinson.

Gothein, Marie (1893), *William Wordsworth, Sein Leben, Seine Werke, Seine Zeitgenossen*, 2 vols. Halle: A. S. Verlag von Max Niemeyer.

—(1914), *Geschichte der Gartenkunst*, 2 vols. Jena.

—(1928), *A History of Garden Art from the Earliest Times to the Present Day*, 2 vols. trans. Mrs Archer Hind, Walter P. Wright (ed.). London: Dent.

—(1931), *Eberhard Gothein. Ein Lebensbild, seinen Briefen nacherzählt*. Stuttgart.

Grimm, Jacob and Grimm, Wilhelm (2005), *Selected Tales*. Joyce Crick (ed.). Oxford: Oxford University Press.

Güttler, Felix (1914), *Wordsworth's politische Entwicklung*. Stuttgart.

Hahn, Franz (ed.) (1901), *Interlinear German Reading Book* by Franz Thimm. London: E. Marlborough & Co.

Hall, C. J. (2005), *An Introduction to Language and Linguistics: Breaking the Language Spell*. London: Continuum.

Hamburger, Michael (1970), *Reason and Energy: Studies in German Literature*. London: Weidenfeld & Nicolson.

—(1983), *A Proliferation of Prophets*. Manchester: Carcanet Press.

—(2004), *Friedrich Hölderlin: Poems and Fragments*. London: Anvil Press.

Hamlin, Cyrus (1973), 'The Poetics of Self-Consciousness in European Romanticism: Hölderlin's *Hyperion* and Wordsworth's *Prelude*', *Genre*, VI, (2), 142–77.

Hanke, Amala M. (1981), *Spatiotemporal Consciousness in English and German Romanticism*. Berne: Peter Lang.

Hartman, Geoffrey H. (1997), *The Fateful Question of Culture*. New York: Columbia University Press.

Hatim, Basil and Ian Mason (1997), *The Translator as Communicator*. London: Routledge.

Haydon, John O. (1971), *Romantic Bards and British Reviewers*. London: Routledge & Kegan Paul.

Heine, Heinrich (1943), *Works of Prose*, Herman Keston (ed.), trans. E. B. Ashton. New York: L. B. Fischer.

Hemans, Felicia (1914), *The Poetical Works*. Oxford: Oxford University Press.

—(2002), *Felicia Hemans Selected Poems, Prose and Letters*, Gary Kelly (ed.). Ontario and Ormskirk: Broadview Press.

Herrig, Ludwig (1851), *The British Classical Authors: Select Specimens of the National Literature of England from Chaucer to the Present Time*. Braunschweig: George Westermann.

Heuval, Jon Vanden (2001), *A German Life in the Age of Revolution: Joseph Görres 1776–1848*. Washington DC: The Catholic University of America Press.

Hill, Alan (2008), 'Wordsworth's Reception in Germany: Some Unfamiliar Episodes and Contacts, 1798–1849', *Review of English Studies*, 59, 241. Oxford: Oxford University Press.

Hill, Rosemary (2007), *God's Architect: Pugin and the Building of Romantic Britain*. London: Penguin Allen Lane Press.

Hirsch, Eric Donald (1960), *Wordsworth and Schelling: A Typological Study of Romanticism*. Newhaven: Yale University Press.

Hohendahl, Peter Uwe (ed.) (2003), *Patriotism, Cosmopolitansim, and National Culture: Public Culture in Hamburg 1700–1933*. Amsterdam: Rodopi.

Hohenhausen, Elise Friederike (1847), *Rousseau, Göthe, Byron: ein kritisch-literarischer Umriss aus ethisch-christlichem Standpunkte*. Kassel: Heinrich Hotop.

Holcroft, Thomas (1926), *Memoirs of Thomas Holcroft*. Oxford: Oxford University Press.

Holes, Clive (2005), 'The Birth of Orientalism', in Stuart Gillespie and David Hopkins (eds), *The Oxford History of Literary Translation in English Volume 3 1660–1790*. Oxford: Oxford University Press, 443–55.

Hopkins, David (2005), 'Dryden and his Contemporaries', in Stuart Gillespie and David Hopkins (eds), *The Oxford History of Literary Translation in English Volume 3 1660–1790*. Oxford: Oxford University Press, 55–66.

Howitt, William (1847i), *Howitt's Journal of Literature and Popular Progress*. London.

—(1847ii), *Homes and Haunts of the Most Eminent British Poets*, 2 vols. London.

Hughes, Gillian (2003), 'Hogg, Gillies, and German Romanticism', *Studies in Hogg and his World*, 14, 62–72.

Hyland, Ken (2005), *Metadiscourse: Exploring Interaction in Writing*. London: Continuum.

Isbell, John Clairborne (1994), *The Birth of European Romanticism: Truth and Propaganda in Staël's 'De l'Allemagne' 1810–1813*. Cambridge: Cambridge University Press.

Jacobsen, Friederich Johann (1820), *Briefe an eine deutsche Edelfrau, über die neuesten englischen Dichter*. Altona.

Kant, Emmanuel (1991), 'An Answer to the Question: "What is Enlightenment?"', in H. S. Reiss (ed.), *Kant: Political Writings*, trans. H. B. Nisbet. Cambridge: Cambridge University Press, 54–60.

Kaplan, Fred (1983), *Thomas Carlyle: A Biography*. Cambridge: Cambridge University Press.

Karl, Frederick (1995), *George Eliot: A Biography*. London: HarperCollins.

Kaul, Suvir (2000), *Poems of Nation, Anthems of Empire: English Verse in the Long Eighteenth Century*. Charlottesville and London: University Press of Virginia.

Kearney, Richard (2006), see Ricoeur (2006).

Kelly, Louis (2005), 'The Eighteenth Century to Tytler', in Stuart Gillespie and David Hopkins (eds), *The Oxford History of Literary Translation in English Volume 3 1660–1790*. Oxford: Oxford University Press, 67–80.

Kennedy, Paul M. (1980), *The Rise of Anglo-German Antagonism 1860–1914*. London: Allen & Unwin.

Kitson, Peter J. (ed.) (2001), *Placing and Displacing Romanticism*. London: Ashgate.

—(2007), *Romantic Literature, Race, and Colonial Encounter*. Basingstoke: Palgrave Macmillan.

Kleist, Heinrich (1978), *The Marquise of O and Other Stories*, trans. David Luke. Harmondsworth: Penguin Books.

Knight, G. (1854), *The New London Echo: Eine Sammlung englischer Redensarten in zusammenhängenden Unterhaltungen*. Leipzig.

Knight, William (1882–6), *The Poetical Works of William Wordsworth*, 8 vols. Edinburgh: William Paterson.

—(1889), *The Life of William Wordsworth*, 3 vols. Edinburgh: William Paterson (published as vols 9–11 of *The Poetical Works*).

Koerner, Joseph Leo (1990), *Caspar David Friedrich and the Subject of Landscape*. London: Reaktion Books.

Kontje, Todd (1998), *Women, The Novel, and the German Nation 1771–1871*. Cambridge: Cambridge University Press.

Kristmannsson, Gauti (2001), *Literary Diplomacy: The Role of Translation Studies in the Construction of National Literatures in Britain and Germany 1750–1830*, 2 vols. Frankfurt, New York and Oxford: Peter Lang.

Laan, J. M. van der (2007), *Seeking Meaning for Goethe's Faust*. London: Continuum.

Lamm, Julia A. (2005), 'The Art of Interpreting Plato', in Jacqueline Mariña (ed.), *The Cambridge Companion to Friedrich Schleiermacher*. Cambridge: Cambridge University Press, 91–108.

Lappenberg, Johann Martin (1834), *A History of England under the Anglo-Saxon Kings*. Hamburg.

—(1857), *A History of England under the Norman Kings*. Hamburg.

Lee, Amice (1955), *Laurels and Rosemary: The Life of William and Mary Howitt*. Oxford: Oxford University Press.

Lee, Stephen J. (1982), *Aspects of European History 1789–1980*. London: Routledge.

Lefevere, André (1977), *Translating Literature: The German Tradition from Luther to Rosenweig*. Amsterdam: Van Gorcum.

—(1992), *Translation/History/Culture*. London: Routledge.

Legouis, Emile (1896/1988), *The Early Life of William Wordsworth 1770–1798*, Introduction by Nicholas Roe. London: Libris.

Lepenies, Wolf (2006), *The Seduction of Culture in German History*. Princeton: Princeton University Press.

Lessing, C. G. (trans.) (1774), *Der Mann von Gefühl. Aus dem Englischen*. Danzig.

Liddell M. F. (1928), 'Ferdinand Freiligrath's Debt to the English Poets', *The Modern Language Review*, April, XXIII.

—(1949), *Ferdinand Freiligrath's Poems*, with a life of the poet. Oxford: Blackwell.

Lienemann, Kurt (1908), *Die Belesenheit von William Wordsworth*. Berlin.

Liptzin, Sol (1924), *Shelley in Germany*. New York: Columbia University Press.

—(1954), *The English Legend of Heinrich Heine*. New York: Black.

Liu, Alan (1989), *Wordsworth: The Sense of History*. Stanford: Stanford University Press.

Lukács, Georg (1964), *Essays on Thomas Mann*, trans. Stanley Mitchell. London: Merlin Press.

Maertz, Gregory (ed.) (1998), *Cultural Interactions in the Romantic Age*. New York: State University of New York Press.

—(1998), 'Reviewing Kant's early Reception in Britain: the Leading Role of Henry Crabb Robinson', in Gregory Maertz (ed.), *Cultural Interactions in the Romantic Age*. New York: State University of New York Press.

Manly, S. (2007), *Language, Custom, and Nation in the 1790s*. London: Ashgate.

Mann, Thomas (1999i), *Doctor Faustus*. London: Vintage.

—(1999ii), *Buddenbrooks*. London: Vintage.

Manz, Stefan (2007), 'Translating Nietzsche, Mediating Literature: Alexander Tille and the limits of Anglo-German Intercultural Transfer', *Neopilologus*, 91, 117–134.

Mariña, Jacqueline (ed.) (2005), *The Cambridge Companion to Friedrich Schleiermacher*. Cambridge: Cambridge University Press.

Marquardt, Hertha (1964), *Henry Crabb Robinson und Seine Deutschen Freunde*. Göttingen: Vanden Hoeck & Ruprecht.

Mason, Eudo (1959), *Deutsche und englische Romantic*. Göttingen (reprinted 1970).

Maurer, Michael, Johanna Sänger and Editha Ulrich (2006), *Im Schaffen geniessen Der Briefwechsel der Kulturwissenschaftler Eberhard und Marie Gothein 1883–1923*. Weimar Wien: Böhlan Verlag Köln.

McCarthy, Justin (1868), 'The Poems of Freiligrath', in *Con Amore; or, Critical Chapters*. London: Tinsley Brothers.

Mellor, Horst (1996), 'The Parricidal Imagination: Schiller, Blake, Fuseli and the Romantic Revolt against the Father', in Burwick (1996).

Melton, James Van Horn (1988), *Absolutism and the Eighteenth-century Origins of Compulsory Schooling in Prussia and Austria*. Cambridge: Cambridge University Press.

Moore, Evelyn K. and Patricia Anne Simpson (eds) (2007), *The Enlightened Eye: Goethe and Visual Culture*. Amsterdam and New York: Rodopi.

Moore, Thomas (1853), *Memoirs, Journal and Correpondence of Thomas Moore*, 6 vols. Lord John Russell (ed.). London.

Moorman, Mary (1965), *William Wordsworth: A Biography*, 2 vols. Oxford: Oxford University Press.

Morgan, Bayard Quincey and A. R. Hohfeld (eds) (1949), *German Literature in British Magazines*. Madison: University of Wisconsin Press.

Morley, Edith J. (1929), *Crabb Robinson in Germany: Extracts from His Correspondence*. Oxford: Oxford University Press.

—(1935), *The Life and Times of Henry Crabb Robinson*. London: Dent.

Morrow, Elsa (1967), *A History of Swanley Horticultural College*. Kent County Library Publication.

Morse, David (1981), *Perspectives on Romanticism: A Transformational Analysis*. London: Macmillan.

Munck, Thomas (2000), *The Enlightenment: A Comparative History*. London: Arnold.

Munday, Jeremy (2001), *Introducing Translation Studies*. London: Routledge.

Nemoianu, Virgil (1984), *The Taming of Romanticism: European Literature and the Age of Biedermeier*. Cambridge, Mass. and London: Harvard University Press.

Nicoll, Henry James (1883), *Landmarks of English Literature*. London: J. Hogg.

—(1888), *Byron: English Men of Letters*. London: Macmillan

Norman, F. (1929), 'Henry Crabb Robinson and Goethe', in *Publications of the English Goethe Society*, J. G. Robinson (ed.). London.

Nutt, David (1905), *English and Scottish Ballads*. London: David Nutt.

O'Kelly, Watanabe (2000), *The Cambridge History of German Literature*. Cambridge: Cambridge University Press.

Owen, W. J. B. and Jane Worthington Smyser (1974), *The Prose Works of William Wordsworth*, 3 vols. Oxford: The Clarendon Press.

Ozment, Steven (2005), *A Mighty Fortress: A New History of the German People*. London: Granta Books.

Paul, Hermann (1901–9), *Grundriss der Germanischen Philologie*. Strasburg.

Paulin, Roger (2003), *The Critical Reception of Shakespeare in Germany 1682–1914*. Hildesheim, Zürich, New York: Georg Olms.

Perkins, Mary Anne (2001), 'The Romantics: Cosmopolitan or Nationalist?' in Kitson (2001).

Pérez, María Calzada (ed.) (2003), *Apropos of Ideology: Translation Studies on Ideology – Ideologies in Translation Studies*. Manchester: St Jerome.

Perteghella Manuella, and Eugenia Loffredo (2006), *Translation and Creativity: Perspectives on Creative Writing and Translation Studies*. London: Continuum.

Perthes, Frederick (1858), *The Life and Times of Frederick Perthes*, Edinburgh.

Piper, Andrew (2006), 'Rethinking the Print Object: Goethe and the Book of Everything', in *PMLA*, 121, (1), 124–38.

Ploennies, Luise von (1843), *Britannia: A Selection of British Poems Ancient and Modern*. Frankfurt: Henry Keller.

—(1863), *Englische Lyriker des neunzehnten Jahrhunderts*. München.

Postgate, Helen B. (1968), *Madame de Staël*. New York: Twayne.

Pound, Ezra (1959), *Ezra Pound: Selected Poems*. London: Faber & Faber.

Prawer, Siegbert (1960), *Mörike und seine Leser*. Stuttgart: Ernst Klett.

—(1961), *Heine, the Tragic Satirist*. Cambridge: Cambridge University Press.

Prawer, Siegbert (ed.) (1970), *The Romantic Period in Germany*. London: Weidenfeld & Nicholson.

Price, Lawrence (1968), *The Reception of English Literature in Germany*. New York and London: Benjamin Blom.

Prickett, Stephen (ed.) (1980), *The Context of English Literature: The Romantics*. London: Methuen.

Pughe, Francis H. (1902), *Byron und Wordsworth*. Heidelberg.

Purdie, Edna (1924), 'German Influence on the Literary Ballad in England during the Romantic Revival', J. G. Robertson (ed.). London: Publications of the English Goethe Society.

Quillinan, Edward (1853), *Poems by Edward Quillinan with a Memoir by William Johnson*. London: Edward Moxon.

—(1891), a reprint of 1853 edn. Ambleside: George Middleton.

Rea, Thomas (1906), *Schiller's Drama and Poems in England*. London: T. Fisher Unwin.

Reiss, Horis (ed.) (1991), *Kant: Political Writings*, trans. H. B. Nisbet. Cambridge: Cambridge University Press.

Reuss, Jeremias David (1804), *Das Gelehrte England oder Lexikon der Jetzlebenden Schriftsteller in Grossbritannien, Irland und Nord-Amerika nebst einem Verzeichniss ihrer Schriften: vom Jahr 1770 bis 1790*, 2 vols. Berlin und Stettin: Friedrich Nicolai.

Richter, Helene (1911), *Gesichte der Englischen Romantik*. Halle.

Richter K. (1899), *Ferdinand Freiligrath als Übersetzer*. Berlin.

Ricoeur, Paul (2006), *On Translation*, with an Introduction by Richard Kearney. London: Routledge.

—(2007), *Reflections on the Just*. Chicago and London: Chicago University Press.

Rivers, David (1796), *The Gospel a Law of Liberty*. Highgate.

—(1798), *Literary Memoirs of Living Authors of Great Britain*, 2 vols. London.

—(1801), *Sermons on Interesting Subjects*. London.

—(1804), *Discourse on Patriotism*. London.

Robertson, J. G. (1953), *A History of German Literature*. London: Blackwood.

Robinson, Douglas (1991), *The Translator's Turn*. Baltimore: John Hopkins University Press.

—(1996), *Translation and Taboo*. De Kalb: Northern Illinois University Press.

—(1997i), *Western Translation Theory from Herodotus to Nietzsche*. Manchester: St Jerome.

—(1997ii), *Translation and Empire*. Manchester: St Jerome.

Robinson, Henry Crabb (1869), *Diary, Reminiscences, and Correspondence of Henry Crabb Robinson*, 3 vols. Thomas Sadler (ed.). London: Macmillan

—(1929), *Crabb Robinson in Germany 1800–1805*, Edith J. Morley (ed.). Oxford: Oxford University Press.

—(1967), *The Diary of Henry Crabb Robinson*, Derek Hudson (ed.). Oxford: Oxford University Press.

Rolleston T. W. (1892), *Lessing and Modern German Literature*. Oxford: Oxford University Press.

Salama-Carr, Myriam (ed.) (2007), *Translating and Interpreting Conflict*. Amsterdam and New York: Rodopi.

Saul, Nicolas (2000), 'Aesthetic Humanism (1790–1830)', in O'Kelly (2000).

Schama, Simon (1996), *Landscape and Memory*. London: Fontana.

Schenk, H. G. (1979), *The Mind of the European Romantics*. Oxford: Oxford University Press.

Scherr, Johannes (1848), *Bildersall der Weltliteratur*, 2 vols. Stuttgart: Kröner.

Schmid, Susanne (1999), 'Martyr? Gentleman? Atheist? Christian? – Nineteenth Century German Constructions of Shelley', in *Anglistentag 1998*, Fritz-Wilhelm Neumann und Sabine Schülting (eds). Trier.

—(2002), 'Reception as Performance: The Case of Shelley in Germany', in *Romantic Poetry*, Angela Esterhammer (ed.). Amsterdam and Philadelphia: John Benjamins.

—(2004), 'The Act of Reading an Anthology', in *Comparative Critical Studies*, 1, (1–2), 53–69.

—(2007), *Shelley's German Afterlives*. Basingstoke: Palgrave Macmillan.

Seeba, Hinrich C. (2003), '*Trostgründe*: Cultural Nationalism and Historical Legitimation in Nineteenth Century German Literary Histories', in *Modern Language Quarterly*, 64, (2), 183–195.

Selincourt, Ernest de (ed.) (1969), *Wordsworth: Poetical Works*. Oxford: Oxford University Press.

Selinker, Larry (1992), *Rediscovering Language*. London: Longman.

Sengle, Friedrich (1971–80), *Beidermeierzeit: Deutsche Literatur im Spannungsfeld zwischen Restauration und Revolution 1815–1848*, 3 vols. Stuttgart: J. B. Metzler.

Shaffer, Elinor and Zuccato, Edoardo (eds) (2007), *The Reception of S. T. Coleridge in Europe*. London: Continuum.

Sharpe, Lesley (1991), *Friedrich Schiller: Drama, Thought, Politics*. Cambridge: Cambridge University Press.

—(1995), *Schiller's Aesthetic Essays: Two Centuries of Criticism*. Columbia: Camden House.

Shields, David S. (1990), *Oracles of Empire: Poetry, Politics, and Commerce in British America 1690–1750*. Chicago: Chicago University Press.

Silz, Walter (1929), *Early German Romanticism: Its Founders and Heinrich von Kleist*. Cambridge, Mass.: Harvard University Press.

Simpson, Patricia Anne (2007), 'Visions of the Nation: Goethe, Karl Friedrich Schinkal, and Ernst Moritz Arndt', in Moore (2007).

Snyder, Alice D. (1928), 'Books borrowed by Coleridge from the Library of the University of Göttingen 1799', in *Modern Philology*, vol. 25, Feb. 1928.

Solomon, Robert C. (1988), *Continental Philosophy since 1750*. Oxford: Oxford University Press.

Spink, Gerald William (1925), 'Freiligrath als verdeutscher der englischen Poesie', in *Germanische Studien*, Berlin.

—(1932), 'Ferdinand Freiligrath's Varbannungsjahr in London', in *Germanische Studien*. Berlin.

Staël, Anne-Louise-Germaine de (1871), *De l'Allemagne*, 2 vols. O. W. Wright (ed.), New York: Hurd & Houghton.

Stahl, E. L. and W. E. Yuill (1970), *German Literature of the Eighteenth and Nineteenth Centuries*. London: Cresset Press.

Stark, Susanne (1999), *"Behind Inverted Commas": Translation and Anglo-German Cultural Relations in the Nineteenth Century*. Clevedon, Philadelphia, Toronto, Sydney: Multilingual Matters Ltd.

Steiner, George (1998), *After Babel: Aspects of Language and Translation*. Oxford: Oxford University Press (first edn. 1975).

Stern, Alfred (1881), *Geschichte der Revolution in England*. Berlin.

Stern, J. P. (1964), *Reinterpretations: Seven Studies in Nineteenth Century German Literature*. Cambridge: Cambridge University Press.

Stokoe, F. W. (1926), *German Influence in the English Romantic Period 1788–1818*. Cambridge: Cambridge University Press.

Strathman, Christopher A. (2006), *Romantic Poetry and the Fragmentary Imperative*. New York: State University of New York Press.

Tang, Jun (2007), 'Encounters with Cross-Cultural Conflicts in Translation', in Salama-Carr (2007).

Taylor, William (1828), *Historic Survey of German Poetry* 3 vols. London: Treutel and Würtz.

Thimm, Franz (1844), *The Literature of Germany from Its Earliest Period to the Present Time*, Henry Farn (ed.). London: D. Nutt; Berlin: A. Asher.

—(1901), see Hahn (1901).

Thorpe, Benjamin trans. (1834 and 1857), see Lappenberg (1834 and 1857). Oxford: Oxford University Press.

Tourey, Gideon (1980), *In Search of a Theory of Translation*. Tel Aviv: Tel Aviv University Press.

Turner, Sharon (1797–1805), *The History of the Anglo-Saxons to the Norman Conquest*, 4 vols. London: Longman.

—(1807), *A Brief Epitome of the History of England from 1066 to the Accession of George III*. London: J. Goodwin.

—(1819), *Prolusions on the Present Greatness of Britain; on Modern Poetry; and on the Present Aspect of the World*. London: Longman.

Tymoczko, Maria (2003), 'Ideology and the Position of the Translator', in Pérez (2003).

Tytler, Alexander F. (1797), *Essay on the Principles of Translation*. London.

Venuti, Lawrence (1998), *The Scandals of Translation: Towards an Ethics of Difference*. London: Routledge.

Wale, William (1902), *What Great Men Have Said of Great Men*. London: Swan & Sonnenschein & Co.

Ward, Thomas Humphrey (1880), *The English Poets. Selections with Critical Introductions by Various Writers*, 4 vols. London: Macmillan.

Weissbort, Daniel and Astradur Eysteinsson (eds), *Translation-theory and Practice: A Historical Reader*. Oxford: Oxford University Press.

Wellek, René (1965), *Confrontations: Studies in the Intellectual and Literary Relations between Germany, England, and the United States during the Nineteenth Century*. Princeton: Princeton University Press.

—(1970), *Discriminations: Further Concepts of Criticism*. New Haven and London: Yale University Press.

Wellek, René and Austin Warren (1949/1963), *Theory of Literature*. London: Peregrine Books.

Wheen, Francis (1999), *Karl Marx*. London: Fourth Estate.

Williams, John (2002), *Critical Issues: William Wordsworth*. Basingstoke: Palgrave Macmillan

—(2005), 'Britain's Nelson and Wordsworth's "Happy Warrior"; a Case of Cautious Dissent', in *Romanticism* 11, (2), 181–198.

—(2007), 'Ferdinand Freiligrath, William Wordsworth, and the Translation of English Poetry into the Conflicts of Nineteenth Century German Nationalism', in Salama-Carr (2007).

Williams, John R. (2001), *The Life of Goethe*. London, Blackwell.

Willoughby L. A. (1930), *The Romantic Movement in Germany*. Oxford: Oxford University Press.

—(1938), 'Wordsworth and Germany', in *German Studies*. Oxford: Clarendon Press.

Wilson, John (1866), *Noctes Ambrosianae*, 5 vols. Revised edn. Shelton Mackenzie, New York.

Wolf, Norbert (2003), *Caspar David Friedrich 1774–1840*. London: Taschen.

Wolff, O. L. B. and C. Schütz (1836–9), *Most Celebrated English Authors, Ancient and Modern*. Velhagen & Klasing.

Wolff, O. L. B. and Dr. H. Doering (1837), *The German Tourist*, trans. H. E. Lloyd. London.

Wolff, O. L. B. (1848), *Hausschatz Englischer Poesie: Chaucer to Bayly*. Leipzig.

Wolfson, Susan J. (1986), *The Questioning Presence: Wordsworth, Keats, and the Interrogative Mode in Romantic Poetry*. Ithaca and London: Cornell University Press.

Wordsworth, Christopher (1851), *Memoir of William Wordsworth*. London.

Wordsworth, Jonathan (1969), *The Music of Humanity: A Critical Study of Wordsworth's Ruined Cottage*. London and Edinburgh: Nelson.

Wordsworth, William (1979), *The Prelude 1799, 1805, 1850*, Jonathan Wordsworth, M. H. Abrams and Stephen Gill (eds). London and New York: W. W. Norton.

—(1983), *Poems in Two Volumes and Other Poems 1800–1807*, Jared Curtis (ed.). Ithaca and New York: Cornell University Press.

—(1988), *The White Doe of Rylstone*, Kristine Dugas (ed.). Ithaca and London: Cornell University Press.

—(1992), *Lyrical Ballads and Other Poems 1797–1800*, James Butler and Karen Green (eds). Ithaca and London: Cornell University Press.

—(2007), *The Excursion*, Sally Bushell, James A. Butler and Michael C. Jaye (eds). Ithaca and London: Cornell University Press.

Wülker, Richard (1896), *Gedichte der englischen Literatur*. Leipzig und Wien.

Wyss, Beat (2008), 'The Whispering Zeitgeist', in *Tate Etc*, (14), Autumn, 52–5.

Yates, W. E. (1972), *Grillparzer, A Critical Introduction*. Cambridge: Cambridge University Press.

Youmans, Charles (2005), *Richard Strauss's Orchestral Music and the German Intellectual Tradition*. Bloomington and Indianapolis: Indiana University Press.

Young, Edward (1971), *The Correspondence of Edward Young*, Henry Pettit (ed.). Oxford: Clarendon Press.

Young, Julian Charles (1871), *A Memoir of Charles Mayne Young*, 2 vols. London: Macmillan.

Young, Julian (2005), *Schopenhauer*. London: Routledge.

Young, Robert (2003), *Post Colonialism*. Oxford: Oxford University Press.

Zonneveld, Jaques (2004), *Sir Brooke Boothby: Rousseau's Roving Baronet Friend*. The Hague: Uitgeverij 'De Nieuwe Haagsche'.

Index

www.ingramcontent.com/pod-product-compliance
Lightning Source LLC
Chambersburg PA
CBHW071522100726

47908CB00004B/1262